T0330373

Theories of Social Innovation

ELGAR INTRODUCTIONS TO MANAGEMENT AND
ORGANIZATION THEORY

Series Editors: Cary L. Cooper, *Alliance Manchester Business School,
University of Manchester, UK* and Stewart R. Clegg, *School of Management,
University of Technology Sydney, Australia*

Elgar Introductions to Management and Organization Theory are stimulating
and thoughtful introductions to main theories in management, organizational
behaviour and organization studies, expertly written by some of the world's
leading scholars. Designed to be accessible yet rigorous, they offer concise and
lucid surveys of the key theories in the field.

The aims of the series are two-fold: to pinpoint essential history, and aspects
of a particular theory or set of theories, and to offer insights that stimulate
critical thinking. The volumes serve as accessible introductions for
undergraduate and graduate students coming to the subject for the first time.
Importantly, they also develop well-informed, nuanced critiques of the field that
will challenge and extend the understanding of advanced students, scholars and
policy-makers.

Titles in the series include:

Elgar Introduction to Organizational Discourse Analysis
Marco Berti

Elgar Introduction to Theories of Organizational Resilience
Luca Giustiniano, Stewart R. Clegg, Miguel Pina e Cunha and Arménio Rego

Theories of Social Innovation
Danielle Logue

Theories of Social Innovation

Danielle Logue

University of Technology Sydney, Australia

ELGAR INTRODUCTIONS TO MANAGEMENT AND ORGANIZATION THEORY

 Edward Elgar
PUBLISHING

Cheltenham, UK • Northampton, MA, USA

Published by
Edward Elgar Publishing Limited
The Lypiatts
15 Lansdown Road
Cheltenham
Glos GL50 2JA
UK

Edward Elgar Publishing, Inc.
William Pratt House
9 Dewey Court
Northampton
Massachusetts 01060
USA

A catalogue record for this book
is available from the British Library

This book is available electronically in the **Elgar**online
Business subject collection
DOI 10.4337/9781786436894

MIX
Paper from
responsible sources
FSC® C013056

ISBN 978 1 78643 688 7 (cased)
ISBN 978 1 78643 689 4 (eBook)

Typeset by Columns Design XML Ltd, Reading

Printed and bound in Great Britain by TJ International Ltd, Padstow, Cornwall

Contents

Preface

This book has emerged from a portfolio of work seeking to theorize and make sense of new ways to solve intractable, social problems, and new ways to finance their solutions. Yet who decides what is socially valuable and 'good', and what is in the public interest after all? This book is driven by a desire to improve the generation, management and organization of public good, and with it our understandings of social value that are embedded in existing institutions, organizations and management practices. It is driven by a desire to see generative and genuine collaborations across public, private and community sectors, and efforts to understand the values and logics of other domains. It is driven by a desire to see us reconceive and recover the role of the state in directing and protecting the public good. It is about developing new meta-narratives on the possible varieties of capitalism, boundaries of markets for producing social value, and alternative ways of organizing to address entrenched inequality. And mainly, writing this book is part of my own thinking and phronetic questioning: where are we going? Is this desirable? Can we do better? Surely we can.

Acknowledgements

There are many dear friends and collaborators who supported the development of this book and my work, to whom I owe much thanks and express my sincere gratitude. I would like to sincerely thank Dr Gillian McAllister and Professor John Gray for their research support, editing, advice and thoughtful feedback on this book. Most importantly, I would like to acknowledge and thank my parents, Pat and Michele, for instilling both a sense of responsibility and optimism – foundational ideals underpinning my writing of this book – and for a lifetime of support and encouragement.

This book was supported through the awarding of an Australian Research Council DECRA.

Introduction: the aim and structure of the book

Social innovation is a contemporary manifestation of historical tensions of the relationship between 'economy' and 'society'. As a concept, it is representative of long-standing debates raised in the works of Adam Smith (1759, 1776) regarding the embeddedness of markets in society, or alternatively the subjugation of society into market-based forms of organizing and the development of civil society. Ultimately, social innovation is concerned with the process and pursuit of both economic and social progress and is underpinned by a fundamental relationship to values and morality, that is, understandings of 'doing good' and 'being good'. As a term, it combines two words that have their own bodies of literature and debates: this makes it a rich multi-disciplinary concept to theorize, and notably prevents (or makes futile) the production of any single theory to capture its manifold effects and possible positions.

So what does this rather obtuse and liberally diffused term mean? Some have attempted to unpack this term by investigating what 'innovation' means, and what 'social' denotes in this usage (Nicholls and Murdock, 2012). Innovation can be both process and outcome, and is both novel and an improvement on a current context or application, or new for a user. As a topic of long-standing interest to a range of disciplines (Fagerberg et al., 2005), it is closely linked to entrepreneurship, and is described by Drucker (1985) as being at the very heart of entrepreneurship in creating focused, purposeful change. What the 'social' in social innovation denotes also varies amongst communities and applications. This ranges from social denoting intentionality and motivation (to be socially 'good'), or participation (for example, of stakeholders in innovation processes), to the social nature of the outcome of the innovation process (addressing a social problem), and distributing the benefits of innovation beyond a single individual or entity (shared value and social impact). According to Nicholls and Murdock (2012), while many innovations may create benefits for society, through providing employment, productivity, economic growth and technological advancement, and some even generate value beyond their initial economic impact, social innovations intentionally seek to address social problems, producing shared value that would otherwise not have been created. This corresponds to a widening rationale and application of innovation beyond that of economic performance and efficiency, to social (Dacin et al., 2011; Miller et al., 2012; Tracey and Stott, 2017) and environmental performance (Jennings and Zandbergen, 1995; York and Lenox, 2014), increasingly considering 'societal consequences' (Greenwood et al., 2017, p. 15) and impact (Gehman and Höllerer, 2019).

Definitions of the term 'social innovation' abound. For example, social innovation is a 'novel solution to a social problem that is more effective, efficient, sustainable or just than existing solutions and for which the value created accrues primarily to society as a whole rather than to private individuals' (Phills et al., 2008, p. 36). It's a term often associated with responses to large-scale social and wicked problems, and transformation or systems change; 'Social innovation is creating capacity to respond to grand challenges' (Benneworth and Cunha, 2015, p. 510; Voltan and De Fuentes, 2016). Others suggest social innovation describes 'the agentic, relational, situated, and multilevel process to develop, promote, and implement novel solutions to social problems in ways that are directed toward producing profound change in institutional contexts' (Van Wijk et al., 2018). Regardless of whether you think social innovation is going to get us to a 'better' version of capitalism or believe that it's more hype than substance, social innovation 'is focused on a set of issues that matter to a shared future'.

This wide-ranging understanding of the term, and its potential wide-ranging applicability, has attracted the attention of many disciplines (discussed further in Chapter 1). Indeed, it has also attracted the attention of many practitioners and policy makers, globally. Much of the early public sense-making of social innovation is in 'grey' literature, published by think tanks, government bodies and other private entities, outside of the academy. This book is developed explicitly for organizational and management scholars, and I would argue that these framings offer a richer and more rigorous approach to social innovation than has occurred in other disciplines so far. Nonetheless, the multiple theoretical lenses suggested are applicable across multiple disciplines and empirical settings.

This book provides a succinct but broad introduction to theories of social innovation. It does not attempt to offer a complete 'map of the jungle', but rather to offer a set of theoretical lenses (and references) that can help to understand the diverse but interconnected nature of this theoretical and empirical ecosystem. The ontological starting positions of these different lenses do differ, ranging from more positivist stances on social value creation and capture to more constructivist positions on the mutual constitution of structure and agency and understandings of social change.

The structure of this book is as follows. I first outline the contemporary evolution of the term 'social innovation', with its emergence often traced to work of management theorist Drucker, and now subject to many multi-disciplinary reviews (Chapter 1). In recent years there has been a proliferation of theorizing across disciplines. This meta-summary identifies key issues that many scholars are grappling with, which I go on to examine in the following chapters. I then take a more positivist stance in considering social innovation as social value creation, capture and distribution (Chapter 2). I draw on strategy literature of value creation and capture, adding a new dimension of 'value distribution' as an important, distinct and necessary mechanism of social innovation. I propose several abstract models for theorizing social value distribution. I then take a different ontological stance, far more social constructivist, in considering social innovation as polysemic (Chapter 3). Social innovation is a concept that means different things to different stakeholders, simultaneously connecting diverse interpretations into a network of meaning. I describe how polysemic concepts are considered in organizational and management studies, and discuss the three main societal domains related to social innovation – private sector, public sector, and the not-for-profit (NFP) sector – and their differing understandings and mobilization of the concept. I argue that it is the polysemic nature of social innovation that provides its grist and capacity for social change. I consequently examine social innovation as social change, specifically institutional change (Chapter 4). As well as being a dominant theoretical approach in organizational and management theory, institutional theory enables theorizing of change across levels: individual, organization, field, and cross-field. Its attention to the mutually constitutive nature of structure and agency, across these levels, is theoretically and empirically valuable, as demonstrated by many existing studies of social innovation using institutional theory. I conclude the book by returning to my original anchoring of social innovation in classical tensions and theorizations of the relationship between the realms of 'economy' and 'society' (Chapter 5). I discuss this in terms of the social construction of markets and their moral legitimacy, and implications for future theories of impact. As social innovation is inherently about morality and values, it also raises the question of how to investigate morality in management by learning more about social innovation, and the value of a phronetic approach for future research. I then detail possible sites for such future empirical investigations by describing core tensions in practice, that of managing hybrids, measuring impact and governing cross-sector collaborations (Chapter 6).

REFERENCES

Benneworth, P. and Cunha, J. (2015). Universities' contributions to social innovation: reflections in theory & practice. *European Journal of Innovation Management*, **18**(4), 508–27.

Dacin, M.T., Dacin, P.A. and Tracey, P. (2011). Social entrepreneurship: a critique and future directions. *Organization Science*, **22**(5), 1203–13.

Drucker, P.F. (1985). The discipline of innovation. *Harvard Business Review*, **63**(3), 67–72.

Fagerberg, J., Mowery, D.C. and Nelson, R.R. (2005). *The Oxford Handbook of Innovation*. Oxford: Oxford University Press.

Gehman, J. and Höllerer, M. (2019). Venturing into the cultural future: research opportunities at the nexus of institutions, innovation, and impact. *Innovation: Organization & Management (IOM)*, forthcoming.

Greenwood, R., Oliver, C., Lawrence, T.B. and Meyer, R.E. (2017). *The Sage Handbook of Organizational Institutionalism*. Thousand Oaks, CA: SAGE Publications.

Jennings, P.D. and Zandbergen, P.A. (1995). Ecologically sustainable organizations: an institutional approach. *Academy of Management Review*, **20**(4), 1015–52.

Miller, T.L., Grimes, M.G., McMullen, J.S. and Vogus, T.J. (2012). Venturing for others with heart and head: how compassion encourages social entrepreneurship. *Academy of Management Review*, **37**(4), 616–40.

Nicholls, A. and Murdock, A. (2012). *Social Innovation. Blurring Boundaries to Reconfigure Markets*. New York: Palgrave Macmillan.

Phills, J.A.J., Deiglmeier, K. and Miller, D.T. (2008). Rediscovering social innovation. *Stanford Social Innovation Review*, **6**(4), 34–43.

Smith, A. (1759[2010]). *The Theory of Moral Sentiments*. Harmondsworth: Penguin.

Smith, A. (1776). *An Inquiry into the Nature and Causes of the Wealth of Nations: Volume One*. London: printed for W. Strahan; and T. Cadell, 1776.

Tracey, P. and Stott, N. (2017). Social innovation: a window on alternative ways of organizing and innovating. *Innovation*, **19**(1), 51–60.

Van Wijk, J., Zietsma, C., Dorado, S., De Bakker, F.G. and Martí, I. (2018). Social innovation: integrating micro, meso, and macro level insights from institutional theory. *Business & Society*.

Voltan, A. and De Fuentes, C. (2016). Managing multiple logics in partnerships for scaling social innovation. *European Journal of Innovation Management*, **1**(4), 446–67.

York, J.G. and Lenox, M.J. (2014). Exploring the sociocultural determinants of de novo versus de alio entry in emerging industries. *Strategic Management Journal*, **35**(13), 1930–51.

1. Social innovation and its contemporary evolution

In this chapter I review the contemporary and multi-disciplinary efforts to define and theorize social innovation. This is not a comprehensive 'map of the jungle' but is more of a meta-review aimed at highlighting the common characteristics across disciplines that many see as defining social innovation: that it is the pursuit of social change, and social change that is significant and consequential, sustainable and ultimately institutionalized. I commence by historically examining when the term first started appearing in literature, and discussing that while this may be a new popular term, it could readily be applied to many historical examples of social change. Social change includes social innovation. I then undertake a meta-review of the many contemporary reviews of social innovation, distilling how different disciplines are conceptualizing social innovation. I interrogate different definitions to identify commonalities and core characteristics of social innovation and use this to develop a defensible construct of social innovation.

EARLY USAGE OF THE TERM 'SOCIAL INNOVATION'

An early reference to the specific term 'social innovation' in organizational and management studies is by Drucker (1987), a management scholar whose work was widely read and adopted by practitioners and industry. In this article titled 'Social innovation – management's new dimension', Drucker emphasizes the impact of non-technological innovations on the economy and society, giving a range of individual, organizational and social movement examples on how positive societal change and development has occurred. His examples of social innovations include 'the research lab; Eurodollar and commercial paper; mass and mass movement; the farm agent; and management itself as an organized function and Discipline' (Drucker, 1987, p. 29). For example, he describes the innovation of research labs by General Electric, in that they brought together multi-disciplinary teams and focused on connecting science to technology. He also cites the rise of farm agents who helped

6

US farmers to improve their productivity (and increase their demand for farm inputs). He argued that social innovation was a novel structural improvement in societal organization, creating new capacities for action and thereby raising overall welfare levels (Benneworth and Cunha, 2015).

Almost ten years later, Kanter, another management scholar, provides the next substantial (and oft-cited) reference to social innovation. In an article in *Harvard Business Review* titled 'From spare change to real change: the social sector as a beta site for business innovation', Kanter extols the value of businesses solving social problems and addressing unmet social needs – for both business and society. The main argument is for companies to move beyond corporate social responsibility (that is, simply avoiding or reducing negative externalities, or undertaking charitable activities), to actively pursuing social sector problems as a business opportunity: that is, from social responsibility to social innovation. Kanter argues that these innovation and R&D efforts are a strategic business investment like any other, and considers that the private sector needs to play a leading role in creating sustainable change to entrenched social problems. Kanter (1999) cites examples such as a mainstream bank opening a community bank to reach under-served minorities, addressing a social need yet also increasing the bank's customer base. Such an approach is reflected in much of the literature on Bottom-of-the-Pyramid (BoP) markets (for example, Anderson and Markides, 2007; Olsen and Boxenbaum, 2009; Prahalad, 2012; Prahalad and Hammond, 2002).

Kanter also connects social innovation as emerging from necessary cross-sector partnerships, between business, government and non-profit organizations, which are difficult given each domain's different goals and responsibilities and also different measures for what constitutes social impact and value.[1] Kanter goes on to suggest that the government and non-profit sectors need to develop more business-like 'institutional infrastructure' (1999, p. 126), and that working with these sectors (I emphasize here from the perspective of business) is similar to the difficulties of working in under-developed markets. For example, Kanter (1999, p. 126) suggests 'six characteristics of successful private-public partnerships: a clear business agenda, strong partners committed to change, investment by both parties, rootedness in the user community, links to other community organizations, and a long-term commitment to sustain and replicate the results', which is also echoed in more recent research on cross-sector partnerships, specifically public–private partnerships (Selsky and Parker, 2005, 2010).

While Drucker and Kanter are amongst the earliest specific references to 'social innovation', other authors argue that 'social innovation' is a new label for historical instances of social change, which could also be described in contemporary terms as social innovation (McGowan and Westley, 2015; Mulgan, 2006; Tracey and Stott, 2017). Mulgan (2006) gives an array of historical examples of individual social innovators and socially innovative organizations. For example, at the individual level, history is rich with examples of individuals who developed ground-breaking ideas to address problems of the day and, perhaps more importantly, successfully diffused these ideas, compelling adoption, and so greater social and often systemic change. Is Thomas Edison therefore a social innovator? Detailed, historical analyses of Edison's efforts to produce and diffuse the electric light show this individual's ability to understand and engage multiple stakeholders (regulators, competitors, consumers) to develop the necessary system and resulting institutional infrastructure for an electricity system (Hargrave and Van de Ven, 2006), having wide-scale technological and arguably, positive, social impact. In another example, Mulgan (2006) describes Florence Nightingale as a social innovator. Known as a social reformer, this statistician reformed nursing and medical care, and was made famous by reports of her nursing efforts during the Crimean War, and efforts to disseminate medical knowledge in plain language. As Lawrence et al. (2014) note, the role of individuals in managing social innovation is a focus in the growing literature on social entrepreneurship, and also civic entre-preneurship (Elkington and Hartigan, 2008).

At an organizational level, while much of the current focus is on finding new means or mechanisms to collaborate and co-create hybrid solutions to social problems or on creating new organizational forms that encourage the pursuit of financial and social value (Battilana and Lee, 2014), there are some historical organizational forms associated with the notion of social innovation and the pursuit of social change. Mulgan (2006) suggests cooperatives and trade unions are social innovations, being historical organizational forms with a central social purpose, designed to pursue a social mission of improving conditions (of work, of pay, of ownership of capital). For example, cooperatives began in 18th-century Britain when workers pooled their income to buy materials and food, and were often common in agriculture and farming sectors. There are debates over the earliest recorded cooperative, with claims that the first cooperative was established in 1791 in Scotland. The Fenwick Weavers' Society was established to sell discounted oatmeal to local workers, later expanding to provide savings and loan services and education. Most famously for the cooperative movement was the estab-lishment in 1844 of the Rochdale Equitable Pioneers Society by mill workers in northern England. As Mulgan (2006) describes, as part of its establishment it devised eight principles of cooperation: open member-ship; democratic control; distributing profits to members in proportion to their spending; paying small amounts of interest on capital; political and religious neutrality; cash trading, no credit; promotion of education; and quality goods and services. At the time, cooperatives represented a novel form of organizing to achieve a social purpose.

Another driver and form of social innovation is social movements (Mulgan, 2006). Social movements are a set of opinions and beliefs in a population that represents preferences for changing some elements of the social structure and/or reward distribution of a society (McCarthy and Zald, 1977). They are 'a major vehicle for ordinary people's participation in public politics' (Tilly, 2004), as they seek to resist, undo or carry out social change. As a form of group action (often with organizational structures and strategies), social movements may enable oppressed populations or non-elites to effectively challenge existing systems and institutions and those who lead them. Examples of histor-ical social movements that resulted in social change (with many arguing much change is still to be achieved) are feminism, race equality and environmentalism.

These earliest references to social innovation raise a number of points. That, coming from the organizational and management literature, social innovation was often seen as a business opportunity and mainly con-cerned with non-technical innovation, to do well and also do good; that social innovation would often involve cross-sector partnerships to address problems but also as the source of innovation itself; and that many historical examples exist of individuals and organizations, and also social movements, that would now be labelled as social innovation. The pursuit of social change is multi-level and often focused on significantly trans-forming existing ways of organizing and managing.

As a term and concept, social innovation has also attracted the attention of other disciplines, as they seek to become involved in the pursuit of social change. I turn now to reviewing the many recent reviews of social innovation and its application across disciplines to further develop the construct.

UNDERSTANDING SOCIAL INNOVATION ACROSS DISCIPLINES

While some of the earliest references to social innovation can be found in the organizational and management literature, much early writing on social innovation is in fact located outside academia, published by foundations and think-tanks (Mulgan, 2006). Practitioners and policy makers, often frustrated with a lack of progress over many years, and being presented with challenges, such as climate change and persistent poverty, that required collaboration across sectors, and a need to mobilize more funding for solutions, have sought new ways to address social problems. Admittedly this is not an uncommon direction of influence in organizational and management studies, when popular concepts are later examined and theorized. Given its association with social change and addressing large-scale problems, the term has more recently attracted much interest in scholarly communities, and also across a wide range of scholarly communities. For example, in organizational and management studies, social innovation is seen as relating to contemporary ideas of social entrepreneurship, social finance, corporate social responsibility, open innovation, public–private partnerships, inclusive innovation and collective impact (Phills et al., 2008). Beyond organization and management studies, theorizing and application also occurs in urban studies, technology management, sociology, not-for-profit and third sector, public administration and public policy (Edwards-Schachter and Wallace, 2017; Lawrence et al., 2014; Moulaert et al., 2013; Pol and Ville, 2009). Figure 1.1 outlines the rise in articles citing 'social innovation' in the title, abstract or keywords across disciplines.

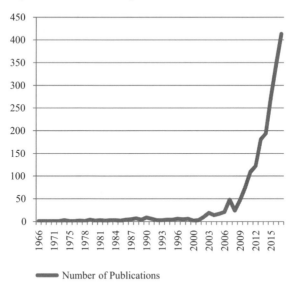

Figure 1.1   Rise in academic publications citing 'social innovation' in title, abstract or keywords 1966–2017

Seeking a Definition of Social Innovation

Like any emerging concept or area of activity, much early work fixated on attaining a singular definition and setting definitional boundaries, based on the assumption that conceptual precision and clarity is necessary for the growth of the field (and in directing its growth).

Systematic reviews of the definition of social innovation identified 76 definitions across academic and grey literature, suggesting the term has become an amalgamation of activities, aspirations, ideologies and rationalities, incorporating normative and instrumental meanings, and structural and behavioural patterns of activity (Edwards-Schachter and Wallace, 2017, p. 64). Table 1.1 is a summary combining definitions included in some of the reviews of social innovation and also frequently cited definitions in 'grey' literature that are referred to in scholarly materials, and from organizations with significant influence on the practical deployment of the term.

Across these and many other definitions of social innovation is a mixed focus on social innovation as a process and/or outcome (Cajaiba-Santana, 2014; Edwards-Schachter and Wallace, 2017; Silveira and Zilber, 2017; Van der Have and Rubalcaba, 2016). Raising confusion – is it about the process of generating social value or good, or the ultimate social value produced? Do the ends then justify the means? One of the earlier and oft-cited definitions (in both grey and academic literature) provided by Mulgan (2006, p. 145) describes social innovation as 'the development and implementation of new ideas to meet social needs'. Westley and Antadze (2010, p. 2) offer a more elaborate definition: 'social innovation is any initiative, product, process, programme, project or platform that challenges and over time contributes to changing the defining routines, resources and authority flows of beliefs of the broader social system in which it is introduced; successful social innovations have durability, scale and transformative impact.' The type of resulting change is also an issue for Van Wijk et al. (2018, p. 3), who focus on social innovation as institutional change: 'Social innovation for us describes the agentic, relational, situated and multi-level process to develop, promote and implement novel solutions to social problems in ways that are directed towards producing profound change in institutional contexts.' Across this compilation of definitions, several characteristics of social innovation are fairly consistent: (1) collectivity and the role of understanding social movements and collective action in generating social value; (2) diversity and the role of multi-disciplinary and cross-sector interactions in generating social value; and (3) what I describe as relationality, the role of creating new relational channels and configurations in generating social value.

Table 1.1   Sample of definitions of social innovation across academic and 'grey' literature (in chronological order)

Source	Definition
Kanter, R.M. (1999). From spare change to real change. The social sector as beta site for business innovation. *Harvard Business Review*, **77**(3), 122–32.	A partnership between private enterprise and public interest that produces profitable and sustainable change for both sides; innovations that have business as well as community payoffs.
OECD (2000). OECD LEED Forum on Social Innovations.	The working definition of social innovation adopted in the framework of the Forum on Social Innovations was that it 'can concern conceptual, process or product change, organisational change and changes in financing, and can deal with new relationships with stakeholders and territories'. 'Social innovation' seeks new answers to social problems by: • Identifying and delivering new services that improve the quality of life of individuals and communities. • Identifying and implementing new labour market integration processes, new competencies, new jobs, and new forms of participation, as diverse elements that each contribute to improving the position of individuals in the workforce. Social innovations can therefore be seen as dealing with the welfare of individuals and communities, both as consumers and producers.
Mumford, M.D. (2002). Social innovation: ten cases from Benjamin Franklin. *Creativity Research Journal*, **14**(2), 253–66.	'The term social innovation ... refers to the generation and implementation of new ideas about how people should organise interpersonal activities, or social interactions, to meet one or more common goals. As with other forms of innovation, the products resulting from social innovation may vary with regard to their breadth and impact.' (p. 253)
Phills, J.A.J., Deiglmeier, K. and Miller, D.T. (2008). Rediscovering social innovation. *Stanford Social Innovation Review*, **6**(4), 34–43.	A novel solution to a social problem that is more effective, efficient, sustainable ... than existing solutions and for which the value created accrues primarily to society as a whole rather than private individuals

Source	Definition
Nicholls, A. and Murdock, A. (eds) (2012). *Social Innovation. Blurring Boundaries to Reconfigure Markets.* New York: Palgrave Macmillan.	Social innovation is defined here as varying levels of deliberative change that aim to address suboptimal issues in the production, availability, and consumption of public goods defined as that which is broadly of societal benefit within a particular normative and culturally contingent context. What is abundantly clear is that social innovation is complex and multi-faceted.
Cajaiba-Santana, G. (2014). Social innovation: moving the field forward. A conceptual framework. *Technological Forecasting and Social Change*, **82**, 42–51.	Social innovations are new social practices created from collective, intentional, and goal-oriented actions aimed at prompting social change through the reconfiguration of how social goals are accomplished. They are 'a collective creation of new legitimated social practices aiming at social change'.
Voorberg, W.H., Bekkers, V.J. and Tummers, L.G. (2015). A systematic review of co-creation and co-production: embarking on the social innovation journey. *Public Management Review*, **17**(9), 1333–57.	Social innovation as the creation of long-lasting outcomes that aim to address societal needs by fundamentally changing the relationships, positions and rules between the involved stakeholders, through an open process of participation, exchange and collaboration with relevant stakeholders, including end-users.
World Economic Forum (2013). Breaking the binary: policy guide to scaling social innovation. WEF.	The application of innovative, practical, sustainable, business-like approaches that achieve positive social and/or environmental change, with an emphasis on low-income or underserved populations.

Crossing Disciplines: Reviewing the Reviews of Social Innovation

In recent years a stream of studies have emerged attempting to review the plethora of other studies (mostly in the academic sphere) which cite the concept of social innovation or report to be theorizing social innovation and mapping the current and future theoretical landscape. As a popular and expanding concept, some early reviews of social innovation highlighted the diversity of disciplines interested in the topic and a consequent and growing fragmentation around the scope and meaning of social innovation (Cajaiba-Santana, 2014; Edwards-Schachter and Wallace, 2017; Phillips et al., 2015; Silveira and Zilber, 2017; Van der Have and Rubalcaba, 2016; see Chapter 1). Many early definitions tried to encompass a variety of views, often sociological in nature and incorporating aspects of both structure and agency (Van der Have and Rubalcaba, 2016). Reviews include Silveira and Zilber's (2017) bibliometric analysis of social innovation, Van der Have and Rubalcaba's (2016) network and bibliometric analysis, Cajaiba-Santana's (2013) structural and institutional summary of social innovation, and content analysis of key terms and understandings associated with social innovation.

In Pol and Ville's (2009) early review and discussion of the term, they describe its mixed emergence in varied academic but especially practitioner literature (as noted in definitions above). This review highlights the concept of social innovation as being related to institutional change, social purposes, the public good, and not necessarily delivered by market mechanisms (as social innovation is often perceived as addressing needs that have been ignored by the market). Pol and Ville (2009) describe social innovation in comparison to business innovation, offering a more economic conceptualization: where the former pursues social impact, the latter pursues increased profitability. They do raise issues with the ultimate outcome of social innovation, that is improved quality of life, noting that there is no agreed definition here, and the complexities that occur when considering the relationship between improvements at the individual level versus the collective level. This starts to raise the issue of social value capture and (re)distribution when it comes to conceptualizing social innovation.

Cajaiba-Santana (2014) is the next academic article to review the growing interest in social innovation, suggesting there exist two main approaches to social innovation: agentic-centred (closely related to the literature on social entrepreneurship and the role of the individual 'hero' change agent), and structuralist (referring to the social structures in which these agents operate). While the review is less systematic and uses a mix of sociological and institutional theories, it does importantly suggest the connection between social innovation and institutional change, and the necessary interactions between structure and agency to make this happen.

Two years later, Van der Have and Rubalcaba (2016) conduct a more systematic network and bibliometric analysis of the expanding scholarly literature on social innovation, focusing on the relationship to innovation studies more generally. They suggest social innovation is more of an innovation paradigm than a separate category of innovation, referring to 'a large revitalization of the social aspects involved in any kind of innovation, technological innovation included' (Van der Have and Rubalcaba, 2016). They review the concept by creating a data set of all articles published between 1986 and 2013, resulting in 172 unique publications.

In their bibliometric study of these articles (where a relationship is constructed between cited references or topic keywords), they produce a map of the relationships and most influential articles, and identify different disciplinary approaches from psychology, sociology, urban studies and management and business. This initially reveals two important foundational articles that are highly cited and therefore shaping the concept of social innovation: Swyngedouw's (2005) paper on grassroots innovation and the need for more innovative and participatory governance structures, and Ramirez's (1999) strategy article on value creation and specifically value co-production as social innovation.

The results of Van der Have and Rubalcaba's (2016) bibliometric study also reveal four main disciplinary clusters for the study of social innovation. First, 'creativity research', a distant and rather unconnected cluster that is predominately based on the one popular article by Mumford (2002). This describes 10 varied empirical examples of social innovations, emphasizing social innovation as about social relationships and social organization. Second, a cluster described as 'community psychology', underpinned by a group of articles examining social innovation and behavioural change (Hazel and Onaga, 2003). Third, a large cluster described as 'local development', encompassing studies of communities or neighbourhoods, cities and regions, and both urban and rural settings (Van der Have and Rubalcaba, 2016, p. 1928). This cluster focuses on empowering citizens, participation and inclusion, and the role of governance. Two influential works underpin this cluster: Swyngedouw (2005) and Moulaert et al. (2005) on local innovation, both published in a special issue of the journal *Urban Studies*.

The largest cluster identified by Van der Have and Rubalcaba's (2016) bibliometric study is labelled as 'social and societal challenges', and focuses on innovative solutions as outcomes to social and technical challenges. Grouped within this cluster is work considering cross-sector alliances and collaborations, social entrepreneurship, and value co-production (Ramirez, 1999). While this review shows that social innovation has a 'young and unsettled history' (2016, p. 1932), the authors identify two core conceptual elements for understanding social innovation, in that 'it encompasses: (1) a change in social relationships, – systems, or – structures, and (2) such changes serve a shared human need/goal or solve a socially relevant problem' (2016, p. 1932).

Another review of social innovation is provided by Edwards-Schachter and Wallace's (2017) content analysis of key terms and understandings. In this study, they produce a data set of 252 definitions of 'social innovation', and use semantic network analysis to identify and examine key terms and connections. Three main clusters emerge, defining social innovation as: processes of social change, sustainable development (linking development and value), and services sector (linking to social need and quality of life). They describe a rough timeline of the changes in discourse surrounding social innovation, beginning with Drucker's description of social innovation and required organizational change, followed by social innovation being discussed in relation to environmental challenges. There is then a period of two decades (up to the mid-1990s) where social innovation is little used as a term. It then emerges again as a policy and normative concept, further growing in interest with the rise of discussions on social entrepreneurship, hybrid forms, and cross-sector partnerships.

Most comprehensive, at the time of writing, is Silveira and Zilber's (2017) review of social innovation. Similar to Van der Have and Rubalcaba's (2016) study, they also produce a bibliometric study, conducting both citation and co-citation analysis on a dataset of 165 articles that mention 'social innovation' as a keyword. The analysis shows a large uptake of the term post-2010, identifying eight fields across which the articles were published: social sciences, business, computer science, engineering, arts and humanities, economy and finance, energy and environmental science, and psychology. In their co-citation analysis, they produce a network map of the most commonly cited keywords, and also a network map of the most commonly cited articles. By also conducting a factor analysis to classify the articles by their focus, the authors divide the set of publications into three main fields: social innovation, consisting of articles concerned with the definition, clarification and application of the concept; social entrepreneurship, consisting of articles that consider social innovation as a result of entrepreneurial effort; and public policy management, consisting of articles concerned with the relationship between the government and other stakeholders and new relational arrangements to address social problems.

This 'review of reviews' provides a comprehensive analysis of a large and growing set of diverse articles that cite and apply 'social innovation'. It also provides the opportunity to identify key themes in contemporary definitions and application. These are set out in the next section.

Identifying Common Insights of Social Innovation as a Construct

Recently, Tracey and Stott (2017) propose typologizing social innovation based on different approaches to social change. Here, they suggest that three types of social innovation can be defined through an analysis of the location of the interaction:

- social entrepreneurship – where social change is created through the founding of new organizations (for example, social enterprises, for profit or non-profit);
- social intrapreneurship – where change is created by leveraging the resources and capabilities of existing or established organizations (that is, inside these organizations);
- social extra-preneurship – where change is created through platforms that support collective effort within and between new and established organizations.

Social entrepreneurship, as defined here, is akin to thinking around individual entrepreneurs with a social mission, often working in the for-profit sector, and developing market-based solutions for social change and positive impact. Social intra-preneurship here is more akin to traditional thinking around corporate social responsibility and shared value (Porter and Kramer, 2011) within corporations and for-profit firms. Within this category, Tracey and Stott (2017) also note the move for public sector agencies to adopt more collective and open processes of innovation when addressing social problems. Such agencies are increasingly using processes of open innovation, where the public and users are involved in co-creation (Randhawa et al., 2017). This may lead to social extra-preneurship as described here, considering the collective and collaborative nature of social innovation, necessary in breaking down silos between the public, private and non-profit sectors and achieving systemic change.

It is the cross-sector work for social innovation, categorized here as social extra-preneurship, that is arguably the most difficult and currently less theorized. What is emphasized in this type of social innovation is that it is an inter-organizational action and activity that 'facilitates alternative combinations of ideas, people, places and resources to address social challenges and make social change' (Tracey and Stott, 2017; see also Algoso, 2015). Activity here may occur between organizations and networks, cultivating the spaces between fields and organizations by building new infrastructure to support social change and social value creation (Logue and Grimes, 2018; see also Chapter 4 in this book).

From across these reviews, and consideration of both academic and 'grey' literature, there are several characteristics that are commonly or frequently attributed to social innovation.[2] These provide a set of elements or issues on which to examine social innovation, and are as follows:

- **Social value:** the main objective of social innovation is improved social outcome that is accrued for collective rather than private benefit.
- **Source:** it can be driven by individuals, organizations or social movements; these individuals and organizations may be located within existing organizations, outside existing organizations or across organizations (Tracey and Stott, 2017).
- **Significance:** while social innovation may pursue large-scale system change (or social problems that require system change), it is acknowledged that incremental change can also be transformative in the longer term (Campbell, 2004).
- **Collectivity:** social innovation often (yet not always) occurs as a collaborative or rather participative process; this is because many of the social (and intractable) problems being addressed cannot be addressed by one organization or one sector alone.
- **Diversity:** given the above, a diversity of actors and disciplines is often involved in a process of social innovation.
- **Relationality:** new relational channels or configurations often need to be established and institutionalized as part of these collaborations; however the coordinating infrastructure to achieve this is varied, temporary, and also under-theorized.

These issues and elements inform a construct of social innovation, appearing in different combination and emphasis in the theoretical lenses outlined in this book.

EMERGING TENSIONS AND DEBATES IN SOCIAL INNOVATION

There are several tensions, some inherent, in this wide-ranging literature theorizing social innovation. I identify the first of these as problem–solution coupling and how decisions are made around problem definition and prioritization, and the consequent selection of solutions to social and environmental problems. This in turn raises the second core tension in social innovation of the power and politics involved in this process of problem and solution identification and action. Another tension is the responsibility for action and change, and the scale of that change. A shift is apparent, moving from a focus on heroic individuals to processes and systems as drivers of social change. This is associated with another tension or issue, the rise of another popular and related term, that of 'inclusive innovation' and 'systems innovation'.

Problem–Solution Construction and Coupling

A common concern in the literature on social innovation is that of solving social problems. The social problems of interest are often large-scale and multi-generational, such as climate change, poverty, obesity and homelessness. Yet, as is increasingly observed in the associated social finance and impact investing literature (for example, Logue et al., 2017), deciding on which problem is the priority (when faced with limited resources) and what counts as social impact is problematic and political. The identification, description (especially boundary setting) and prioritization of social problems is in and of itself socially constructed. This means that what constitutes a problem, its boundaries, its effects, and its importance is a process of social negotiation and is not given (Clegg et al., 2006; Lawrence et al., 2014). As such, values, norms and power relations all impact problem and solution definition and their associated coupling. For example, in the charity sector we already see struggles to gain donations for causes that are less 'attractive', widespread or comparatively lack awareness, such as different types of diseases. 'There are particular moral assumptions about who is and is not "worthy" of support – which tend to reflect the values of elites – and shape whether issues become categorized as "problems"' (Tracey and Stott, 2017, p. 56). Within the construction of the problem are understandings of responsibility (for example, is it the individual or the failure of the system), resources (does addressing homelessness require more resources for mental health or temporary shelters or public housing stock), and value, such as how much is it worth to society to reduce recidivism rates of prisoners (how to calculate this, and does this contribute to political elections), and so on. Therefore, an important consideration in social innovation is to consider not only the novel solution, but the construction of the problem, and its coupling (relationship) to the solution. 'This shifts the question of what counts as a social problem from being a boundary condition of social innovation scholarship to an integral element of managing social innovation, and consequently a necessary part of the processes and practices examined' (Lawrence et al., 2014, p. 4).

Embeddedness, Power and Politics

Accompanying the recognition that the social construction of social problems is at the core of social innovation literature and activity, is the recognition of the embeddedness of individuals, organizations and governments in institutionalized social systems and mental models. We know from volumes of innovation literature (see Rogers, 1962 for a classic overview) that diffusing a new product, service or way of organizing is extremely difficult as existing incumbents may resist or challenge novel ideas (especially when these challenge the status quo or power relations). More broadly, as Lawrence et al. (2014) describe, 'resistance to change is rooted in people's investments – material (time and money), cognitive (assumptions and values), and relational (social capital and networks) to existing arrangements' and so maintaining the status quo (Lawrence et al., 2014, p. 323). Any process of social innovation is conducted within existing social, organizational and technological structures that may both enable and constrain them. While seemingly abstract, this reinforces the understanding that a novel solution to a social problem is likely to involve (or invoke) a connected set of actors, processes and practices, achieving change or the creation of social value by reconfiguring social, discursive and material relations (Lawrence et al., 2014). Furthermore, that the social value created, and its distribution, is also a negotiated and so inherently political process; 'the impacts of social innovation are never "ethically neutral"' (Lawrence et al., 2014, p. 325). As will be discussed in detail in Chapter 4, an institutional theory lens is valuable for examining social innovation, as it highlights the importance of the established social arrangements and the institutions and institutional infrastructure that enable and reinforce them. These institutions may be the source of intractable social problems, such that novel solutions will require associated change in these institutions and deeply held meaning and power structures.

From the Social Innovation 'Hero' Individual to Cross-sector Processes and Systems Thinking

Social innovation as a concept has been rapidly embraced across business and management literature and is often associated with broader processes of innovation and entrepreneurship. As such, the more dominant and current understandings of social innovation have viewed the phenomenon through this lens, in particular associating social innovation with product innovation processes and the conceptualization of the 'hero' and lone operating entrepreneur. However, just as the entrepreneurship literature has moved away from worshipping individual entrepreneurs (the likes of Richard Branson, Virgin CEO Founder, or even US President Donald Trump) and considering entrepreneurship as based on personality traits, to adopting more of a process and systems change approach, a similar shift has occurred (or is occurring) in social innovation. As entrepreneurship has moved from being about personality and serendipity, to an increasingly scientized and standardized process (with universal start-up methodologies and practices), a similar shift has occurred in more contemporary understandings of social innovation.

In the past decade, examples of 'hero' social entrepreneurs (and their associated stories of how they addressed social problems and generated social value) were common in the social innovation literature. A leading example is Nobel Prize winner Muhammad Yunus and his work in microfinance. Yet as the shift in entrepreneurial thinking started to occur, coupled with a desire to scale impact, a similar move in the social innovation literature can be observed, towards processes and systems and away from the cult of individual personalities (Elkington and Hartigan, 2008). It has also shifted from market-oriented approaches to innovation and entrepreneurship (and consequently only market-based solutions to social problems) to a greater focus on cross-sector collaborations and broader institutional change (Seelos and Mair, 2017; Van Wijk et al., 2018).

Social Innovation and Inclusive Innovation

A related concept to social innovation is the notion of inclusive innovation (George et al., 2012; Moulaert et al., 2013). Linked to inclusive growth, inclusive innovation refers to innovations that create or enhance opportunities to improve wellbeing for those at the 'bottom of the pyramid' (BoP). It can include any form of innovation – product, service, business model – and can represent the recombining of existing resources in new ways, or be completely new to a context (George et al., 2012). The issue of extreme inequality facing global society has seen a complementary increase in public policy attention (or at least discourse) on the issue of inclusive growth. Inclusive growth is about improvements in the social and economic prosperity of those members of society who have been 'structurally denied access to resources, capabilities and opportunities' (George et al., 2012, p. 661).

Similar to social innovation, inclusive innovation is often described as referring to both a process and outcome of innovation. However, distinct from social innovation is its focus on removing or overcoming the structural barriers for marginalized or the poorest members of society, those at the bottom of the income pyramid, with many examples focusing on developing-country contexts. This focus on the BoP often sees inclusive innovation transforming the poor into entrepreneurs and being innovative with minimal resources (also referred to as 'frugal innovation') or involves multinational firms in producing products and services appropriate for BoP markets. As for social innovation, the paradoxical tension between generating financial and social value, or in this case the tension between growth (economic) and equality (or avoiding harm), persists, making not all efforts of inclusive innovation 'good'. For example, Hall et al. (2012) show the negative impact of government efforts to drive social inclusion through entrepreneurship in examining state-backed tourism developments in Brazil that neglect local history and local craft. Others also note the dark side of inclusive innovation, when multinationals do not understand and as a result disrupt local community relations and social structures, doing more harm than good (for example, see Ansari et al., 2012; Halme et al., 2012).

The discourse on inclusive innovation converges, at this point in time, on removing structural barriers to participation in marketplaces and access to capital for entrepreneurial activities. Scholars note, similarly to social innovation, that any innovations attempting to deliver inclusive growth are created and implemented within a broader institutional system that can both enable or constrain activities and growth. Existing structures, norms, values, sources of legitimacy, and regulatory systems all shape the process and outcome of inclusive innovation. The questions over actually measuring when inclusivity has been achieved are inherently difficult, as is the issue of who is included versus who benefits.

CHAPTER SUMMARY

It has not been the aim of this chapter to aggregate the many definitions and reviews and deliver an all-compassing definition. A review of the academic and grey literature, across disciplines, has revealed some common characteristics as to understandings of innovation that are useful in developing the construct of social innovation. What it also reveals is the plurality of views and how maintaining this plurality is actually a source of innovation (for example, bringing different voices and values about problem definition and solution to discussions), as well as a necessary part of understanding how problems and solutions are (and may be) worked out across different disciplines and sectors. In this sense, the plurality is to be embraced.

As a construct, there are several well identified elements of social innovation that scholars of social innovation need to be attentive to, based on existing literature: social value, source and significance. Yet extending this, as shown in this review, is a necessary focus on elements' collectivity of process, diversity of actors, and relationality whereby new relational channels or configurations often need to be established; however, the coordinating infrastructure to achieve this is varied, temporary and also under-theorized. These elements of social innovation lend themselves to three theoretical lenses of social innovation, appearing with different emphasis.

In each of the following chapters, I explore in detail what I identify as three lenses for theorizing social innovation, with varying ontological positions: social innovation as social value creation, capture and distribution (Chapter 2); social innovation as polysemous and irreducible to a single definition (Chapter 3); and social innovation as institutional change (Chapter 4). As noted in the Introduction, I then conclude with a discussion of how social innovation is a contemporary manifestation of long-examined tension between the economy and society and theorizing of justice and social and economic progress.

In what follows, Chapter 2, I theorize social innovation as social value creation, capture and distribution. Existing bibliometric reviews of social innovation reveal a core citation on value co-production (Ramirez, 1999) anchoring much theorizing on social innovation. This theoretical approach takes a more positivist view of social innovation, in assuming that there can be some objectivity around calculating, measuring and observing value. I draw on key articles from mainstream management and business literature on value creation and capture, and develop the process of value distribution as a way of theorizing social innovation more comprehensively.

NOTES

1. Chapter 3 explores in greater detail the different perspectives and understandings of each of these societal domains of activity, and what this means for social innovation.
2. Noting that whilst they are common, they are also in need of further exploration, which I do in Chapters 2, 3 and 4.

REFERENCES

Algoso, D. (2015). Feeling frustrated by your job in development? Become an extrapreneur. *The Guardian*, 1 September.
Anderson, J. and Markides, C. (2007). Strategic innovation at the base of the pyramid. *MIT Sloan Management Review*, **49**(1), 83–8.
Ansari, S., Munir, K. and Gregg, T. (2012). Impact at the 'bottom of the pyramid': the role of social capital in capability development and community empowerment. *Journal of Management Studies*, **49**(4), 813–42.
Battilana, J. and Lee, M. (2014). Advancing research on hybrid organizing: insights from the study of social enterprises. *Academy of Management Annals*, **8**(1), 397–441.

Benneworth, P. and Cunha, J. (2015). Universities' contributions to social innovation: reflections in theory & practice. *European Journal of Innovation Management*, **18**(4), 508–27.

Cajaiba-Santana, G. (2013). Image construction in non-profit organizations: a discursive analysis. *Academy of Management Proceedings*, **2013**(1).

Cajaiba-Santana, G. (2014). Social innovation: moving the field forward. A conceptual framework. *Technological Forecasting and Social Change*, **82**, 42–51.

Campbell, J.L. (2004). *Institutional Change and Globalization*. Princeton, NJ: Princeton University Press.

Clegg, S.R., Courpasson, D. and Phillips, N. (2006). *Power and Organizations*. Thousand Oaks, CA: SAGE Publications.

Drucker, P.F. (1987). Social innovation – management's new dimension. *Long Range Planning*, **20**(6), 29–34.

Edwards-Schachter, M. and Wallace, M.L. (2017). 'Shaken, but not stirred': sixty years of defining social innovation. *Technological Forecasting and Social Change*, **119**, 64–79.

Elkington, J. and Hartigan, P. (2008). *The Power of Unreasonable People: How Social Entrepreneurs Create Markets that Change the World*. Boston, MA: Harvard Business Press.

George, G., McGahan, A.M. and Prabhu, J. (2012). Innovation for inclusive growth: towards a theoretical framework and a research agenda. *Journal of Management Studies*, **49**(4), 661–83.

Hall, J., Matos, S., Sheehan, L. and Silvestre, B. (2012). Entrepreneurship and innovation at the base of the pyramid: a recipe for inclusive growth or social exclusion? *Journal of Management Studies*, **49**(4), 785–812.

Halme, M., Lindeman, S. and Linna, P. (2012). Innovation for inclusive business: intrapreneurial bricolage in multinational corporations. *Journal of Management Studies*, **49**(4), 743–84.

Hargrave, T.J. and Van de Ven, A.H. (2006). A collective action model of institutional innovation. *Academy of Management Review*, **31**(4), 864–88.

Hazel, K.L. and Onaga, E. (2003). Experimental social innovation and dissemination: the promise and its delivery. *American Journal of Community Psychology*, **32**(3–4), 285–94.

Kanter, R.M. (1999). From spare change to real change. The social sector as a beta site for business innovation. *Harvard Business Review*, **77**(3), 122–32.

Lawrence, T.B., Dover, G. and Gallagher, B. (2014). Managing social innovation. In M. Dodgson, D. Gann and N. Phillips (eds), *The Oxford Handbook of Innovation Management*. Oxford: Oxford University Press, pp. 316–34.

Logue, D. and Grimes, M. (2018). Platforms for the people: the cultivation of institutional infrastructure for social innovation. Working paper.

Logue, D., McAllister, G. and Schweitzer, J. (2017). Social entrepreneurship and impact investing report. Report prepared for innovationXchange, Department of Foreign Affairs and Trade by the University of Technology Sydney. Accessed at: https://www.uts.edu.au/sites/default/files/article/downloads/UTS%20SEIII%20Research%20Report_2017.pdf.

McCarthy, J.D. and Zald, M.N. (1977). Resource mobilization and social movements: a partial theory. *American Journal of Sociology*, **82**(6), 1212–41.

McGowan, K. and Westley, F. (2015). At the root of change: the history of social innovation. In A. Nicholls, J. Simon and M. Gabriel (eds), *New Frontiers in Social Innovation Research*. London: Palgrave Macmillan.

Moulaert, F., MacCallum, D., Mehmood, A. and Hamdouch, A. (2013). *Handbook of Social Innovation*. Cheltenham, UK and Northampton, MA, USA: Edward Elgar Publishing.

Moulaert, F., Martinelli, F., Swyngedouw, E. and Gonzalez, S. (2005). Towards alternative model(s) of local innovation. *Urban Studies*, **42**(11), 1969–90.

Mulgan, G. (2006). The process of social innovation. *Innovations*, Spring, pp. 145–62.

Mulgan, G., Tucker, S., Ali, R. and Sanders, B. (2007). *Social Innovation: What it is, why it matters and how it can be accelerated*. Accessed at: https://youngfoundation.org/publications/social-innovation-what-it-is-why-it-matters-how-it-can-be-accelerated/.

Mumford, M.D. (2002). Social innovation: ten cases from Benjamin Franklin. *Creativity Research Journal*, **14**(2), 253–66.

Nicholls, A.M. and Murdock, A. (2012). *Social Innovation. Blurring Boundaries to Reconfigure Markets*. New York: Palgrave Macmillan.

OECD (2000). *OECD LEED Forum on Social Innovations*. Accessed at: http://www.oecd.org/fr/cfe/leed/forum-social-innovations.htm.

Olsen, M. and Boxenbaum, E. (2009). Bottom-of-the-pyramid: organizational barriers to implementation. *California Management Review*, **51**(4), 100–125.

Phillips, W., Lee, H., Ghobadian, A., O'Regan, N. and James, P. (2015). Social innovation and social entrepreneurship: a systematic review. *Group & Organization Management*, **40**(3), 428–61.

Phills, J.A.J., Deiglmeier, K. and Miller, D.T. (2008). Rediscovering social innovation. *Stanford Social Innovation Review*, **6**(4), 34–43.

Pol, E. and Ville, S. (2009). Social innovation: buzz word or enduring term? *The Journal of Socio-Economics*, **38**(6), 878–85.

Porter, M. and Kramer, M. (2011). Creating shared value: how to reinvent capitalism – and unleash a wave of innovation and growth. *Harvard Business Review*, January–February, 1–17.

Prahalad, C.K. (2012). Bottom of the pyramid as a source of breakthrough innovations. *Journal of Product Innovation Management*, **29**(1), 6–12.

Prahalad, C.K. and Hammond, A. (2002). Serving the world's poor, profitably. *Harvard Business Review*, **80**(9), 48–59.

Ramirez, R. (1999). Value co-production: intellectual origins and implications for practice and research. *Strategic Management Journal*, **20**(1), 49–65.

Randhawa, K., Josserand, E., Logue, D. and Schweitzer, J. (2017). Knowledge collaboration between organizations and online communities: the role of open innovation intermediaries. *Journal of Knowledge Management*, **21**(6), 1293–318.

Rogers, E.M. (1962). *Diffusion of Innovation*. New York: Free Press.

Seelos, C. and Mair, J. (2017). *Innovation and Scaling for Impact: How Effective Social Enterprises do it*. Stanford, CA: Stanford University Press.

Selsky, J.W. and Parker, B. (2005). Cross-sector partnerships to address social issues: challenges to theory and practice. *Journal of Management*, **31**(6), 849–73.

Selsky, J.W. and Parker, B. (2010). Platforms for cross-sector social partnerships: prospective sensemaking devices for social benefit. *Journal of Business Ethics*, **94**(Suppl.), 21–37.

Silveira, F.F. and Zilber, S.N. (2017). Is social innovation about innovation? A bibliometric study identifying the main authors, citations and co-citations over 20 years. *International Journal of Entrepreneurship and Innovation Management*, **21**(6), 459–84.

Swyngedouw, E. (2005). Governance innovation and the citizen: the janus face of governance-beyond-the-state. *Urban Studies*, **42**(11), 1991–2006.

Tilly, C. (2004). *Social Movements, 1768–2004*. London: Routledge.

Tracey, P. and Stott, N. (2017). Social innovation: a window on alternative ways of organizing and innovating. *Innovation*, **19**(1), 51–60.

Van der Have, R.P. and Rubalcaba, L. (2016). Social innovation research: an emerging area of innovation studies? *Research Policy*, **45**(9), 1923–35.

Van Wijk, J., Zietsma, C., Dorado, S., De Bakker, F.G. and Martí, I. (2018). Social innovation: integrating micro, meso, and macro level insights from institutional theory. *Business & Society*.

Voorberg, W.H., Bekkers, V.J. and Tummers, L.G. (2015). A systematic review of co-creation and co-production: embarking on the social innovation journey. *Public Management Review*, **17**(9), 1333–57.

Westley, F. and Antadze, N. (2010). Making a difference: strategies for scaling social innovation for greater impact. *Innovation Journal*, **15**(2), 1–19.

World Economic Forum (2013). Breaking the binary: policy guide to scaling social innovation. WEF. Accessed at: https://www.weforum.org/reports/breaking-binary-policy-guide-scaling-social-innovation-2013.

2. Social innovation as social value creation, capture and distribution

In this chapter I take a more positivist view of social innovation and theorize it as the pursuit of social value generation, capture and distribution, through a range of organizational and inter-organizational activities to realize social change. I say positivist as I base my theorizing on the assumption that value can be captured and distributed, and so observed, directed, organized and objectively measured and quantified. Theorizing social innovation in this way addresses two issues: it enables distinction between processes and outcomes of social value creation and capture that are often implicit, explicit or conflated across the literature. It also extends insights from existing bibliometric reviews of social innovation that reveal a common core citation on value co-production (Ramirez, 1999), which anchors much of the later theorizing on social innovation, as described in the previous chapters.

Importantly, in conceptualizing social innovation in this way, it identifies the issue of social value distribution as a key mechanism that makes social innovation distinct from traditional approaches to value creation in management, organization and strategy studies. In this chapter I develop this dimension of value distribution, presenting three abstract models for further testing and elaboration. I conclude by connecting these discussions to related contemporary discourse on 'public value creation and capture' in economics and public policy (Mazzucato, 2018) that heightens attention on value distribution and the sharing of value across members and sectors of society.

SOCIAL INNOVATION AS PROCESS AND OUTCOME

From its early anchoring in value co-production (Ramirez, 1999), theorizing on social innovation has focused on both the process of creating (social) value and also (social) value as the ultimate outcome. For example, in an early and oft-cited definition on the topic in the Special Issue in *Urban Studies*, Moulaert et al. (2005) proposed three dimensions of social innovation (that interact): satisfaction of human needs that are currently unmet, changes in social relations, and increased socio-political capability and access to resources. Others emphasized that the outcome of social innovation was the core thread across different disciplinary discussions, and could be considered as any 'new idea that has the potential to improve either the quality or quantity of life' (Pol and Ville, 2009, p. 881). Others tried to encompass a focus both on processes and outcome, defining social innovations as 'new social practices created from collective, intentional, and goal-oriented actions aimed at prompting social change through the reconfiguration of how social goals are accomplished' (Cajaiba-Santana, 2014, p. 44).

In attempting to further synthesize across disciplines, account for both process and outcome, yet also provide some anchoring in management and organization studies, I suggest that these existing definitions and debates could be approached with a new lens – social value. What is difficult about social innovation is that it necessarily conflates social value as both relating to a set of ethics and morals (doing 'good', social change for the better) and as a measure of benefit that may be gained (both economic benefit and also social benefit – the latter relating to values as ethically derived). It produces an ontological situation where social value is understood as being able to be objectively produced, measured and quantified. As Mulgan, a practitioner and policy maker, describes the challenge of understanding social innovation by measuring social value:

> [M]ost metrics assume that value is objective, and therefore discoverable through analysis. Yet as most modern economists now agree, value is not an objective fact. Instead, value emerges from the interaction of supply and demand, and ultimately reflects what people or organizations are willing to pay. Because so few of the tools reflect this, they are inevitably misaligned with an organization's strategic and operational priorities. (Mulgan, 2010, p. 40)

Practitioner networks, such as Social Value UK, describe social value as: 'the quantification of the relative importance that people place on the changes they experience in their lives' (http://www.socialvalueuk.org), such quantification being necessary to make investment and policy decisions for the allocation of scarce resources in the face of many social problems.

In drawing on existing management, organization and strategy literature, conceptualizing social innovation in terms of social value creation, capture and distribution offers a new and integrative perspective on the agency and structures that seemingly comprise social innovation. It also emphasizes social value distribution as underlying and interlinking processes, relevant across disciplinary perspectives.

Traditional Understandings of Value Creation and Capture

Value creation and capture are central concepts in management literature, key to attaining competitive advantage through innovation (Adner and Kapoor, 2010; Barringer and Harrison, 2000; Bowman and Ambrosini, 2000; Kivleniece and Quelin, 2012; Lepak et al., 2007; Ramirez, 1999). While an extensive historical treatment of value is beyond the scope of this book, given it necessitates deep historical analysis and requires consideration of its roots both in moral philosophy and economic history (Douglas, 1986; Mazzucato, 2018; Morrell, 2012; Ramirez, 1999), several summative points are described in what follows. Ramirez notes two definitions of value that have become separated over time: 'Etymologically, "value" originally denoted both (i) what people have done and become, and the actions they could perform; and (ii) how they traded goods with each other' (1999, p. 50). Moving beyond notions of utility value to exchange value that dominated in the industrial era, Mazzucato (2018) provides a rich economic history of value, describing the shift from the seventeenth century and calculating national wealth in terms of accumulations of gold and silver, and the role of mercantilists in trading, to the mid-eighteenth century where economists saw value arising from the amount of labour going into production. The industrial era and economic theories of value were further propelled by the work of Adam Smith, David Ricardo and Karl Marx, resulting in economists by the nineteenth century 'measuring the market value of a product in terms of the amount of work that had gone into its production', and a labour theory of value. This was a shift from having exchange (and what was gained from it) at the centre of value production, to now linking value creation with production (Mazzucato, 2018). Certain jobs and activities were then classed as productive or unproductive; with society comprising three classes – framers, manufacturers and an unproductive 'distributive' class (landlords, nobility and clergy) who accumulated and distributed value to themselves (Mazzucato, 2018, p. 30). Unsurprisingly, concerns were then raised that if labour was providing the value, then it should receive more from the sale, contributing to the rise of the cooperative movement (and worker participation in ownership), and eventually a new theory of value proposed based on marginal utility. Here, the emergence of neo-classical economics calculated that 'the value of things is measured by their usefulness to the consumer'.

In management literature broadly, there is a blend of economic and sociological roots in understandings of value and value creation. Much strategy literature relies on the cost of production and marginal utility theory to theorize value (Helfat et al., 2007; Peteraf and Barney, 2003). For example, taking an economic view of value creation and capture, Bowman and Ambrosini (2000) describe use value and exchange value – the former referring to the perceived value or contribution of a new product, model or innovation by the target user; the latter referring to the monetary amount the target user is willing to exchange to acquire this (perceived) value. Yet incorporating a more sociological view, Pitelis suggests that value is based on perceived worthiness and that '[p]erceived worthiness can be due to rarity, aesthetic appeal, a perceived satisfactory price for what is on offer or "value for money" (Pitelis and Taylor, 1996), their combination and/or other attributes of the subject matter, perceived by others to be worthy' (2009, p. 1118). While this seems to align with basic economic and market fundamentals, the perception of value and the process by which it is created are far more complicated and vary depending on the level of analysis and focal source (Lepak et al., 2007).

Conceptually, there is much variation as to the sources and targets of value creation, from individuals (customers) to society (Lepak et al., 2007). Understanding value creation raises important sociological questions as to how to define what is valuable (content), who decides what is valuable, and also where value resides. Lepak et al. (2007) argue that value creation and value capture 'should be viewed as distinct processes, since the source that creates a value incremental may or may not be able to capture or retain the value in the long run' (2007, p. 181). In business terms, value created by one actor or organization may be captured by another actor, or the value created by one organization may provide greater value to the broader market or society itself, rather than the organization. A multi-level understanding of value creation emerges, as summarized by Lepak et al. (2007), with sources of value creation including:

- individuals: including employees through knowledge creation and creativity, producing something that is novel or appropriate for employer or customer;
- organizations: by developing or inventing new products, services, knowledge or distinct processes (or capabilities or routines), often targeting the consumer's valuation or that of other stakeholders;
- societal: as a source of innovation and entrepreneurship, role of government in creating conditions for innovation and new value creation, includes both intentional and unintentional value creation

(for example, organizational-level value creation may result in new jobs, providing a source of value creation at societal level).

In economic and strategic terms, if a firm is unable to capture the value it creates, why would it pursue value creation at all? Capturing or appropriating value is central to firm viability and competitiveness, and arguably the main objective of firms (Brandenburger and Nalebuff, 1995). Yet often firms that create value 'will lose or need to share this value with other stakeholders, such as employees, competitors or society' (Lepak et al., 2007, p. 187; see also Coff, 1999), sometimes described as 'value slippage'. When a firm is successful in creating new value (product, service and so on), other firms will enter the market to compete for this new value (market share, profits). In economic terms, this competition may keep prices down, yet also stimulate new sources of value creation. To prevent others (especially competitors) from capturing the created value, individuals and organizations may create barriers or mechanisms to block any such 'value slippage' or loss; this is an important part of value capture. For example, at an individual level, an employee may try and keep their knowledge tacit, to prevent other employees being able to deliver on a particular product or service, forcing the employer to increase their salary. At an organization level, a firm may use a patent to protect the value it has created and to create a barrier against other firms who may attempt to compete or secure (or create) valuable and inimitable resources. More recently, it has been suggested that business models both create value yet also operate as mechanisms for capturing value, where new activities may be added, connected in different ways or governed in different ways (Amit and Zott, 2011). At a societal level, governments may use regulation to protect and restrict resource use, or (co)invest in certain technologies and markets, attempting to create national competitive advantages (Porter, 1990; see also Mazzucato, 2018).

A welcome addition to the more strategic and economic views of value creation is proposed by Ramirez (1999), who conceptualizes value creation as a process of co-production, arguing for understanding value creation as occurring in a constellation of activities across actors, and not a linear sequence of activities in a so-called 'value chain'. Value is therefore not simply an economic function of utility and rarity. This requires scholars to 'rethink organizational structures and managerial arrangements for value creation inherited from the industrial era … and value creation itself' (Ramirez, 1999, p. 49; see also Norman and Ramirez, 1993). While this argument was proposed in the 1990s, it has been a 'sleeping beauty' in the strategy and innovation space. It is arguable that recognition has been delayed due to a more overwhelming industrial and positivist view of value chains and value production and consumption until more recent times, when attention has shifted to multi-stakeholder understandings of value creation and business eco-systems (Teixeira et al., 2017). 'Value' is considered as not simply 'added' but mutually co-created among actors with different values, and often co-produced with the customer over time (Ramirez, 1999).

A more socio-technical view of value creation (Trist, 1981) proposes 'value creation as synchronic and interactive, not linear and transitive' (Ramirez, 1999, p. 50). Importantly, Ramirez highlights that this idea is not new – and indeed can be traced back over 300 years to scholars such as De Boisguilbert (1707[1966]) and Storch (1823) who detailed the inter-dependence and necessary cooperation between different actors in producing value. Here, value does not come from use (as per traditional economic understandings of utility value) but from interaction itself, which often involves complex social relations, as different actors hold different roles in relation to different counterparts (the ecosystem), but also in relation to a single counterpart (where a firm may be a competitor to one firm, a supplier to another, a customer to another). This multi-stakeholder and interactive understanding of value creation also renders the 'make-buy organizational boundary definitions less relevant assuming organizational boundaries are more permeable, overlapping and change-able' (Ramirez, 1999, p. 56). A focus on interactions as a unit of analysis in value creation was overlooked until recent years as understandings of 'open innovation' (Chesbrough, 2010) emerged – a unit of analysis highly useful for theorizing social innovation.

Relating these traditional economic understandings of value creation to social innovation raises several issues in terms of processes of social value creation and social value capture, in that social innovation is multi-level, subjective, contingent, contextually embedded, and com-prises interlinked processes (that may be conceptually distinct but empirically entangled). Understanding social innovation through these organizational and inter-organizational processes of value creation and capture provides a lens to view and digest the growing, fragmented, multi-disciplinary research on social innovation, offering opportunity for theoretical integration. Yet it also raises several questions when applying this approach for social innovation. What happens when value capture is needed to address, sustain and institutionalize socially innovative solu-tions to some of the world's most pressing societal problems, such as inequality, climate change and poverty (George et al., 2016; Phills et al., 2008)? What happens when an individual or organization's socially innovative goal is 'value slippage', or rather, value distribution?

SOCIAL VALUE CREATION AND CAPTURE

Despite a rapidly growing and expanding interest in social innovation, limited research in management and organizational studies (or more broadly for that matter) examines value creation and capture from a social innovation perspective (Cajaiba-Santana, 2014; Silveira and Zilber, 2017). The term 'social' has several different, albeit related meanings in the social sciences (Barman, 2016; see also Calhoun, 1998; Mansbridge, 1998; Durkheim 1895[2014]). For example, Barman (2016) describes how 'social' can refer to a specific societal space, civil society, networks or quality of relations between individuals (social capital) and can also 'invoke the notion of collectivity that stands distinct from and analytically above its constituent members' (Barman, 2016, p. 7). Importantly, it can also refer to an orientation of organized action with positive or beneficial consequences for the wellbeing of others (for example, social welfare, social security). For the purposes of this book, I take 'social' as referring to the positive, shared outcome (or intended outcome) of a process of innovation, and not only as indicating the involvement of many or diverse actors (although it may well be) or organizations in the 'social' or third not-for-profit (NFP) sector.

'Value' also has a long genealogy in the social sciences, as Barman rightly points out, encapsulating 'a decision about quality and an act of assessment' (Barman, 2016, p. 8; see also Dewey, 1939; Stark, 2011). Value is about making decisions regarding 'what counts' and 'how to count', and doing so by determining and making claims using criteria relevant to a specific situation. These criteria may come from existing 'orders of worth' (Boltanski and Thevenot, 2006) or 'institutional logics' (Thornton et al., 2012). For example, Barman (2016) explores how a market logic produces (and legitimizes) the use of market-calculating devices in the social sector, including rankings and rating systems, to quantify the amount of social good or benefit an organization creates, and how it is distributed. This is a complex sociological issue that requires further theorization, especially given the increasing demand to demonstrate social impact (value) by governments, philanthropists, investors, consumers, from corporations, NFPs and citizens.

Some recent work has explored this matter of social value creation and its measurement, focusing on calculating units of positive social impact to quantitatively compare interventions across social problems (Kroeger and Weber, 2014; see also Chapter 6). In related work, others have focused on organizational roles in value creation, appropriation and wealth distribution as it relates to inequality, and specifically the skewing of value via shareholder dividends, taxation and philanthropy (Bapuji et al., 2018; see Chapter 5). Similarly, a disconnected line of inquiry in not-for-profit literature has examined value creation and capture in collaborations between corporations and not-for-profits (Austin and Seitanidi, 2012a, 2012b), outlining different rationales and incentives for collaborating in terms of value creation by association, interaction and also synergies between partners where they can achieve more by working together. Many articles on public (government) and private sector collaborations also highlight how these arrangements, whilst seeking to create value, are often ridden with tradeoffs and tensions, 'highlighting the different value-creating rationale and capacities in public-private ties' (Kivleniece and Quelin, 2012, p. 295). This suggests the need for further theorizing when it comes to tripartite value-creating arrangements (public, private, social sector), which are often observed in social innovation.

These studies suggest important questions remain unanswered, hindering both theoretical and empirical progress: What are the sources of value creation in the pursuit of social innovation? How is such value captured and appropriated (and by whom)? Social innovation goes beyond the notion of corporate shared value, strategic corporate social responsibility and the central role of a corporation, focusing more on democratically organized multi-stakeholder processes of social value production (Crane et al., 2014). In this section I outline how social value has been considered in existing management-related literature.

Three Perspectives on Social Value: Social Entrepreneurship, Shared Value, BoP Markets

Existing literature in organization and management studies considers 'social value', often implicitly, from three broad, and mainly for-profit, perspectives:

- social entrepreneurship: social value or social returns being the driver and outcomes of the operation of social enterprises and the efforts of social entrepreneurs;
- shared value: social value as 'shared value' between business and society in the operations and outputs of a business;
- bottom of the pyramid markets: social value in the context of international development and 'benefits' for those living at the 'bottom of the pyramid' (BoP) as the poor are regarded as consumer market segments.

Social value and social entrepreneurship: individuals and organizational forms

Social value is a concept central to discussions of social entre-preneurship; its meaning, however, is often assumed rather than explicitly analysed. As an organizational form, for-profit social enterprises are one of the most studied forms for social value creation in the organizational and management literature, despite the many other organizational forms and processes implicated in social innovation (Tracey and Stott, 2017). In an early review of definitions of social entrepreneurship, Austin et al. (2006, p. 2) note that: 'Common across all definitions of social entre-preneurship is the fact that the underlying drive for social entre-preneurship is to create social value, rather than personal and shareholder wealth' and that '[t]he fundamental purpose of social entrepreneurship is creating social value for the public good, whereas commercial entre-preneurship aims at creating profitable operations resulting in private gain' (Austin et al., 2006, p. 3). Peredo and McLean (2006) ask what makes social entrepreneurship social. They conclude that social entre-preneurs aim in some way to increase social value, that is, to contribute to the welfare or wellbeing in a given human community. Dzisi and Otsyina also note that 'generating social value is the explicit, central driving purpose and force for social entrepreneurship' (2014, p. 233).

According to Austin et al. (2006), social-purpose organizations emerge when there is social-market failure – that is, commercial forces do not meet a social need. This is often due to the inability of those needing the services to pay for them; here social entrepreneurship often focuses on serving basic, long-standing needs more effectively through innovative approaches. This focus on anchoring social value in terms of addressing market failure is echoed by Felicio et al. (2013, p. 2140): 'Social value refers to the necessary goods and services provided by organizations with social purposes such as promoting community development, advocating for more inclusive and fairer policies, or dealing with a variety of other social problems.'

The generation of social value is implicitly considered by (Dees and Anderson, 2003) who consider for-profit social ventures as those expli-citly designed to serve a social purpose while making a profit. 'Having a social purpose involves a commitment to creating value for a community or society rather than just wealth for the owners or personal satisfaction for customers' (Dees and Anderson, 2003, p. 2). It follows that for-profit social ventures must measure their success in terms of social impact while also addressing the creation of economic value. This is the 'double bottom line' (Dees and Anderson, 2003, p. 2), and later the 'triple bottom line' (Elkington, 1994). It's important to note that whilst this initial argument for a triple bottom line has become common parlance amongst scholars and practitioners, the original proponent had hoped it would lead to systemic change rather than management appropriation into 'another measure' (Elkington, 2018).

More closely aligned with understandings of value capture are the activities that Dees and Anderson (2003) outline, where social enterprises (and all enterprises for that matter) can create (or expand) and capture value.

- Procurement: entrepreneurs can purchase from disadvantaged suppliers or engage in environmentally friendly purchasing.
- Employment: enterprises can employ disadvantaged or marginalized people with the goal of providing training and development opportunities.
- Product or service: Dees and Anderson (2003) argue that certain products or services have inherent social value. These include basic education, environmentally sustainable products or products aimed at alleviating a major social problem such as hunger, crime or drug addiction.
- Production: entrepreneurs can use their methods of production and delivery to serve a social purpose. The most common example here is environmentally friendly production practices.
- Marketing to target customers: entrepreneurs can target a particularly disadvantaged market in a way that benefits not only individuals in that market but also society. Micro-finance as developed by the Grameen Bank and Mohammed Yunus is a suggested example here.

A variation on social value is the notion of social wealth, as examined by Zahra et al. (2009), who review and integrate different definitions of social entrepreneurship to propose '[s]ocial entrepreneurship encompasses the activities and processes undertaken to discover, define, and exploit opportunities in order to enhance social wealth by creating new ventures or managing existing organizations in an innovative manner' (2009, p. 522), noting that 'social wealth' is not explicitly defined.

Acs et al. (2013) examine the different organizational forms that can generate social value, beyond the for-profit social enterprise. Acs et al. (2013, p. 789) compare social enterprise with charity and philanthropy in terms of the creation of social value. They argue that each type of organization is responsible for a different type of social value creation, be that income redistribution (charity), reconstitution of wealth (philanthropy) or as change agents and social innovators (social enterprise), operating on a continuum of implementing incremental to more radical change in social structures. While this is an oversimplified representation of these organizational forms or sectors that pursue social value (Tracey and Stott, 2017), both Zahra et al. (2009) and Acs et al. (2013) view social value as being delivered at different levels (individual, organizational, societal) and by different forms of organizations, including partnerships and other multi-stakeholder collaborations. For example, in their study of hybridity and social value, Quelin et al. (2017) juxtapose traditional studies in economics and management – which emphasize the accrual of economic value to the individual economic actor (usually a firm) – with studies on hybrids, social enterprises and not-for-profit organizations which use broader conceptualizations of value. In this latter literature, social value becomes about 'the creation of benefits or reduction of costs for society' (citing Phills et al., 2008) through, for example, concentrating on the positive change in the subjective wellbeing of specific population targets, innovations that foster inclusiveness and the impact on societal groups at the bottom of the pyramid (Quelin et al., 2017). Similarly, in their study of public–private partnerships and the nature of social value creation, Caldwell et al. (2017) simply stated that '[s]ocial value is created when the hybrid organizational form generates positive societal outcomes beyond that created by either actor working alone or within its sector' (p. 907). Like others, though, Quelin et al. (2017) see a need for more work to understand the criteria that distinguish economic, social, and blended/shared value creation.

Social value as shared value: the role of the corporation in society
In the recent decade, post the Global Financial Crisis (GFC) of 2007–08, there has been increasing discourse and debate around the role of business in society, public purpose and its social contract more broadly. This social contract, especially as it relates to large corporations, has changed over the past century, where corporations provided secure jobs, lifetime employment and often were key anchors and contributors in the life of communities (Davis, 2010). Yet as corporations pursued a goal of maximizing shareholder value – to the detriment of other values – this social contract changed, and some would argue, substantially diminished (Munir, 2011). The debate on the relationship between business and the society in which it operates began to go further than previous decades of discussion on corporate social responsibility, which pervaded the corporate world globally (Meyer and Höllerer, 2010). Post GFC, with the legitimacy of big business at an all-time low, academics Porter and Kramer again argued for companies to pursue shared value now more than ever: '[P]olicies and operating practices that enhance the competitiveness

of a company while simultaneously advancing the economic and social conditions in the communities in which it operates' (Porter and Kramer, 2011, p. 6).

Shared value in this sense involves companies moving beyond what Porter and Kramer see as their traditional function of generating profit and economic value and focusing on the 'right kind of profits – profits that create societal benefits rather than diminish them' (Porter and Kramer, 2011, p. 17). Shared value is about how companies can share value with consumers, employees and society. Porter and Kramer (2011) articulate three ways of creating shared value:

● conceiving products and markets to produce (for example) healthier food and environmentally friendly products;
● redefining productivity in the value chain to take into account broader social and environmental costs;
● enabling local cluster development so that various developmental goals can be achieved in cooperation with local suppliers and institutions.

As one element making up the concept of shared value, social value is only loosely defined. Although it involves the creation of societal benefits, its scope is limited to societal benefits that are connected to the organization's products and will contribute to the organization's economic success: 'An ongoing exploration of societal needs will lead companies to discover new opportunities for differentiation and repositioning in traditional markets, and to recognise the potential of new markets they previously overlooked' (Porter and Kramer, 2011, p. 8).

As a management concept, the idea of shared value as societal benefit that also provides economic benefit to the firm has been criticized for its narrow scope (Crane et al., 2014; Dembek et al., 2016). Crane et al. (2014) argue that a true societal perspective would take a systemic view and would focus on the common good of society rather than the creation of additional profit opportunity on a corporation-by-corporation basis. This view is shared by Dembek et al. (2016):

> [I]t is indeed unlikely that any social problems will be solved through shared value. Instead it may be possible to address some unmet needs through shared value. For example, shared value may contribute to increasing income within a poor community, but it is very unlikely to solve poverty, which is a much more complex and multifaceted problem. (Dembek et al., 2016, p. 244)

In terms of social value creation, capture and distribution, these concerns over the transformational capacity of 'shared value' underlie other questions as to the role of management as a profession, and the consideration of managers as stewards of business (as an alternative to principal–agent approaches and incentives). Understanding organizational processes of social value creation, capture and distribution now become embedded in the moral-relational judgements and decision-making of managers (Jarvis and Logue, 2016).

Bottom of the pyramid

In 2002, Prahalad and Hammond produced a seminal paper in the *Harvard Business Review* that focused on how the world's poorest people could be served – profitably. This was referred to as 'bottom of the pyramid' markets, at that stage an untapped population of billions of possible consumers that large corporations could target with the right products at the right price point. In short, that poverty can be alleviated through financially profitable activity. Stimulating such commerce in these 'markets' was seen as offering the chance to radically improve the lives of billions of people and make for a less dangerous world (Prahalad and Hammond, 2002, p. 4). This wasn't about corporations having to act charitably, but about them acting in their own interest, pursuing these new markets for growth that also offered opportunity for experimentation and innovation. Furthermore, by doing so, they would be contributing towards alleviating the economic ills of the poor in developing countries.

This idea of the 'bottom of the pyramid' is consistent with 'a long tradition in economic thought, from Adam Smith (1776) to Milton Friedman (Friedman and Friedman, 1990), [which] argues that market forces and private ownership of productive assets lead to a prosperous society' (Kolk et al., 2014, p. 339). In reviewing a decade of application of the concept, Kolk and colleagues (2014) see a growing number of examples that involve small and medium-sized firms (as compared to initial arguments about the role of multinational corporations (MNCs)) as well as BoP initiatives being instigated by non-profit firms. Interestingly, when it comes to understanding the outcomes of BoP initiatives (social, environmental and financial), the empirical evidence is somewhat limited. Calculating social impact (social value) is a predominant focus, yet there is a lack of clarity on how to achieve this, and even less so when it comes to calculating environmental impact (value) (Kolk et al., 2014). Assessing the overall impact of the BOP approach is difficult given the wide variety of measures used across the many studies.

International development scholars have also taken up this concept, and more explicitly define social value creation. For example, Singh and Kathuria (2017, p. 76) define social value in relation to the achievement of global development goals:

> We adopt the definition of social value creation as an activity that leads to the
> realisation of any of the three core values of development, i.e., sustenance;
> self-esteem; and freedom from servitude ... Sustenance can be defined as
> ability to meet basic needs such as food, shelter, healthcare, etc. Self-esteem
> touches upon dimensions such as dignity and legitimacy; whereas freedom
> from servitude refers to ability to choose from a wide range of options in
> wide range of areas in one's life such as education, products, housing, etc.
> (Todaro and Smith, 2011)

Writing in a development context, Sinkovics et al. (2015) also conceptualize social value creation as social constraint alleviation. They also use
Todaro and Smith (2011) and their three core values of development –
sustenance, self-esteem and freedom from servitude – to anchor their
definition of social value. Social value is therefore measured in relation
to the position and wellbeing of the individual but could involve breaking
down economic, social or structural barriers that impede the achievement
of individual wellbeing.

> Following on from this definition of the 'social', social constraints can be
> delineated as the root causes that prevent a group of individuals from making
> use of their human right to sustenance, self-esteem and freedom from
> servitude. The universality of these rights ensures that social value creation
> defined as the alleviation of social constraints is comparable across different
> contexts. (Sinkovics et al., 2015, p. 355)

The role of entrepreneurs in social value creation in BoP markets is also
explored by Sundaramurthy et al. (2013) in a study of Indian social
entrepreneurs. They identified three patterns of social value creation
which they saw as relevant to emerging markets. First, social enterprises
add value by creating markets and adding new products and services.
Second, value is generated by social entrepreneurs as *system innovators*,
who address specific inefficiencies in current systems. They seek to
remedy these inefficiencies by identifying opportunities to cater to
marginalized groups. Third, social value is generated (or rather distributed) through innovative campaigns. Awareness-raising and education are
their primary means of creating social value and their focus is on
multiple actors rather than looking to deliver a specific solution to a
defined set of stakeholders.

What these three brief descriptions of approaches to social value reveal
in existing management literature is an implicit rather than explicit focus
on social value and consequently a missed opportunity to integrate ideas
across literature and studies. In addition, the focus of much of this work
is on for-profit models of organization and the role of individual
entrepreneurs, as compared to broader systems change to achieve social

value. While value creation and capture processes are somewhat addressed, what is missing is a clear articulation of value distribution – the distribution of social good being a central purpose to socially innovative activities.

THEORIZING SOCIAL VALUE CREATION, CAPTURE *AND* DISTRIBUTION

A central premise of this book is that social innovation is fundamentally about the distribution of value and collective impact to address social problems. Yet traditional frameworks of industrial value creation and capture (for example, Bowman and Ambrosini, 2000; Lepak et al., 2007; Peteraf and Barney, 2003; Pitelis, 2009; Priem, 2007; Zott et al., 2011) are limited in their ability to explain this important dimension of 'value distribution'. Importantly, in seeking to understand value distribution, the earlier idea of value co-production is most relevant as it 'requires that we consider a multiplicity of values, held in relations with multiple actors, which cannot be reduced to a single metric' (Dean et al., 1997, p. 423; in Ramirez, 1999, p. 55).

On Theorizing Social Value Distribution

In drawing on existing literature on value creation and capture, recent discussions on value distribution in terms of business's role in increasing inequality in society, and implicit theorizing in existing social innovation on social value creation, capture and distribution, I defined and typologize these as follows (see Table 2.1):

- *Social value creation*: as the sourcing of ideas, practices, relations and models that generate, or have the potential to generate social impact.
- *Social value capture*: the organizing of resources and relations to enact, embed and enable sources to generate social impact.
- *Social value distribution*: the sharing of the captured social value, either automatically and directly through value capture mechanisms, or through additional mechanisms to ensure distribution and collective impact.

Table 2.1 Social value creation, capture and distribution

	Social Value Creation	Social Value Capture	Social Value Distribution
Focus of activity	*Sourcing*	*Organizing*	*Sharing*
Examples of Organizational processes	New firm New technology New product/ service New organizational model (enterprise, co-op, NFP, combination) Leveraging resources/ capabilities of established org	Connecting disparate groups (supply/demand) Org model Co-produce with users/ consumers/ beneficiaries/ others/	Via value creation itself (or often assumed) Via consumption (of products/ services) Via participation in capture Secondary distribution (philanthropy, employment)
Examples of Inter-organizational processes	New partnership, collaborations and combinations of people, resources, ideas	Via policy, standards, agreements, public–private partnerships, other coordinating architecture enabling and sustaining cross-field collaboration	Via platform effects (rules for participating) Measurement practices Systems change, rule change Via governance mechanisms

Value distribution is traditionally considered as the distribution of retained earnings to shareholders and occasionally employees, often neglecting the many other claimants on the value produced (Bapuji et al., 2018; Ostrom, 2015). Bapuji (2015) argues for scholars, and especially organizational scholars, to urgently study economic inequality, given firms are the primary sources of wealth creation and distribution, and that current levels of extreme economic inequality being observed around the world 'are a result of value distribution being skewed toward some actors at the expense of others' (Bapuji et al., 2018, p. 984). Drawing on traditional understandings of value creation and capture, Bapuji and colleagues theorize value distribution based on the key insight that many stakeholders contribute to the generation of value by an organization, and so the value produced should be more equally shared (distributed) as compared to current distributions to shareholders (under the mantra of maximizing shareholder value). This (re)distribution is particularly necessary given that value (knowledge) is produced through intra-firm and inter-firm (social) interactions – with employees, suppliers, customers and governments. So while most of this activity is conducted within firm boundaries, many other actors provide indirect assistance, yet have limited bargaining power in claiming or accessing some of the produced value (see for example Mazzucato, 2018).[1]

Models of Social Value Distribution

In conceptualizing social innovation in this way, it identifies the issue of social value distribution as a key mechanism that makes social innovation distinct from traditional approaches to value creation in management, organization and strategy studies. In what follows, I present three abstract models for further testing and elaboration. While this may be readily applicable or realizable at an organizational level (such as for social enterprises), it is also relevant for applying to cross-sector collaborations and arrangements. For example, early work on value distribution at the organizational level indirectly raises the idea of different mechanisms and models of a value distribution based relationship between customers and beneficiaries (Battliana et al., 2012). For some social enterprises, the customers are the beneficiaries, such as the case for micro-finance organizations who provide small low-cost loans to women; at other times the beneficiaries are the employees in an organization. For others, there is less integration between customers and beneficiaries, and customers may pay full price for a product or service to enable beneficiaries to have the product or service for free, or greatly subsidized. Here, value distribution (and ultimate impact) is shaped by the integration of customers and beneficiaries in an organizational model, and where these are separate presents greater risk of mission-drift.

However, when moving beyond just customers and beneficiaries, value distribution is a 'complex socio-political process that various claimants (i.e., those who provided direct and/or indirect resources for value creation and appropriation) engage in' (Bapuji et al., 2018, p. 988), and cannot simply be assumed to occur within or via processes of value capture. As per the mainstream value creation and capture literature, there is often empirical difficulty in separating the processes of value creation and capture, and in the case of social innovation, value distribution. There are different organizational and inter-organizational combinations of these elements, some of which are described below.

In Figure 2.1, the very existence of the (inter) organizational or business model provides or increases the sharing of social value and

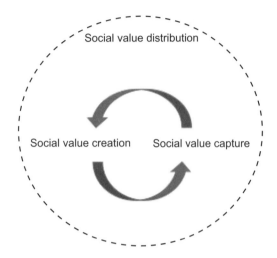

Figure 2.1   Implicit social value distribution

positive impact. This may be in the form of secondary effects, such as employment or the production of a particular product (such as medicine or medical devices). There is the greatest risk of 'mission drift' here (Ebrahim et al., 2014; Grimes et al., 2018) if the model is a social enterprise and the value produced is more of a by-product than integral to the activity; positive social value is assumed to occur.

In contrast, in Figure 2.2, additional value distribution mechanisms or processes are needed to ensure sharing of value or positive impact for desired beneficiaries. An example of a social enterprise may be organizations based on the 'buy one, give one' model, where a consumer (in a developed country or market) purchases a pair of shoes, and the company also gives a pair of shoes to a beneficiary often in another less developed country or market. Depending on the social problem being addressed (or the social value being created), this additional process or transaction may be required to ensure the beneficiary or target group is reached. In a corporate, for-profit setting, this may include corporate social responsibility (CSR) or philanthropic initiatives that are somewhat separate from the core business. The benefit of this model is that it may make it easier to calculate or measure social value distribution, at least when it comes to outputs (as opposed to outcomes).

Figure 2.3 sets out what I describe as an integration model of social value distribution. This is where there is mission-lock (possibly asset lock) for an organization or collaboration, making it difficult or unlikely that mission drift will occur. This is related to Battliana et al.'s (2012)

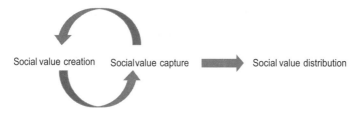

Figure 2.2   Explicit social value distribution

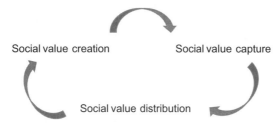

Figure 2.3   Integrated social value distribution

'hybrid ideal', a hypothetical organization that is fully integrated, in that everything it does produces social value and commercial revenue. This may occur in organizations (social enterprises) where customers and beneficiaries are the same, and so the 'growth of sales and fulfillment of mission are inseparable' (Battliana et al., 2012, p. 53). An example may be microfinance organizations, serving customers at the bottom of the pyramid. Another example is cooperative organizations, where members are also customers, employees and owners, and so the value created and then captured is also distributed as an inherent part of the functioning of the shared-ownership of this model.

These abstract, simplified models provide a start to theorizing social value distribution; they highlight the need to theorize and account for social value distribution as a set of mechanisms and processes that are not always inherent in organizational models or collaborations that are seeking a social purpose. This focus also raises the opportunity for further theorizing on the complex socio-political processes that may comprise (or need to inform) value distribution to ensure that these arrangements or models of organizing are accessible for all claimants who contributed to the value creation and capture process (Bapuji et al., 2018). Future research would do well to investigate when, how and why there may be transitions between models, or if certain models of social value distribution are found (or more successful) in certain sectors or social problem areas. As social innovation often occurs through a decentralized, open, multi-actor process, understanding how social value can or will be distributed to a variety of claimants will also be a particularly important area to theorize and it is in need of empirical investigation.

SOCIAL VALUE DISTRIBUTION AND IMPACT MEASUREMENT

Central to understanding if value has indeed been distributed is the consequent issue of then measuring its ultimate impact; for example, how do we know this value has been distributed? Underlying these discussions of social value distribution and impact measurement is a strong sociological position, that value is sociologically constructed by actors using specific calculating devices. While social value cannot be reduced to a single metric, especially if we assume it comes from interactions and is co-produced (Ramirez, 1999), the operations of many organizations, governments, corporations and collaborations often require measurement of social value to secure (or continue) funding support, market certification, trading and so on (Barman, 2016; Grimes, 2010). In this section I examine three examples of the distribution of social value and impact measurement, and distil insights for understandings of social innovation (noting that measuring impact is a core tension in practice that I discuss in further detail in Chapter 6).

First, Barman (2016) analyses market-based approaches to social problems, investigating the types of measuring devices that social purpose organizations use to measure and demonstrate their value and contribution, in order to understand how they construct and define 'social value'. She investigates how the measure and meaning of social value changes when a range of organizations, not just traditional NFPs, are seeking to produce social value and address social problems (including hybrid and for-profit organizations), and social value and economic value goals come into conflict or blend. The monetization of social value does limit what gets to count as social value. She looks at the role of measuring frameworks such as 'social returns on investment' (SROI) and ESG performance measures (environmental impact, social consequences, and its model of governance) and how they reflect and blend with financial measures (such as shareholder returns). She also looks at those who create and promote such measures, comparing the development of 'inclusive business' fields and impact investing. Here easily observed are varying understandings of social impact from simple job creation for the poor and development of consumer products suitable for those at the bottom of the pyramid in the 'inclusive business' field, to impact investing, where diverse actors are trying to build a market.

Building such a market relies on the creation of a single measure of social value in order for the market to function, as investors need to 'engage in commensurability as to the social return of their investments' (Barman, 2016, p. 202). A global leader in the field, Global Impact Investing Network (GIIN) was set up to solve this value problem, and even it has moved away from attempting to find a single measure, instead now seeking to develop individual investor capacity for calculation, based on the criteria that it decides is important for them. These devices, however, go a long way towards developing the 'value infrastructure' (Barman, 2016, p. 206) or institutional infrastructure for the impact investing field (Hinings et al., 2017, p. 175; see also Chapter 4 in this book). Overall, Barman (2016, p. 215) shows how the 'embrace of market actors and market-based methods to solve social problems ... has shaped the valuation of social good'. Important to an understanding of social innovation is the recognition that social value 'is multivocal in meaning and measure' with its proponents holding 'competing and contradictory conceptions of the meaning of that quality, how it can be achieved, and how judgment can be made – it is polymorphous in practice and perception' (Barman, 2016, p. 218). I take up this conception of social innovation as polysemous in Chapter 3.

In contrast, and taking a far more positivist and quantitative stance on social value, (Kroeger and Weber, 2014) respond to this challenge of developing a conceptual framework for comparing social value creation – across all and any type of social problem or issue – using the concept of 'subjective wellbeing'. They explore social value creation in terms of measurement of outcomes, focusing on calculating units of positive social impact to quantitatively compare interventions across social problems (Kroeger and Weber, 2014). Kroeger and Weber argue that 'the very intangibility of social value creation raises problems with comparing various forms of it' (Kroeger and Weber, 2014, p. 518; see also Dacin et al., 2010). At the basis of their model is their definition of social value: '[W]e understand social value as created as the positive change, initiated by a social intervention in the subjective well being of disadvantaged individuals' (Kroeger and Weber, 2014, p. 518; Clark et al., 2004; Nicholls, 2009). Subjective wellbeing is proposed as the unit of measurement, accepted in economics and psychology as a valid and reliable unit, and defined as 'primarily concerned with the respondents' own internal [perceptional] judgment of well-being, rather than what policy makers, academics, or others consider as important' (Diener and Suh, 1997, p. 201; in Kroeger and Weber, 2014, p. 519). Using this measure, against overall measures of satisfaction, the authors provide an equation for calculating social value creation or improvements across different social problem domains. This relies on statistical satisfaction measures, drawn from personal perceptions, and belief in the equivalency of measures of wellbeing across areas of one's life.

Offering another take on social value measurement and distribution is Mazzucato's (socio)economic analysis of value creation and measurement as it relates to the wellbeing and wealth of nations, and 'public value'. As social value distribution is considered as the collective sharing of value, Mazzucato (2018) presents an economically and historically rich argument as to who and how value is created in economies. She argues that in recent decades, much of the economic (and social) value created has been due to government investment (public investment) yet has been captured by private interests, and is far from being collectively shared or distributed. She explains how many national (and global) innovation systems have led to some oft-described hero entrepreneurs as actually extracting value from the system, neglecting the cumulative and systemic nature of innovation, that is backed by deep and expansive public investments in research, science and technology. For example, she described much activity in the pharmaceutical industry as 'unproductive entrepreneurship' (2018, p. 206), that restricts growth, benefits the few, to the actual physical and social harm of many. Mazzucato proposes a rethink of the role of the public sector in innovation and economic development, from addressing market failures, to a role in 'collective value creation', where the public sector leads investment for inclusive growth, and socializes both risk and rewards. This draws from Ostrom's (2010) ideas around the need for 'public entrepreneurship' by the state, and new ways of governing the commons. These require institutional arrangements that are beyond that solely of the market or hierarchy (Ostrom, 2010), and extend across different societal domains and diverse stakeholders. This matter is explored further in Chapter 3.

CHAPTER SUMMARY

This chapter makes the case for viewing the diverse literature on social innovation by using the lens of social value creation, capture and distribution. This approach enables distinction between processes and outcomes of social value creation and capture that are often implicit, explicit or conflated across the literature. It builds off traditional understandings of value creation and capture in existing literature, and also implicit (mainly for-profit) conceptualizations of social value. While recognizing the underlying and ultimate social constructivist position of social value, it takes a more positivist view when conceptualizing social value creation, capture and distribution models. Importantly, in conceptualizing social innovation in this way, it identifies the issue of social value distribution as a key mechanism that makes social innovation distinct from traditional approaches to value creation in management, organization and strategy studies. In doing so, it offers opportunity for further theorizing, outlining a set of models available for future testing. It also highlights the empirical and conceptual arguments around social value distribution and associated impact measurement frameworks that also need to be considered in any models of social value, and so understandings of social innovation.

This lens also provides insight into the multi-vocal and polysemous nature of social innovation when empirically applied (Chapter 3), the role of institutional infrastructure in many social innovation arrangements (Chapter 4), and the inherent tensions in the literature (Chapter 5 and Chapter 6).

In what follows, Chapter 3, I suggest that it is theoretically generative to consider social innovation as polysemous. That the different interpretations of social innovation are valuable in that they can maintain plurality, which can be a source of innovation, but also be a way of connecting diverse stakeholders with differing motivations under a common concept. I describe the notion of polysemy and how it has been applied in existing organizational and management studies. I then demonstrate this polysemy by describing how three main societal sectors – public, private and not-for-profit – understand social innovation, their differing guiding logics, and how this can still create a productive network of meaning.

NOTE

1. I also attend to the issue of value capture by corporations of public investment at the end of this chapter.

REFERENCES

Acs, Z.J., Boardman, M.C. and McNeely, C.L. (2013). The social value of productive entrepreneurship. *Small Business Economics*, **40**(3), 785–96.
Adner, R. and Kapoor, R. (2010). Value creation in innovation ecosystems: how the structure of technological interdependence affects firm performance in new technology generations. *Strategic Management Journal*, **31**(3), 306–33.

Amit, R. and Zott, C. (2011). The business model: a growing domain of scholarly inquiry. In G. Markman and P.H. Phan (eds), *The Competitive Dynamics of Entrepreneurial Market Entry*. Cheltenham, UK and Northampton, MA, USA: Edward Elgar Publishing, pp. 465–7.

Austin, J.E. and Seitanidi, M.M. (2012a). Collaborative value creation: a review of partnering between nonprofits and businesses: Part I. Value creation spectrum and collaboration stages. *Nonprofit and Voluntary Sector Quarterly*, **41**(5), 726–58.

Austin, J.E. and Seitanidi, M.M. (2012b). Collaborative value creation: a review of partnering between nonprofits and businesses. Part 2: Partnership processes and outcomes. *Nonprofit and Voluntary Sector Quarterly*, **41**(6), 929–68.

Austin, J., Stevenson, H. and Wei-Skillern, J. (2006). Social and commercial entrepreneurship: same, different, or both? *Entrepreneurship Theory and Practice*, **30**, 1–22.

Bapuji, H. (2015). Individuals, interactions and institutions: how economic inequality affects organizations. *Human Relations*, **68**(7), 1059–83.

Bapuji, H., Husted, B.W., Lu, J. and Mir, R. (2018). Value creation, appropriation, and distribution: how firms contribute to societal economic inequality. *Business & Society*, **57**(6), 983–1009.

Barman, E. (2016). *Caring Capitalism*. New York: Cambridge University Press.

Barringer, B.R. and Harrison, J.S. (2000). Walking a tightrope: creating value through interorganizational relationships. *Journal of Management*, **26**(3), 367–403.

Battliana, J., Lee, M., Walker, J. and Dorsey, C. (2012). In search of the hybrid ideal. *Stanford Social Innovation Review*, Summer, 51–5.

Boltanski, L. and Thevenot, L. (2006). *On Justification: Economies of Worth*. Princeton, NJ: Princeton University Press.

Bowman, C. and Ambrosini, V. (2000). Value creation versus value capture: towards a coherent definition of value in strategy. *British Journal of Management*, **11**(1), 1–15.

Brandenburger, A.M. and Nalebuff, B.J. (1995). *The Right Game: Use Game Theory to Shape Strategy*. Boston, MA: Harvard Business Press.

Cajaiba-Santana, G. (2014). Social innovation: moving the field forward. A conceptual framework. *Technological Forecasting and Social Change*, **82**, 42–51.

Caldwell, N.D., Roehrich, J.K. and George, G. (2017). Social value creation and relational coordination in public–private collaborations. *Journal of Management Studies*, **54**(6), 906–28.

Calhoun, C. (1998). The public good as a social and cultural project. In W.W. Powell and E. Clemens (eds), *Private Action and the Public Good*, New Haven, CT: Yale University Press, pp. 20–35.

Chesbrough, H. (2010). Business model innovation: opportunities and barriers. *Long Range Planning*, **43**, 354–63.

Clark, C., Rosenzweig, W., Long, D. and Olsen, S. (2004). *Double Bottom Line Project Report: Assessing Impact in Double Bottom Line Ventures*. New York: Research Initiative on Social Entrepreneurship, Columbia Business School.

Coff, R.W. (1999). When competitive advantage doesn't lead to performance: the resource-based view and stakeholder bargaining power. *Organization Science*, **10**(2), 119–212.

Crane, A., Palazzo, G., Spence, L.J. and Matten, D. (2014). Contesting the value of 'creating shared value'. *California Management Review*, **56**(2), 130–53.

Dacin, P.A., Dacin, M.T. and Matear, M. (2010). Social entrepreneurship: why we don't need a new theory and how we move forward from here. *Academy of Management Perspectives*, **24**(3), 36–56.

Davis, G.F. (2010). After the ownership society: another world is possible. In Michael Lounsbury and Paul M. Hirsch (eds), *Markets on Trial: The Economic Sociology of the U.S. Financial Crisis*. Bingley: Emerald Group Publishing, pp. 331–56.

De Boisguilbert, P.L. (1707[1966]). *Factum de la France*, reprinted in *Pierre de Boisguilbert, II*. Paris: INED.

Dean, J.W., Ottensmeyer, E. and Ramirez, R. (1997). An aesthetic perspective on organizations. In C.L. Cooper and S.E. Jackson (eds), *Creating Tomorrow's Organizations: A Handbook for Future Research in Organizational Behavior*. Chichester: Wiley, pp. 419–38.

Dees, J.G. and Anderson, B. (2003). Sector-bending: blurring lines between nonprofit and for-profit. *Society*, May/June, 16–27.

Dembek, K., Singh, P. and Bhakoo, V. (2016). Literature review of shared value: a theoretical concept or a management buzzword? *Journal of Business Ethics*, **137**(2), 231–67.

Dewey, J. (1939). *Theory of Valuation*. Chicago, IL: Chicago Press.

Diener, E. and Suh, E. (1997). Measuring quality of life: economic, social, and subjective indicators. *Social Indicators Research*, **40**, 189–216.

Douglas, M. (1986). *How Institutions Think*. Syracuse, NY: Syracuse University Press.

Durkheim E. (1895[2014]). *The Division of Labour in Society*. New York: Free Press.

Dzisi, S. and Otsyina, F.A. (2014). Exploring social entrepreneurship in the hospitality industry. *International Journal of Innovative Research & Development*, **3**(6), 233–41.

Ebrahim, A., Battilana, J. and Mair, J. (2014). The governance of social enterprises: mission drift and accountability challenges in hybrid organizations. *Research in Organizational Behavior*, **34**, 81–100.

Elkington, J. (1994). Towards the sustainable corporation: win–win–win business strategies for sustainable development. *California Management Review*, **36**(2), 90–100.

Elkington, J. (2018). 25 years ago I coined the phrase Triple Bottom Line: here's why its time to rethink it. *Harvard Business Review*, 25 June. Accessed at: https://hbr.org/2018/06/25-years-ago-i-coined-the-phrase-triple-bottom-line-heres-why-im-giving-up-on-it.

Felicio, J.A., Goncalves, H.M. and Goncalves, V. (2013). Social value and organizational performance in non-profit social organizations: social entrepreneurship, leadership, and socioeconomic context effects. *Journal of Business Research*, **66**(10), 2139–46.

Friedman, M. and Friedman, R. (1990). *Free to Choose: A Personal Statement.* New York: Houghton Mifflin Harcourt Publishing.

George, G., Howard-Grenville, J., Joshi, A. and Tihanyi, L. (2016). Understanding and tackling societal grand challenges through management research. *Academy of Management Journal*, **59**(6), 1880–95.

Grimes, M. (2010). Strategic sensemaking within funding relationships: the effects of performance measurement on organizational identity in the social sector. *Entrepreneurship Theory and Practice*, **34**(4), 763–83.

Grimes, M.G., Gehman, J. and Cao, K. (2018). Positively deviant: identity work through B Corporation certification. *Journal of Business Venturing*, **33**(2), 130–48.

Helfat, C.E., Finkelstein, S., Mitchell, W., Peteraf, M., Singh, H., Teece, D. and Winter, S.G. (2007). *Dynamic Capabilities: Understanding Strategic Change in Organizations.* Oxford: Wiley-Blackwell.

Hinings, C.R., Logue, D.M. and Zietsma, C. (2017). Fields, institutional infrastructure and governance. In R. Greenwood, C. Oliver, T.B. Lawrence and R.E. Meyer (eds), *The SAGE Handbook of Organizational Institutionalism.* Thousand Oaks, CA: SAGE Publications.

Jarvis, W.P. and Logue, D. (2016). Cultivating moral-relational judgement in business education: the merits and practicalities of Aristotle's phronesis. *Journal of Business Ethics Education*, **13**, 349–72.

Kivleniece, I. and Quelin, B.V. (2012). Creating and capturing value in public–private ties: a private actor's perspective. *Academy of Management Review*, **37**(2), 272–99.

Kolk, A., Rivera-Santos, M. and Rufin, C. (2014). Reviewing a decade of research on the 'base/bottom of the pyramid' (BOP) concept. *Business & Society*, **53**(3), 338–77.

Kroeger, A. and Weber, C. (2014). Developing a conceptual framework for comparing social value creation. *Academy of Management Review*, **39**(4), 513–40.

Lepak, D.P., Smith, K.G. and Taylor, M.S. (2007). Value creation and value capture: a multilevel perspective. *Academy of Management Review*, **32**(1), 180–94.

Mansbridge, J. (1998). On the contested nature of the public good. In W. Powell and E.S. Clemens (eds), *Private Action and the Public Good.* New Haven, CT: Yale University, pp. 3–19.

Mazzucato, M. (2018). *The Value of Everything: Making and Taking in the Global Economy.* Harmondsworth: Penguin.

Meyer, R.E. and Höllerer, M.A. (2010). Meaning structures in a contested issue field: a topographic map of shareholder value in Austria. *Academy of Management Journal*, **53**(6), 1241–62.

Morrell, K. (2012). *Organization, Society and Politics: An Aristotelian Perspective.* London: Palgrave Macmillan.

Moulaert, F., Martinelli, F., Swyngedouw, E. and Gonzalez, S. (2005). Towards alternative model(s) of local innovation. *Urban Studies*, **42**(11), 1969–90.

Mulgan, G. (2010). Measuring social value. *Stanford Social Innovation Review*, **8**(3), 38–43.

Munir, K.A. (2011). Financial crisis 2008–2009: what does the silence of institutional theorists tell us? *Journal of Management Inquiry*, **20**(2), 114–17.

Nicholls, A. (2009). 'We do good things, don't we?': 'blended value accounting' in social entrepreneurship. *Accounting, Organizations and Society*, **34**(6), 755–69.

Norman, R. and Ramirez, R. (1993). From value chain to value constellations: designing interactive strategy. *Harvard Business Review*, July–August, 65–77.

Ostrom, E. (2010). Beyond markets and states: polycentric governance of complex economic systems. *American Economic Review*, **100**(3), 641–72.

Ostrom, E. (2015). *Governing the Commons*. Cambridge: Cambridge University Press.

Peredo, A.M. and McLean, M. (2006). Social entrepreneurship: a critical review of the concept. *Journal of World Business*, **41**(1), 56–65.

Peteraf, M.A. and Barney, J.B. (2003). Unravelling the resource-based tangle. *Managerial and Decision Economics*, **24**(4), 309–23.

Phills, J.A.J., Deiglmeier, K. and Miller, D.T. (2008). Rediscovering social innovation. *Stanford Social Innovation Review*, **6**(4), 34–43.

Pitelis, C.N. (2009). The co-evolution of organizational value capture, value creation and sustainable advantage. *Organization Studies*, **30**(10), 1115–39.

Pitelis, C. and Taylor, S. (1996). From generic strategies to value for money in hypercompetitive environments. *Journal of General Management*, **21**(4), 45–61.

Pol, E. and Ville, S. (2009). Social innovation: buzz word or enduring term? *The Journal of Socio-Economics*, **38**(6), 878–85.

Porter, M.E. (1990). New global strategies for competitive advantage. *Planning Review*, **18**(3), 4–14.

Porter, M. and Kramer, M. (2011). Creating shared value: how to reinvent capitalism – and unleash a wave of innovation and growth. *Harvard Business Review*, January–February, 1–17.

Prahalad, C.K. and Hammond, A. (2002). Serving the world's poor, profitably. *Harvard Business Review*, **80**(9), 48–59.

Priem, R.L. (2007). A consumer perspective on value creation. *Academy of Management Review*, **32**(1), 219–35.

Quelin, B., Kivleniece, I. and Lazzarini, S. (2017). Public–private collaboration, hybridity and social value: towards new theoretical perspective. *Journal of Management Studies*, **54**(6), 763–92.

Ramirez, R. (1999). Value co-production: intellectual origins and implications for practice and research. *Strategic Management Journal*, **20**(1), 49–65.

Silveira, F.F. and Zilber, S.N. (2017). Is social innovation about innovation? A bibliometric study identifying the main authors, citations and co-citations over 20 years. *International Journal of Entrepreneurship and Innovation Management*, **21**(6), 459–84.

Singh, A. and Kathuria, L.M. (2017). Role of innovation in social value creation at bottom of the pyramid. *International Journal of Business Innovation and Research*, **13**(1), 68–91.

Sinkovics, N., Sinkovics, R.R., Hoque, S.F. and Czaban, L. (2015). A reconceptualisation of social value creation as social constraint alleviation. *Critical Perspectives on International Business*, **11**(3/4), 340–63.

Smith, A. (1776). *An Inquiry into the Nature and Causes of the Wealth of Nations*. London: W. Strahan and T. Cadell.

Stark, D. (2011). What's valuable. In P. Aspers and J. Beckert (eds), *The Worth of Goods: Valuation and Pricing in the Economy*. Oxford: Oxford University Press.

Storch, H. (1823). *Cours D'Economie Politique*. Paris: Aillaud.

Sundaramurthy, C., Musteen, M. and Randel, A.E. (2013). Social value creation: a qualitative study of Indian social entrepreneurs. *Journal of Developmental Entrepreneurship*, **18**(2).

Teixeira, A.A., Vieira, P.C. and Abreu, A.P. (2017). Sleeping beauties and their princes in innovation studies. *Scientometrics*, **110**(2), 541–80.

Thornton, P.H., Ocasio, W. and Lounsbury, M. (2012). *The Institutional Logics Perspective: A New Approach to Culture, Structure, and Process*. Oxford: Oxford University Press.

Todaro, M. and Smith, S. (2011). *Economic Development*. Boston, MA: Addison-Wesley, Pearson.

Tracey, P. and Stott, N. (2017). Social innovation: a window on alternative ways of organizing and innovating. *Innovation*, **19**(1), 51–60.

Trist, E. (1981). *The Socio-technical Perspective: The Evolution of Socio-technical Systems as a Conceptual Framework and as an Action Research Paradigm*. New York: Wiley & Sons.

Zahra, S.A., Gedajlovic, E., Neubaum, D.O. and Shulman, J.M. (2009). A typology of social entrepreneurs: motives, search processes and ethical challenges. *Journal of Business Venturing*, **24**(5), 519–32.

Zott, C., Amit, R. and Massa, L. (2011). The business model: recent developments and future research. *Journal of Management*, **37**(4), 1019–42.

3.   Social innovation as polysemous

In this chapter I explore social innovation as polysemous. There are two main arguments in this chapter. First, that social innovation itself as a term is polysemic, and that it is therefore valuable to embrace this polysemy as this actually provides the grist for the associated action. Second, understanding social innovation as polysemous increases attention to how three domains in society associated with social innovation (public, private and not-for-profit sectors) bring different meanings, values and structures, particularly important when examining social innovation empirically and navigating cross-sector settings and collaborations. For social innovation, the difference in understanding is both a source and a barrier for social innovation.

WHY THEORIZE SOCIAL INNOVATION AS POLYSEMOUS?

As demonstrated in Chapter 1, social innovation as a term and concept is of interest to many academic disciplines, and also many sectors of society given its perceived role in addressing social and environmental problems. As such, social innovation has multiple meanings, and as a concept is polysemous. Social innovation is susceptible to polysemy, but this need not be a constraint. In this chapter I make three arguments as to the benefits of theorizing social innovation as polysemous: (1) it recognizes core characteristics of social innovation across fields in contrast to pursuing definitional precision; (2) some plurality and variation in meaning actually is generative for the practice (and purpose) of social innovation; and (3) this recognition highlights the social construction of social innovation, and so the role that multi-vocal power plays in constructing and prioritizing social problems and their solutions. After all, innovation often comes from the borrowing, translation and contestation of different ideas from different groups, and this is particularly so when trying to address societal 'wicked' problems that are cross-sectoral, multi-level and multi-disciplinary.

In this chapter I describe the idea of polysemous concepts. I then look at three main societal sectors engaging in social innovation from across the literature: private sector, public sector and not-for-profit sector. In examining how these sectors approach social innovation, I compare and argue how recognizing these differences in meaning and approach can be generative for theorizing social innovation. I then examine what this may mean for social innovation as it occurs in the cross-sectoral partnerships often necessary to address social and environmental problems. I conclude with a discussion on how conceptualizing social innovation as polysemous also requires attention to the multi-constructions of social problems and solutions (and their prioritizations) and the role of power in whether multiple meanings or views of problems and solutions are manifested.

POLYSEMY AND POLYSEMIC CONCEPTS

Polysemy is the phenomenon whereby a single word form is associated with two or several related meanings. Polysemy is a topic of relevance to linguistic and philosophical debates regarding lexical meaning representation and compositional semantics, and is the subject of renewed study and focus in psycholinguistics (Vincente, 2018). According to the *Oxford Research Encyclopedia of Linguistics*,[1] polysemy is pervasive in natural languages, and affects both content and function words. Linguists have long examined the lexical component of language systems that makes them susceptible to polysemy, and why users use the same word to refer to different things or properties. While it may not be difficult when using polysemous words during verbal communication to ascertain a particular intent or meaning, given the context in which it is spoken, for linguists, philosophers and psycholinguists, polysemic words present other theoretical and empirical difficulties. For example, this raises the questions of: '(i) the representation, access, and storage of polysemous senses in the mental lexicon; (ii) how to deal with polysemous words in a compositional theory of meaning; and (iii) how novel senses of a word arise and are understood in the course of communication'.[2] Important for understanding and theorizing 'social innovation' as a polysemous concept is the linguistic focus on how lexical meanings get extended into different senses, and the processes and mechanisms involved, and indeed, in the case of social innovation, the ultimate impacts on action (Evans, 2009; Falkum and Vincente, 2015).

A polysemous concept is one with a central origin yet which produces varied interpretations, thereby forming a network of meaning across different groups (Fillmore and Atkins, 2000). It is this 'network of meaning' – its production and sustainability – that is important in cross-sector and cross-discipline settings of social innovation in particular. It is also important in highlighting the different views that may (or may not) be held on particular definitions and prioritizations of perceived social problems and their perceived solutions.

APPLICATIONS OF POLYSEMY

Scholars in business, management, information and knowledge management, and marketing and advertising, have recognized the application and role of polysemy (Puntoni et al., 2013). For example, in marketing, Puntoni et al. (2013) describe polysemy as occurring when people generate basic understandings of the same message, specifically that 'polysemy can be synchronic – where an advertisement means different things to different groups at a particular point in time – or diachronic – where the meaning of an advertisement changes for the same audience over time' (Puntoni et al., 2013, p. 58). Importantly, for theorizing social innovation, the authors argue that polysemy can be purposeful or strategic, where advertisers deliberately design advertisements to support multiple interpretations.

Application of the concept of polysemy has particularly resonated with those examining organizational change (Brown and Humphreys, 2006; Brown, 1998; Collins and Rainwater, 2005; Currie and Brown, 2003). Polysemy is used to demonstrate and explain how the same organizational change event can be interpreted differently by groups within the organization, who then use their 'story' of the event for political purposes and legitimation of their position. For example, in Brown's (1998) study of a hospital implementing a new IT system, three groups' narratives are identified to illustrate how those involved in an IT system implementation sought retrospectively to make sense of events in ways that legitimated their actions and protected their interests. Brown uses interview data to construct a narrative about the change from the perspective of each group, unpacking espoused and latent motivations. For example, the espoused motivation of each group centres on the idea of 'quality care' and improving quality of care for patients and clinical and financial outcomes for the hospital. However, their latent motivations are recognized as the ward (save doctor and nursing staff time while making minimal adjustments to work practices); the laboratory (retain existing IT systems, retain existing work practices); and the IT project team (advance careers, and increase the dependency of the hospital on IT under our control).

While we can see here a version of polysemy, as different meanings are attached to the concept of 'quality of care', we can also see how researchers need to identify the plurality of views in their investigations. Similar studies by Brown and Humphreys (2006) and Currie and Brown (2003) – all case studies of organizational change processes – also call on researchers to recognize the role of polysemy methodologically, arguing that 'interpretive researchers require to incorporate pluri-vocal understandings of events in ways that encourage polysemy to be read back into case study research' (Currie and Brown, 2003, p. 583). In other disciplines such as accounting, concerns over polysemous notions such as 'internal audit quality' are also raised (Roussy and Brivot, 2016). Practically unpacking the different perspectives that surround this notion is considered to assist in developing better governance roles and rules to coordinate quality control – the ultimate aim of the practice.

Another line of related research on polysemy in organizational and management studies is that of organizational story telling (Boje, 1991, 1994, 1995), which theorizes organizations as learning sites and as a struggle between multiple voices (polyvocal), multiple discourses (polydiscursive) and multiple meanings (polysemous). These issues are of interest for social innovation scholars and theorists, as we examine how social problems are defined, solutions proposed and implemented, and also how impact (or outcomes of those actions) is validated. There are increasing demands for social enterprises and not-for-profits, for example, to demonstrate and validate their social impact, especially in social problem settings where quantifying impact is difficult or inappropriate.

In contrast, a number of studies raise concerns in relation to polysemous concepts, arguing that having multiple meanings simply requires further effort to develop precision in the study of that (polysemous) concept. For example, Aernoudt (2004) argues that 'incubation' as a concept has become an umbrella term for a range of completely different approaches. It is important to understand the different types of incubators if you are to evaluate the impact of incubators accurately. He also makes the point that, when a concept becomes fashionable, candidates try to appropriate it in order to use it as a brand, 'even if the underlying referee is miles away from what the concept incubator might refer to' (p. 127). Gomes et al. (2016) raises similar concerns over the polysemous concept of 'innovation ecosystem', after conducting a bibliometric review on how the concept was being applied across contexts and for different purposes. While revealing fragmentation of the literature, and presenting a challenge to consolidate knowledge, they also identified key shifts in meaning from a business ecosystem construct (focusing on value capture) to the innovation ecosystem construct (focusing on value creation). The polysemous nature of some words and phrases can also allow for strategic manoeuvring in relation to those terms.

Sustainability is another polysemous concept. Bolis et al. (2014) argue that this polysemy has *undermined the credibility of the concept, leading, among other effects, to the inability to translate discourse into practical actions and to distortive appropriations of the term* (Bolis et al., 2014, p. 7). Similar to Aernoudt's (2004) concerns over 'incubator', they also suggest further research and theorizing to demarcate the term. Quelin et al. (2017) raise similar concerns over the multi-faceted and polysemous concept of 'hybridity'. They argue that it is critical for scholars to recognize two theoretically distinct approaches to hybridity, in terms of hybridity in governance, and hybridity in terms of institutional logics.

Conceptually, and to summarize, there are advantages and disadvantages of terms and concepts being polysemous or being considered by scholars as polysemous. The advantages include:

- it brings different groups together into a network of meaning – especially needed when cross-sector;
- it recognizes some concepts as irreconcilable to a single definition (avoiding wasting time to get to precision);
- it generates plural vocality and discourses; and
- through variety/diversity, it is generative for innovation by bringing in a diversity of actors and maintaining a 'broad tent' by including rather than excluding.

Disadvantages of a concept being polysemous include:

- confusion;
- it undermines credibility;
- it is difficult to implement; and
- a lack of precision enables hijacking of the concept for strategic manoeuvring.

In the following section, I examine how social innovation is made polysemous, often due to the three main societal domains (or sectors) involved in this space or activity: public, private and non-profit sectors. I consider the disadvantages and advantages of such a conceptualization, and how recognizing social innovation as polysemous can be generative both theoretically and in practice, especially for cross-sector collaborations.

SECTORAL UNDERSTANDINGS OF SOCIAL INNOVATION: PUBLIC, NOT-FOR-PROFIT AND PRIVATE SECTORS

For social innovation, both 'social' and 'innovation' are polysemous terms, relying on context and much definition (as discussed in Chapter 1). There already exist broad definitions for 'social innovation' as a concept (Chapter 2) that can be mobilized for scholars. What I suggest here is that conceptually, it is theoretically generative to not become overwhelmed by precision to the detriment of actually being socially innovative! The conundrum is that, for social innovation, the polysemous aspect of the concept is what also drives its meaning. As social innovation is often generated by different fields or sectors coming together in new ways via new relational configurations, I review how three main sectors understand social innovation. I do this with the aim of understanding how social innovation is considered in each sector but also to later theorize what may happen when these different fields come together. Social innovation can take place within governments, corporations or the NFP sector, but usually and increasingly 'social innovation happens in space between these three sectors' (Mulgan, 2006).

As such, I consider how social innovation is understood in three sectoral streams of work in the not-for-profit sector, public sector and private sector. In examining how these sectors approach social innovation, I then compare and argue how recognizing these differences in meaning and approach can be generative for theorizing social innovation. To review each of these sectors, I developed a corpus of the most highly cited articles using the term 'social innovation' in the abstract and keywords. These articles were identified first by developing a list of the most highly ranked journals in each of the three fields and then by conducting a search for articles within those journals.

Fundamental to this analysis is the recognition that these sectors or domains are guided by three distinct logics: state, market and welfare. Logics are institutionalized belief systems that shape cognition and guide decision-making by providing categories of knowledge, social prescriptions and shared understandings of what constitutes legitimate action in a field or sector (Friedland and Alford, 1991; Thornton et al., 2012). In arrangements such as inter-institutional collaborations that bridge multiple sectors and domains, there is significant risk of conflict, contestation and power struggles due to the divergent rationales and logics that actors bring to the collaboration from each domain. The plurality of institutional logics will most likely convert into considerable institutional complexity

(Greenwood et al., 2011), having major consequences for interaction, decision-making, and agency of the various organizational actors involved in such collaborative arrangements. In what follows I describe the logics of the key institutional domains relating to social innovation, adapted from Thornton et al. (2012, p. 56) (see Table 3.1).

Table 3.1   Logics of each domain

	Government	Business	Not-for-Profit
Institutional domain	State	Private sector/Market	Civil society
Root metaphor	Redistribution	Transaction	Equity
Sources of legitimacy	Democratic participation	Share price	Service provision
Sources of authority	Bureaucratic domination	Shareholder activism	Social justice
Basis of norms	Citizen membership	Self-interest	Morality
Basis of attention	Status of interest group	Status in market	Status with funders
Basis of strategy	Increase community good	Increase profit	Increase service provision
Economic system	Welfare capitalism	Market capitalism	Welfare/Market capitalism

Source: Adapted from Thornton et al., 2012.

Social Innovation and the Public Sector

Logic of the state

One of the institutional logics, or institutional orders, as originally described by Friedland and Alford (1991), is that of the bureaucratic state. As a material and symbolic governance system, the logic of the state draws upon a root metaphor of the state as a central redistribution system, securing legitimacy from democratic participation and exercising authority by virtue of bureaucratic domination (Thornton et al., 2012). The governing rationale of a Weberian-style bureaucratic state administration has these twin pillars of legitimate consent and bureaucratic domination fused in authority. The bureaucratic state, as a key institutional sector with its own logic, is potentially influenced by the contending logics of other societal sectors. For example, the healthcare field is shaped not only by the institutional logic of the bureaucratic state and its allocative economy but also by encroachment from the logic of the market for elective surgery and treatment as well as the professional logic of medical care (Reay and Hinings, 2009; Scott et al., 2000). Within the bureaucratic state, government agencies have increasingly adopted the neo-liberal approach of New Public Management, through which features of the market logic have increasingly penetrated the organization of activities and decision-making in terms of an increased attention to efficiency, effectiveness, outcome/impact orientation, contract management, or public–private partnerships (for an overview see Pollitt and Bouckaert, 2011). I discuss the implications of this for understandings of social innovation.

Why now? Wicked problems and new public management

Increasing attention to social innovation, as a concept, in the public sector literature is driven by a number of forces. The complexity and wickedness of problems facing societies (Rittel and Webber, 1973), requires the mobilization of capital from sources other than the public sector to fund solutions to social problems. This need for greater financing comes after decades of neo-liberal approaches have pursued a diminished role for the state in the provision of social services, coupled with the prolific diffusion of 'new public management' as a market-based approach to social service delivery (Hood, 1991) and the privatization of public assets. In this paradigm, there is a reduced and much diminished role for the public sector, and social innovation is often associated with social entrepreneurship and more market-based approaches to solving social problems. Some also consider that social innovation is on the rise as many governments suffer from a 'democracy deficit' (Bekkers et al., 2007), with entrenched economic inequality in many societies leading to the public sector seeking ways to engage citizens via a social innovation approach. The early focus on social innovation in the public sector as about mobilizing other funds led to it developing with little explicit reference to the role of government per se (Toepler, 2018). Yet, eventually, with the recognition of the complexity of problems came the recognition of the need for multi-actor responses and the need to find new forms of collaboration (Hood, 1991; Pollit and Bouckaert, 2004; Voorberg et al., 2015), and for the public sector, new ways of governing those collaborations.

Social innovation as civic participation: addressing a democracy deficit

Much discussion of social innovation in the scholarly literature on the public sector and public sector management has focused on social innovation as civil participation and co-creation. For example, social innovation is described as:

> the creation of long-lasting outcomes that aim to address societal needs by fundamentally changing the relationships, positions and rules between the involved stakeholders, through an open process of participation exchange and collaboration with relevant stakeholders, including end users, thereby crossing organizational boundaries and jurisdictions. (Voorberg et al., 2015, p. 1334)

Co-creation is considered as a cornerstone for social innovation in the public sector. This emerges from trends in (technology and business) innovation literature that also describe a paradigm shift from closed to open innovation (Chesbrough, 2006), where participation from stakeholders (suppliers, employees, customers) is considered to be a source of idea generation and acceleration in producing improved or new products and services, often providing additional cost efficiencies (Edwards et al., 2015; Randhawa et al., 2016).

Yet for the public sector, civic involvement has traditionally been seen as uncontrollable and unreliable (Voorberg et al., 2015), so it did not seek to incorporate citizens in public service delivery. Improving public services was done through competition and quasi-markets; in this view, service users or end-users had no role in adding value to services, they were customers and not co-creators (Osborne, 2006). However, involving service users, end-users or citizens raises the issue of equality of participation. Not all citizens have the resources, social capital and willingness to participate and contribute – nor should they. For example, Logue and Grimes (2019) describe how a civic crowdfunding platform in the UK resulted in some communities, with which local councils desired to engage, being unable to participate because participation required access to computers, the internet, a level of internet literacy and so on. Civic participation may be used for political legitimacy and to address perceptions of a 'democratic deficit' (Bekkers et al., 2007).

Opening up processes of decision-making and implementation changes the distribution of roles and responsibility, and ultimately power, in deciding what social problems are a priority, what solutions are the most appropriate, and how these solutions are implemented. For example, Toepler (2018) describes how, in the context of reduced public funds, philanthropic actors have gained more influence on public decision-making; specifically raising concerns as to the role of foundations in shaping American democracy and State priorities.

Social innovation as country and policy problem dependent

A stream of inquiry in public sector literature considers in what countries and for what (social) problems social innovation (especially when conceived as co-creation) is most suitable or appropriate (Loughlin and Peters, 1997; Pollitt and Bouckaert, 2004). There are fundamental historical and institutional issues that need to be considered here, specifically the tradition of sharing authority across governments and with non-government entities, the culture of governance and how these and other characteristics culminate in a particular variety of capitalism or societal organization (Hall and Soskice, 2001). For example, Voorberg et al. (2017) describes Pierre's (1995) distinction between 'Reichtsstaat-oriented states', where state actions are often focused on the preparation and enforcement of laws, and 'public-interest' countries, where the government's role is considered as a referee for the fair distribution of resources. For example, similar governance traditions stimulate co-creation in Estonia, yet also hamper co-creation in Germany (Voorberg et al., 2017). Jing and Gong (2012) describe social innovation in China as a tension between a top-down managed process, often driven by local councils with engineered civic engagement, and citizen driven needs. Their examination of venture philanthropy in Shanghai, a rather Western import, provides mixed results on how ideas of social innovation interact with existing social and institutional structures and relations. Gawell (2014) looks at how ideas of social entrepreneurship are taken up in Sweden, where a large public sector dominates the provision of social services. At the same time, policy shifts have opened this up to competition from private and not-for-profit service providers, which has changed recipients of social services into 'clients' and 'customers'. This again changes the relationship and power structures amongst those providing social services.

Understandings and applications of social innovation also vary depending on the social problem being addressed. For example, the emergence of impact investing markets has seen investors move into funding solutions to social problems, sometimes through government supported mechanisms such as social impact bonds (Logue et al., 2019). This type of investment, which seeks both financial and social return, is often attractive (and easier to manage) for government and NFP interventions where social outcomes can be more readily quantified. Consequently, this has seen a surge in social impact bonds in areas such as recidivism, where reoffending rates can be readily and easily measured, without minimal debate across stakeholders and for a comparatively low cost (Logue et al., 2017). In this regard, there is increasing attention from governments to impact measurement frameworks and outcomes measurement for service providers such as NFPs, in seeking to mobilize more private capital and fund outcomes rather than inputs or even outputs.

Public entrepreneurship and governing cross-sector collaborations

Surprisingly less considered in the public sector literature on social innovation is the responsibility of the public sector not only in responding to complex, multi-stakeholder problems, but also in managing the commons (Ostrom, 1990). While many have studied the transformation of the public sector in terms of the ideological rise of New Public Management (NPM) and the diffusion of Public Private Partnerships (PPPs) in the building of public infrastructure (Dunleavy and Hood, 1994; Lynn, 2006; Pollitt and Bouckaert, 2011), less is understood about public entrepreneurship in more contemporary settings of social innovation. Some describe social innovation in the public sector as part of a New Public Governance (NPG) paradigm 'in which relatively autonomous, but interdependent actors try to shape the content and results of policy programs' (Osborne, 2006). This means that governing cross-sector relational configurations and networks of activity becomes a crucial skill set and area of attention – empirically and theoretically. Such a lack of attention is surprising given the work of Nobel prize-winning political scientist Ostrom (1990), yet I predict it is an area that will be revisited with increasing vigour.

As a political economist, Ostrom's work on public water resource management argued for the injection of private entrepreneurial energy in the management of natural resources for the collective good (Roper and Cheney, 2005). This led to a lifelong portfolio of work on the governance of the commons and examination of the institutional arrangements developed and sustained for the management of natural resources (Klein et al., 2010; see also Chapter 6 in this book). For Ostrom, the problem of providing and producing public goods – for example, health, education, safety – as well as the problem of devising governance mechanisms for sustaining natural resources requires institutional arrangements that are beyond those of the market (Ostrom, 2005): 'Institutions to encourage collective action and discourage free-riding are needed' (Ostrom, 2005, p. 1).

A major discussion throughout Ostrom's work was how insights from private sector entrepreneurship (the discovery of new ways of combining factors of production) could be transferred into the public sector (and the discovery of new ways of combining the factors of production to provide, produce and co-produce public goods and services). Entrepreneurs, in either public or private spheres of activity, 'are decision makers in the allocation of scarce resources under uncertainty' (Klein et al., 2010). Public entrepreneurs may pursue 'public interests in light of, and sometimes in concert with private resources in pursuit of social object-ives' (Ostrom, 1990, in Klein et al., 2010).

In economics, public entrepreneurship is described as 'the creation or definition of property rights in ways that make private and political action more efficient and effective' (Klein et al., 2010, p. 4; Foss and Foss, 2005). More broadly, as Ostrom initially conceptualized, public entre-preneurship involves allocating resources over time for the collective good, establishing the rules of the game, possibly establishing new public organizations, and the creative management of public resources (Klein et al., 2010). While this was referred to as 'public entrepreneurship' in the works of Ostrom, it very much resonates with contemporary under-standings of social innovation in the public sector today. Indeed, Ostrom (2005) argued for precisely this unlocking of local citizen potential and empowerment to take action to solve local problems and concerns, having significant implications for the role of the State in positioning itself in a polycentric system of public entrepreneurship.[3]

A key argument in the work of Ostrom (1996) was the 'conceptual trap' in separating the market and the State, and the Government and civil society, in examinations of institutional arrangements used to manage common resources in society. Ostrom uses case studies of water and sanitation infrastructure in Brazil and the provision of primary education in Nigeria to show how a single public agency is not truly responsible for outcomes, and that local application of policy varies depending on local bureaucratic motivations. The production of a public service needs the participation of recipients to be effective (Ostrom, 1996). For example, in Brazil in the 1980s, the planning and building of water pipes went from being federally centralized to being administered at a neighbourhood level, with each neighbourhood block involving citizens in the planning and sometimes the digging of water pipelines. Being in their own backyards, this participation reduced costs, secured local commitment (reducing protests), and also involved citizens in the longer-term moni-toring of performance of the infrastructure. In contrast, Ostrom reports that in the case of primary school education in Nigeria in the 1970s, active discouragement of citizen involvement in the education system led to teachers in village schools lacking the necessary support from parents and community members. The community feeling that the schools were not 'theirs' consequently incapacitated teachers and contributed to lower educational outcomes for students. How citizens, public officials and private sector providers are coordinated and incentivized, and how they participate initially and on an ongoing basis in the co-production of public goods and services, generates what Ostrom refers to as a poly-centric system. Understanding how stakeholders from public, private and community fields come together is 'crucial for achieving higher levels of welfare in developing countries, particularly for those who are poor' (Ostrom, 1996, p. 1083).

Social Innovation and the NFP Sector

Logic of the non-profit sector

The institutional logic of the non-profit sector resembles Thornton et al.'s (2012) description of a community logic, drawing legitimacy from equality of participation, authority from collective action and advocacy, united in the pursuit of social justice for all, especially those marginal-ized in some way (see also Marquis et al., 2011). The logic reflects the guiding values and rationales of social justice and advocacy (Nicholls, 2010), development (Battilana and Dorado, 2010) and care (Dunn and Jones, 2010). There also exist underlying principles and tensions in the NFP sector, in balancing social mission with the goals and requests of philanthropists and donors, in fundamental assumptions of recipient agency and responsibility.

While commitment to community values and ideologies persist, market logic has entered the non-profit domain, via the growth in competition for funding. The reduced availability of public funds as well as the emergence of social enterprises and venture philanthropy (Battilana and Lee, 2014; Dees, 1998; Hwang and Powell, 2009; Letts et al., 1997) is creating significant 'market' pressures for non-profit organizations. These pressures have had significant organizational and (sometimes dysfunc-tional) practical effects on the non-profit sector, including increased professionalization, commercialization, and 'managerialization' of non-profit organizations (Hwang and Powell, 2009; Meyer et al., 2013).

Drivers of (social) innovation

Innovation in the NFP sector raises tensions, seen as confirmation that the need to do things differently is based on a reputation for being more languid than its commercial counterpart or under-performing. Austin et al. (2006) describe the profound changes in the structure of the social economy that elevate the importance of entrepreneurship and innovation within the sector. They too argue that this has come from market-based approaches pervading the sector, generating greater competition within the sector, requiring innovation to develop alternative streams of funding (especially earned income or revenue), resourcing and competitive advantage. Innovation is also driven, perhaps counter-intuitively, by the withdrawal of the State, necessarily requiring local communities and social entrepreneurs to create new ways of providing local services, often via bottom-up collaborations and social movements (Austin et al., 2006; Bornstein, 2004; Waddock and Post, 1991). While innovation may arise via new collaborations with other types of organizations, a growing line of research demonstrates the difficulties in conducting such work (Smith et al., 2010), including identity tensions and power imbalances. Market-based innovation is met with resistance, challenging the fundamental logic that underpins the NFP form, and collective understanding on the position and role of the sector in broader society.

Social innovation as social enterprise
In the current literature search, there is little explicit discussion as to social innovation and NFPs. Instead, social innovation is inextricably linked to the notion of social enterprise, a radical innovation (in organizational form) in the NFP sector due to its representing different strategy, structure, norms and values compared to traditional NFP organizations. It was also associated or attributed to individual social entrepreneurs, and an individualistic view of social change that is also in contrast to the often collective pursuits (management and delivery) of NFPs (for example Grohs et al., 2017).

A volume of literature, beyond the scope of this book, theorizes the purpose of the NFP sector (for example Salamon, 1995; Weisbrod, 1988), often arguing that the NFP sector exists because of government or market failures in the provision of social services and welfare support. Similarly, social enterprise is often explained as a rational and functional solution to public-sector funding and philanthropic resource constraints, or it is said to represent a strategically better option for organizations to fulfil their pro-social mission (Dees, 2003; Emerson and Twersky, 1996). These rationalist explanations ignore or overshadow some of the socio-logical basis and cultural or political origins of the non-profit sector (and of its recent innovation in developing the social enterprise form). These explanations lead us to search for narrow economic or strategic reasons for the existence and structure of these organizations when in fact they may have emerged in response to much broader and more complex contexts.

Over a decade ago Dart (2004) sought to make sense of the emergence of social enterprise as a new and prominent form of organization in the NFP sector. Unsatisfied with its emergence being rather simply attributed to reductions in public sector or philanthropic funding or suggestions that this organizational form allowed NFPs to better fulfil their social goals

(Dees, 2003; Emerson and Twersky, 1996), Dart (2004) situated the emergence of social enterprise in a richer socio-political context. He attributed its development to the decline of the welfare-state ideology, especially in the UK, the US and across many OECD nations, and a renewed and pervasive belief in the market and business-based approaches and solutions, including for social problems. Dart (2004) posits that adopting such market-based language, goals and structures provided the NFP sector, and especially social enterprise as a form, with much legitimacy, reflecting the broader socio-political environment. As a result, as Zimmerman and Dart (1998, p. 16) note, this marketization 'has put management at the centre of our organizations, corporate business at the centre of society and defined government and nonprofit organizations as nonproductive and burdensome'.

It is this notion of social enterprise as competition for the NFP sector (in terms of funds) and as challenging the NFP sector that pervades the NFP literature when it comes to theorizing (and engaging in) social innovation. In the practitioner literature, or grey literature, there is a greater focus on what social innovation means for the NFP sector, or the 'grant economy' as it has been described (Mulgan et al., 2010). Suggestions on how to be more socially innovative include engaging in new forms of grant giving (competitions and challenges), improving accountability by including users and beneficiaries on boards and using new metrics, considering incorporating new organizational and corporate forms for some activities, developing and contributing to civil society networks to share ideas. It's important to note here that Mulgan, as a leading practitioner and policy advocate, makes suggestions for social innovation in all sectors (private sector, government), seeing this as necessary for systems transformation and improved societal outcomes (Mulgan et al., 2010).

Resisting social innovation
It is important to recognize the counter-narratives and critical reflections that exist in relation to the market-based view and understanding of social innovation in the NFP sector. Some see that service providers taking the form of social enterprises have detrimental effects on clients and the ultimate social good they are trying to produce. For example, Garrow and Hasenfeld (2014) see social enterprises as the ultimate expression of the neo-liberal welfare logic that challenges social rights. They analyse work integration social enterprises, hybrid organizations attempting to balance market and social justice logics. They find that when a market logic dominates, this results in the commodification of clients as production workers, further blurring the boundary between the

market and the welfare state (see also Nicholls and Murdock, 2012; Nicholls and Teasdale, 2017). Tracey and Stott (2017) also highlight the work of Dey and Teasdale (2016, p. 56), who 'show how social sector actors engage in "tactical mimicry" – publically identifying with the discourse of social enterprise in order to acquire resources, while at the same time privately expressing disdain for it and characterizing its core ideas as neoliberal bullshit'.

Social Innovation and the Private Sector

Logic of the market
The institutional logic of the market is focused 'on the accumulation, codification, and pricing of human activity' (Thornton et al., 2012, p. 44) in interaction with natural, social and material reality. Accordingly, the logic of the market draws from a root metaphor of transaction and competition in the struggle for profit as a value, with its organizational legitimacy deriving from price competition, supply and demand, driven by self-interest, status and the reproduction of capital (Thornton et al., 2012). With the rise of neo-liberalism, the capitalist market logic has been pervasive in its infusion into other institutional domains and sectors of society, such as health (Reay and Hinings, 2005), education (Logue, 2014), professional services (Greenwood and Hinings, 1996; Suddaby and Greenwood, 2005), wind energy (York et al., 2016) as well as social innovation.

Social innovation and the evolution from CSR: the role of business in society
Current conceptions of social innovation from the business sector emerge from a longer history in corporate social responsibility (CSR), and also the belief in entrepreneurship and the application of market mechanisms to addressing social problems. One of the earliest references to 'social innovation', as noted in Chapter 1, was by Kanter (1999), in arguing the case for corporations to consider the value – both social and financial – of working in and for the social sector in developing innovations and products that not only serve new markets but provide community payoffs.

Corporate scandals resulting in environmental and social damage and the undermining of public wellbeing (Locke and Spender, 2011; Pfeffer and Fong, 2004), coupled with the relentless and myopic pursuit of shareholder value and financial conceptions of control (Dobbin and Zorn, 2005; Fligstein, 1990), have led to a growing line of literature and activity in managing, encouraging and ensuring CSR. The interpretation of CSR may vary across countries (Djelic, 2001; Meyer and Höllerer,

2010); however, overwhelmingly it points to a questioning of dominant business and management ideologies, and also management education (Jarvis and Logue, 2016). Others go as far as to argue that the overall legitimacy of and trust in big business is at an all-time low, and that management suffers from an outdated view of value creation (Bartunek, 2002; Porter and Kramer, 2011). This sees companies prospering at the expense of their communities, ignoring the wellbeing of their employees and customers, and the depletion of natural resources vital to their businesses and that of their suppliers (Porter and Kramer, 2011).

Social innovation is part of the evolution of this thinking, or rather questioning, of the role of business in society (Davis, 2013), and in particular the assumption that generating financial and social returns are mutually exclusive pursuits. In addition to notions of social intrapreneurship – that existing corporations can be changed from the inside out – there are movements that centrally position business as drivers of social change, such as 'for-purpose' or benefit corporations (Gehman and Grimes, 2017). While CSR activities may often be separate from an organization's main business activities, perhaps even compensating for the negative impact of those business activities, social innovation begins to integrate conceptions of business purpose and position into broader social structures and relations, and a wider and more distributive conception of value creation and capture. Within a neo-liberal economic context this is seen as contributing to the financial and social viability of a business or corporation.

Social innovation and its relationship to social entrepreneurship[4]

Dominant in the literature in management, business and entrepreneurship is – unsurprisingly – a focus on the role of enterprise in delivering social value and benefit, and specifically the role (and belief) of 'social entrepreneurs' in driving change (Elkington and Hartigan, 2008). A key characteristic of the literature on social entrepreneurs is an overwhelming focus on the individual, the 'hero' entrepreneurs, who would create a novel product or business model, and drive broader system change (Austin et al., 2006; Dacin et al., 2011; Nicholls, 2010). This reflects a similar pattern in the mainstream literature on commercial entrepreneurship, but while there was once a focus on individuals and their personalities and often genetic competencies, this has subsequently shifted to understanding entrepreneurship more as process and an activity embedded in wider systems.

From a process point in the social enterprise domain, there are many parallels between commercial innovation processes and social innovation processes. This is mainly because social enterprises are conceived and observed as for-profit business models that pursue financial return (or at least financial sustainability) in addition to social return or providing some social benefit shared and distributed beyond the organization itself. Some argue that Garud et al.'s (2013) description of commercial innovation as occurring via initiation, development and implementation, reflects social innovation processes of initiation, development and scaling, given that social entrepreneurs are seeking larger, systems change (Bhatt and Ahmad, 2017). A central focus of social entrepreneurship is the role of market-based models to address social problems and drive social change (Mair and Martí, 2006). This is in developed and developing economies alike, and readily observed in emerging markets where 'Bottom of the Pyramid' strategies are pursued to turn the poorest members of society into consumers and engage them in market-based trading (Mair et al., 2012) to stimulate economic development. In moving beyond social enterprises as one organizational model to pursue social innovation, Tracey and Stott (2017) instead situate social entrepreneurship as an activity that occurs in different organizational locations (from new organizations, inside existing organizations, or from inter-organizational collaborations). While they use this location-based categorization to define social innovation (in a rather limited way), it helpfully highlights social innovation as comprising organizational and inter-organizational activity (see also Chapter 4).

Complementing the body of work on social entrepreneurship is a growing line of inquiry that examines the funding of social innovations, and often social enterprises, variously described as 'social finance', 'venture philanthropy' or 'impact investing' (Hinings et al., 2017; Mair and Hehenberger, 2014; Moore et al., 2012). This is coupled with an increase in the range of actors who are interested in financing solutions to social problems, and also the development of novel financial arrangements to do so, such as social impact bonds, development impact bonds, blended finance, venture philanthropy, and civic crowd funding.

By explicating the dominant societal domains involved in social innovation and their guiding logics, it can be seen how these different value systems and understandings could be (and have proven to be) a significant barrier to collaboration and to achieving any social innovation or impact. Alternatively, these different meaning systems and ways of organizing also provide opportunity for ideas and practices to be borrowed, reinterpreted and recombined into new ways of organizing and managing when addressing social problems.

CHAPTER SUMMARY

In this chapter I have argued that social innovation is a polysemous concept, and while the words 'social' and 'innovation' have their own varied interpretations, together 'social innovation' provides another layer of semantic complexity. In being polysemous, these differences in meaning and understanding, and how they may 'hang together', are both a source of social innovation itself, and also a challenge in application.

Theoretically, social innovation is focused on changing and transforming social relations and structures, bringing diverse actors and fields together into new configurations to address social problems. The natural extension of this is that actors from across different societal domains are interacting. These different domains have their own understandings and interpretations of 'social innovation'. I have described three societal domains of activity involved in social innovation, namely public sector, NFP sector and business sector, and the general source, perspective and common application of social innovation in each domain. Whilst this contributes to our theoretical understanding, it does raise the issue of what occurs empirically in such cross-sector partnerships for social innovation, where institutional plurality and complexity arise and necessitate navigation. This is a conundrum: it is the difference in understanding that is both a source and barrier for social innovation.

Recognizing the polysemous nature of social innovation requires scholars and practitioners to give greater attention to the multi-constructions of social problems and solutions (and their prioritizations) and the role of power in determining how multiple meanings (or views) of problems and solutions are manifested (Lawrence et al., 2014; Tracey and Stott, 2017). Like other polysemous concepts, it affords opportunity to investigate more critical questions as to what sector or actor is defining the problem. How did consensus on a particular solution arise? Which voices were part of this process? What set (or whose set) of values underpin this configuration? What are the unintended consequences of organizing in this way or changing social structures in this way?

In the following chapter, Chapter 4, I examine cross-sector collaborations in further detail through an institutional lens, by theorizing social innovation as institutional change. I examine how we can understand social innovation through institutional theory at the level of individual, organization, field and field-to-field interactions.

74   *Theories of social innovation*

NOTES

1. http://linguistics.oxfordre.com/view/10.1093/acrefore/9780199384655.001.0001/acrefore-9780199384655-e-325
2. Ibid.
3. See Chapter 6 for further discussion on the role of the State in governing cross-sector collaborations.
4. Social enterprises are often described as hybrid organizations (Battilana and Lee, 2014). See Chapter 4 and Chapter 6 for further discussions of hybrids.

REFERENCES

Aernoudt, R. (2004). Incubators: tool for entrepreneurship? *Small Business Economics*, **23**(2), 127–35.

Austin, J., Stevenson, H. and Wei-Skillern, J. (2006). Social and commercial entrepreneurship: same, different, or both? *Entrepreneurship Theory and Practice*, **30**, 1–22.

Bartunek, J.M. (2002). Corporate scandals: how should Academy of Management members respond? *Academy of Management Perspectives*, **16**(3), 138.

Battilana, J. and Dorado, S. (2010). Building sustainable hybrid organizations: the case of commercial microfinance organizations. *Academy of Management Journal*, **53**(6), 1419–40.

Battilana, J. and Lee, M. (2014). Advancing research on hybrid organizing: insights from the study of social enterprises. *Academy of Management Annals*, **8**(1), 397–441.

Bekkers, V.J.J.M., Dijkstra, G., Edwards, A. and Fenger, M. (2007). Governance and the democratic deficit: an evaluation. In *Governance and the Democratic Deficit: Assessing the Democratic Legitimacy of Governance Practices*. Farnham: Ashgate Publishing, pp. 295–312.

Bhatt, P. and Ahmad, A.J. (2017). Financial social innovation to engage the economically marginalized: insights from an Indian case study. *Entrepreneurship & Regional Development*, **39**(5–6), 391–413.

Boje, D. (1991). The storytelling organization: a study of story performance in an office-supply firm. *Administrative Science Quarterly*, **36**, 106–26.

Boje, D. (1994). Organizational storytelling: the struggles of pre-modern, modern and postmodern organizational learning discourses. *Management Learning*, **25**(3), 433–61.

Boje, D. (1995). Stories of the storytelling organization: a postmodern analysis of Disney as 'Tamara-land'. *Academy of Management Journal*, **38**(4), 997–1035.

Bolis, I., Morioka, S.N. and Sznelwar, L.I. (2014). When sustainable development risks losing its meaning. Delimiting the concept with a comprehensive literature review and a conceptual model. *Journal of Cleaner Production*, **83**, 7–20.

Bornstein, E. (2004). *The Spirit of Development: Protestant NGOs, Morality, and Economics in Zimbabwe*. New York: Routledge.

Brown, A.D. and Humphreys, M. (2006). Organizational identity and place: a discursive exploration of hegemony and resistance. *Journal of Management Studies*, **43**(2), 231–57.

Brown, J.B. (1998). Management control in the hospitality industry: behavioural implications. In P.J. Harris (ed.), *Accounting and Finance for the International Hospitality Industry*. Woburn, MA: Butterworth-Heinemann, pp. 183–201.

Chesbrough, H.W. (2006). *Open Innovation: The New Imperative for Creating and Profiting from Technology*. Boston, MA: Harvard Business School Press.

Collins, D. and Rainwater, K. (2005). Managing change at Sears: a sideways look at a tale of corporate transformation. *Journal of Organizational Change*, **18**(1), 16–30.

Currie, G. and Brown, A.D. (2003). A narratological approach to understanding processes of organizing in a UK hospital. *Human Relations*, **56**(5), 563–86.

Dacin, M.T., Dacin, P.A. and Tracey, P. (2011). Social entrepreneurship: a critique and future directions. *Organization Science*, **22**(5), 1203–13.

Dart, R. (2004). The legitimacy of social enterprise. *Nonprofit Management & Leadership*, **14**(4), 411–24.

Davis, G.F. (2013). After the corporation. *Politics & Society*, **41**(2), 283–308.

Dees, J.G. (1998). Enterprising nonprofits. *Harvard Business Review*, **76**(1), 55–66.

Dees, J.G. (2003). Social entrepreneurship is about innovation and impact, not income. *SocialEdge Online*.

Dey, P. and Teasdale, S. (2016). The tactical mimicry of social enterprise strategies: acting 'as if' in the everyday life of third sector organizations. *Organization*, **23**(4), 485–504.

Djelic, M.L. (2001). *Exporting the American Model: The Post-war Transformation of European Business*. Oxford: Oxford University Press.

Dobbin, F. and Zorn, D. (2005). *Corporate Malfeasance and the Myth of Shareholder Value* (Vol. 17). Bingley: Emerald Group Publishing.

Dunleavy, P. and Hood, C. (1994). From old public administration to new public management. *Public Money & Management*, **14**(3), 9–16.

Dunn, M.B. and Jones, C. (2010). Institutional logics and institutional pluralism: the contestation of care and science logics in medical education, 1967–2005. *Administrative Science Quarterly*, **55**(1), 114–49.

Edwards, M., Logue, D. and Schweitzer, J. (2015). Towards an understanding of open innovation in services: beyond the firm and towards relational co-creation. In R. Agarwal, W. Selen, G. Roos and R. Green (eds), *The Handbook of Service Innovation*. London: Springer.

Elkington, J. and Hartigan, P. (2008). *The Power of Unreasonable People: How Social Entrepreneurs Create Markets that Change the World*. Boston, MA: Harvard Business Press.

Emerson, J. and Twersky, F. (1996). *New Social Entrepreneurs: The Success, Challenge, and Lessons of Non-profit Enterprise Creation*. San Francisco, CA: Roberts Foundation.

Evans, V. (2009). *How Words Mean: Lexical Concepts, Cognitive Models and Meaning Construction*. Oxford: Oxford University Press.

Falkum, I.L. and Vincente, A. (2015). Polysemy: current perspectives and approaches. *Lingua*, **157**, 1–16.

Fillmore, C.J. and Atkins, B.T. (2000). Describing polysemy: the case of 'crawl'. In Y. Ravin and C. Laecock (eds), *Polysemy: Theoretical and Computational Approaches*. Oxford: Oxford University Press, pp. 91–110.

Fligstein, N. (1990). *The Transformation of Corporate Control*. Cambridge, MA: Harvard University Press.

Foss, K. and Foss, N.J. (2005). Resources and transaction costs: how property rights economics furthers the resource-based view. *Strategic Management Journal*, **26**(6), 541–53.

Friedland, R. and Alford, R. (1991). Bringing society back in: symbols, practices, and institutional contradictions. In W.W. Powell and P.J. DiMaggio (eds), *The New Institutionalism in Organizational Analysis*. Chicago, IL: University of Chicago Press, pp. 232–66.

Garrow, E.E. and Hasenfeld, Y. (2014). Social enterprises as an embodiment of a neoliberal welfare logic. *American Behavioral Scientist*, **58**(11), 1475–93.

Garud, R., Tuertscher, P. and Van de Ven, A.H. (2013). Perspectives on innovation processes. *Academy of Management Annals*, **7**(1), 775–819.

Gawell, M. (2014). Social entrepreneurship and the negotiation of emerging social enterprise markets: re-considerations in Swedish policy and practice. *International Journal of Public Sector Management*, **27**(3), 251–66.

Gehman, J. and Grimes, M. (2017). Hidden badge of honor: how contextual distinctiveness affects category promotion among certified B corporations. *Academy of Management Journal*, **60**(6), 2294–320.

Gomes, L.A.V., Facin, A.L.F., Salerno, M.S. and Ikenami, R.K. (2016). Unpacking the innovation ecosystem construct: evolution, gaps and trends, *Technological Forecasting and Social Change*, **136**, 30–48.

Greenwood, R. and Hinings, C.R. (1996). Understanding radical organizational change: bringing together the old and the new institutionalism. *Academy of Management Review*, **21**(4), 1022–54.

Greenwood, R., Raynard, M., Kodeih, F., Micelotta, E.R. and Lounsbury, M. (2011). Institutional complexity and organizational responses. *Academy of Management Annals*, **5**(1), 317–71.

Grohs, S., Schneiders, K. and Heinze, R.G. (2017). Outsiders and intrapreneurs: the institutional embeddedness of social entrepreneurship in Germany. *VOLUNTAS: International Journal of Voluntary and Nonprofit Organizations*, **28**(6), 2569–91.

Hall, P.A. and Soskice, D. (2001). *Varieties of Capitalism: The Institutional Foundations of Comparative Advantage*. Oxford: Oxford University Press.

Hinings, C.R., Logue, D.M. and Zietsma, C. (2017). Fields, institutional infrastructure and governance. In R. Greenwood, C. Oliver, T.B. Lawrence and R.E. Meyer (eds), *The SAGE Handbook of Organizational Institutionalism*. London: SAGE Publications.

Hood, C. (1991). A public management for all seasons? *Public Administration*, **69**(1), 3–19.

Hwang, H. and Powell, W.W. (2009). The rationalization of charity: the influences of professionalism in the nonprofit sector. *Administrative Science Quarterly*, **54**(2), 268–98.

Jarvis, W.P. and Logue, D. (2016). Cultivating moral-relational judgement in business education: the merits and practicalities of Aristotle's phronesis. *Journal of Business Ethics Education*, **13**, 349–72.

Jing, Y. and Gong, T. (2012). Managed social innovation: the case of government-sponsored venture philanthropy in Shanghai. *Australian Journal of Public Administration*, **71**(2), 233–45.

Kanter, R.M. (1999). From spare change to real change: the social sector as a beta site for business innovation. *Harvard Business Review*, **77**(3), 122–32.

Klein, P.G., Mahoney, J.T., McGahan, A.M. and Pitelis, C.N. (2010). Toward a theory of public entrepreneurship. *European Management Review*, **7**(1), 1–15.

Lawrence, T.B., Dover, G. and Gallagher, B. (2014). Managing social innovation. In M. Dodgson, D.M. Gann and N. Phillips (eds), *The Oxford Handbook of Innovation Management*. Oxford: Oxford University Press.

Letts, C., Ryan, W. and Grossman, A. (1997). Virtuous capital: what foundations can learn from venture capitalists. *Harvard Business Review*, **75**(2), 36–44.

Locke, R.R. and Spender, J.C. (2011). *Confronting Managerialism: How the Business Elite and Their Schools Threw Our Lives out of Balance*. London: Zed Books.

Logue, D.M. (2014). Adoption and abandonment: global diffusion and local variation in university top management teams. In G.S. Drori, M.A. Höllerer and P. Walgenbach (eds), *Global Themes and Local Variations in Organization and Management: Perspectives on Globalization*. New York: Routledge, pp. 175–88.

Logue, D.M. and Grimes, M. (2019). Platforms for the people: enabling civic crowdfunding through the cultivation of institutional infrastucture. Working Paper.

Logue, D.M., McAllister, G. and Schweitzer, J. (2017). Social entrepreneruship and impact investing: doing aid differently. Report prepared for Australian Department of Foreign Affairs and Trade. Accessed at: https://www.uts.edu.au/node/273516/social-entrepreneurship-and-impact-investing-report.

Logue, D.M., Höllerer, M.A., Millner, R., Jebali, J. and Clegg, S. (2019). Navigating institutional complexity in cross-sector collaboration: interweaving work and the case of social impact bonds. Working paper.

Loughlin, J. and Peters, B.G. (1997). State traditions, administrative reform and regionalization. In M. Keating and J. Loughlin (eds), *The Political Economy of Regionalism*. London: Frank Cass.

Lynn, L.E. (2006). *Public Management: Old and New*. New York, USA and London, UK: Routledge.

Mair, J. and Hehenberger, L. (2014). Front-stage and backstage convening: the transition from opposition to mutualistic coexistence in organizational philanthropy. *Academy of Management Journal*, **57**(4), 1174–200.

Mair, J. and Martí, I. (2006). Social entrepreneurship research: a source of explanation, prediction, and delight. *Journal of World Business*, **41**(1), 36–44.

Mair, J., Martí, I. and Ventresca, M. (2012). Building inclusive markets in rural Bangladesh: how intermediaries work institutional voids. *Academy of Management Journal*, **55**(4), 819–50.

Marquis, C., Lounsbury, M. and Greenwood, R. (2011). *Communities and Organizations* (Vol. 33). Bingley: Emerald Group Publishing.

Meyer, M., Buber, R. and Aghamanoukjan, A. (2013). In search of legitimacy: managerialism and legitimation in civil society organizations. *Voluntas*, **24**(1), 167–93.

Meyer, R.E. and Höllerer, M.A. (2010). Meaning structures in a contested issue field: a topographic map of shareholder value in Austria. *Academy of Management Journal*, **53**(6), 1241–62.

Moore, M., Westley, F. and Nicholls, A. (2012). The social finance and social innovation nexus. *Journal of Social Entrepreneurship*, **3**(2), 115–32.

Mulgan, G. (2006). The process of social innovation. *Innovations*, Spring, 145–62.

Mulgan, G., Caulier-Grice, J., Kahn, L., Pulford, L. and Vasconcelos, D. (2010). Study on social innovation. Paper prepared by the Social Innovation eXchange and the Young Foundation for the Bureau of European Policy Advisors.

Nicholls, A. (2010). Fair trade: towards an economics of virtue. *Journal of Business Ethics*, **92**(2), 241–55.

Nicholls, A. and Murdock, A. (2012). *Social Innovation: Blurring Boundaries to Reconfigure Markets*. New York: Palgrave Macmillan.

Nicholls, A. and Teasdale, S. (2017). Neoliberalism by stealth? Exploring continuity and change within the UK social enterprise policy paradigm. *Policy & Politics*, **45**(3), 323–41.

Osborne, S.P. (2006). The new public governance. *Public Management Review*, **8**(3), 377–87.

Ostrom, E. (1990). *Governing the Commons: The Evolution of Institutional Forms of Collective Action*. Cambridge: Cambridge University Press.

Ostrom, E. (1996). Crossing the great divide: coproduction, synergy, and development. *World Development*, **24**(6), 1073–87.

Ostrom, E. (2005). *Unlocking Public Entrepreneurship and Public Economies*. Helsinki: EGDI.

Pfeffer, J. and Fong, C.T. (2004). The business school 'business': some lessons from the US experience. *Journal of Management Studies*, **41**(8), 1501–20.

Pierre, J. (1995). *Bureaucracy in the Modern State: An Introduction to Comparative Public Administration*. Cheltenham, UK and Northampton, MA, USA: Edward Elgar Publishing.

Pollitt, C. and Bouckaert, G. (2004). *Public Management Reform: A Comparative Analysis*. New York: Oxford University Press.

Pollitt, C. and Bouckaert, G. (2011). *Continuity and Change in Public Policy and Management*. Cheltenham, UK and Northampton, MA, USA: Edward Elgar Publishing.

Porter, M. and Kramer, M. (2011). Creating shared value: how to reinvent capitalism – and unleash a wave of innovation and growth. *Harvard Business Review*, January–February, 1–17.

Puntoni, S., Schroeder, J.E. and Ritson, M. (2013). Meaning matters. *Journal of Advertising*, **39**(2), 51–64.

Quelin, B., Kivleniece, I. and Lazzarini, S. (2017). Public–private collaboration, hybridity and social value: towards new theoretical perspective. *Journal of Management Studies*, **54**(6), 763–92.

Randhawa, K., Wilden, R. and Hohberger, J. (2016). A bibliometric review of open innovation: setting a research agenda. *Journal of Product Innovation Management*, **33**(6), 750–72.

Reay, T. and Hinings, C.R. (2005). The recomposition of an organizational field: health care in Alberta. *Organization Studies*, **26**(3), 351–84.

Reay, T. and Hinings, C.R. (2009). Managing the rivalry of competing institutional logics. *Organization Studies*, **30**(6), 629–52.

Rittel, H.W. and Webber, M.M. (1973). Dilemmas in a general theory of planning. *Policy Sciences*, **4**, 155–69.

Roper, J. and Cheney, G. (2005). The meanings of social entrepreneurship today. *Corporate Governance*, **5**(3), 95–104.

Roussy, M. and Brivot, M. (2016). Internal audit quality: a polysemous notion? *Accounting, Auditing and Accountability Journal*, **29**(5), 714–38.

Salamon, L. (1995). *Partners in Public Service: Government–Nonprofit Relations in the Modern Welfare State*. Baltimore, MA: Johns Hopkins University Press.

Scott, W.R., Ruef, M., Mendel, P.J. and Caronna, C.A. (2000). *Institutional Change and Healthcare Organizations: From Professional Dominance to Managed Care*. Chicago, IL: University of Chicago Press.

Smith, W.K., Binns, A. and Tushman, M.L. (2010). Complex business models: managing strategic paradoxes simultaneously. *Long Range Planning*, **43**(2–3), 448–61.

Suddaby, R. and Greenwood, R. (2005). Rhetorical strategies of legitimacy. *Administrative Science Quarterly*, **50**(1), 35–67.

Thornton, P.H., Ocasio, W. and Lounsbury, M. (2012). *The Institutional Logics Perspective: A New Approach to Culture, Structure and Process*. Oxford: Oxford University Press.

Toepler, S. (2018). Public philanthropic partnerships: the changing nature of government/foundation relationships in the US. *International Journal of Public Administration*, **41**(8), 657–69.

Tracey, P. and Stott, N. (2017). Social innovation: a window on alternative ways of organizing and innovating. *Innovation*, **19**(1), 51–60.

Vincente, A. (2018). Polysemy and word meaning: an account of lexical meaning for different kinds of content words. *Philosophical Studies*, **175**, 947–68.

Voorberg, W.H., Bekkers, V.J. and Tummers, L.G. (2015). A systematic review of co-creation and co-production: embarking on the social innovation journey. *Public Management Review*, **17**(9), 1333–57.

Voorberg, W., Bekkers, V., Timeus, K., Tonurist, P. and Tummers, L. (2017). Changing public service delivery: learning in co-creation. *Policy and Society*, **36**(2), 178–94.

Waddock, S.A. and Post, J.E. (1991). Social entrepreneurs and catalytic change. *Public Administration Review*, **51**(5), 393–401.

Weisbrod, B.A. (1988). *The Nonprofit Economy*. Cambridge, MA: Harvard University Press.

York, J.G., Hargrave, T.J. and Pacheco, D.F. (2016). Converging winds: logic hybridization in the Colorado wind energy field. *Academy of Management Journal*, **59**(2), 579–610.

Zimmerman, B. and Dart, R. (1998). *Charities doing Commercial Ventures: Societal and Organizational Implications.* Toronto: Canadian Policy Research Network and the Trillium Foundation.

4. Social innovation as institutional change

In this chapter, I examine social innovation as a process and outcome of institutional change. The social problems that social innovation seeks to address frequently involve multiple and diverse actors, from different fields, across systems with multiple interdependencies (Van Wijk et al., 2019). Furthermore, social innovations, be they new products, processes or business models, require change in or affect existing relational and social structures, including routines, resource and authority flows, governance and values (Parés, 2015; Westley and Antadze, 2010). This makes institutional theory a compelling lens through which to advance theorizing and understandings of social innovation given it involves 'the re-negotiating of settled institutions or the building of new ones' (Van Wijk et al., 2019, p. 887).

It also gives due attention to issues of structuration (Giddens, 1984) and thus takes seriously the idea that 'rules, norms, and beliefs are socially constituted, negotiated orders (Martí et al., 2013; Strauss, 1978), which can be renegotiated to promote social innovations' (Van Wijk et al., 2013, and that 'social innovators are central but so are the social orders that influence and pattern their action' (Van Wijk et al., 2019). Using the lens of institutional theory, I examine what this means for understanding social innovation at different levels of analysis: individual, organizational, field and field-to-field interactions.

WHY USE AN INSTITUTIONAL THEORY LENS TO THEORIZE SOCIAL INNOVATION?

Institutional theory examines social structure and meaning systems, including the processes by which structures, including rules, norms and routines, become established and guide behaviour and action. Scott describes institutions as 'composed of cultural-cognitive, normative, and regulative elements that, together with associated activities and resources, provide stability and meaning to social life. Institutions are transmitted by various types of carriers, including symbolic systems, relational systems, routines, and artifacts' (Scott, 2001, p. 48).

Institutional theory provides opportunity to understand social structure (and change and stability) at different levels of analysis, emphasizing rational myths, isomorphism and legitimacy in doing so.

Related to social innovation, a growing line of research in a broad base of institutional theory examines efforts to address social, environmental and economic problems (Amis et al., 2017; Fan and Zietsma, 2017; George et al., 2016). For example, embedding new water and sanitation infrastructure in Indian villages (Mair et al., 2016), and the inclusion and exclusion of women in the emergence of microfinance (Zhao and Wry, 2016). I say broad base of institutional theory to convey the multi-level analytical opportunities and the focus on both structure and agency. Institutional theory foregrounds a macro-perspective, the primary concept of fields, directing scholarly attention to relational systems in which individuals and organization are embedded (Zietsma et al., 2017). Despite long-held concerns that it is a theory of stability and not change (Greenwood et al., 2017), institutional theory also provides conceptual purchase for understanding the role of individuals in driving change (Battilana et al., 2009; Dacin et al., 2011) and processes of change across micro, meso and macro levels (Smets et al., 2012). As Van Wijk et al. (2019, p. 891) succinctly describe it: 'Social innovation efforts then depend not only on the will of actors to see them through but also on the institutional conditions that frame them.' In foregrounding context (institutional conditions) and processes of institutional change, it offers potential to examine social innovation across settings, time and levels of analysis. Below I describe institutional theorizing of social innovation at four levels of analysis: individual, organization, field and field-to-field.

A MULTI-LEVEL INSTITUTIONAL VIEW OF SOCIAL INNOVATION

The Individual Social Entrepreneur as an Institutional Entrepreneur

As noted in previous chapters, much previous work on social innovation is often associated with individual social entrepreneurs. These 'change agents' set out to disrupt and transform systems (Elkington and Hartigan, 2008). These social entrepreneurs can often be equated with 'institutional entrepreneurs' (Dacin et al., 2011), who are trying to scale innovations within existing fields and systems. Yet similar to the move away from 'hero entrepreneurs' in mainstream entrepreneurship and social entrepreneurship literature, there is a move away from heroic conceptions of institutional entrepreneurs (Battilana et al., 2009; Levy and Scully, 2007). Institutional entrepreneurship refers to 'activities of actors who have a particular interest in particular institutional arrangements and who leverage resources to create new institutions or change existing ones' (Battilana et al., 2009; Maguire et al., 2004, p. 657). Institutional entrepreneurs are associated with identifying and solving problems within a field (Greenwood and Suddaby, 2006).

Although institutional entrepreneurs are often associated with change in institutions and fields, they also work to maintain institutions and the status quo (Lawrence and Suddaby, 2006). As Hardy and Maguire (2017) describe, the concept of institutional entrepreneurship connects to the broader paradox in institutional theorizing on embedded agency. In short, the issue is how can an actor, who is embedded in an institution or field, even be able to 'see' possibilities for change, and indeed generate change (Battilana, 2006; Battilana et al., 2009; DiMaggio and Powell, 1991; Seo and Creed, 2002)? Investigation of this paradox has seen a move away from attributing significant agency to individuals, and towards considering institutional entrepreneurship as also involving disruptive collective efforts to generate change incrementally or radically, and the possible multi-level affects (Hardy and Maguire, 2017).

In further trying to understand this paradox, much has also been written on where these institutional entrepreneurs are located in a field and their capacity to drive change. For example, 'dominant central actors have the means to drive institutional change, yet lack the motivation and vision to be institutional entrepreneurs; while peripheral actors have both motivation and vision, but lack the resources and networks to bring about field level change' (Hardy and Maguire, 2017, p. 262), or in the case of social entrepreneurs and social innovation, systems change. On this paradox, a recent line of inquiry explores the role of emotions in generating change at the micro level for social innovation. Van Wijk et al. (2019) suggest that as actors interact with others, 'they experience emotions which enable them to hear and understand others' viewpoints, stimulating reflexivity, challenging their taken-for-granted perspectives, and partially (or wholly) disembedding them from their governing institutional environment, creating room for new, innovative perspectives to enter their thinking and acting'. As Van Wijk et al. (2019) argue, this enables entrepreneurs to gain 'at least partially, a disembedded perspective for their efforts to bring about the radical institutional changes required for social innovation'.

Institutional entrepreneurship can seek change in field-level institutional infrastructure, rules and structures, and can also lead to battles over power, position and meaning systems. Meaning systems are both a constraint and resource, as are institutional logics and the infrastructure of fields, and many times the source or object of a discursive struggle through which institutional entrepreneurship succeeds or fails. The work of Zilber (2006, 2007) and Maguire and Hardy (2006, 2009) show examples of how institutional entrepreneurs struggle to reframe or (re)construct narratives to change or protect institutional orders and meaning systems in fields as diverse as the Israeli IT sector and global gatherings regarding the use of DDT pesticide. Many institutional entrepreneurs employ political and social skills to generate change (or maintain the status quo) (Fligstein, 2001).

Looking across the literature on institutional entrepreneurship, it focuses both on specific actors (and their position, legitimacy, resources and power) and the broader struggle of institutional entrepreneurship as a process of change. A growing line of literature examines the emotions and emotional work of individuals in socially innovative situations (entrepreneurs and intra-preneurs), or when they are striving to drive social change (Martin de Holan et al., 2017; see also Battilana and Dorado, 2010; Fan and Zietsma, 2017; Voronov and Vince, 2012).

Conceptualizing social entrepreneurs as institutional entrepreneurs highlights how social entrepreneurs face a variety of competing pressures, often because they are working across fields, between fields, generating new fields or introducing or generating change in existing fields. This (institutional) complexity is generated because, as described by Dacin et al. (2011), entrepreneurs must of necessity draw on multiple logics (for example, both for-profit and non-profit institutional logics), which may be in conflict with one another. Navigating institutional plurality and complexity, building and elaborating institutional infrastructure becomes a necessary skill set of social entrepreneurs (Fligstein, 1997; Mair and Marti, 2006), especially as they develop (or change) organizations to pursue their mission. This lens of individual social entrepreneurs as institutional entrepreneurs is theoretically generative in shifting attention to the systems change pursued by social entrepreneurs. It also provides a rich understanding of how being embedded in existing structures and values is both constraint and opportunity.

Organizations: Social Innovation as Hybrid Organizing

At the organizational level, a key focus of social innovation has been on new organizational forms generating and delivering socially innovative solutions and services. In addition to changing existing organizational forms (described as social intra-preneurship) to address both financial and social goals (Tracey and Stott, 2017), the bulk of attention at the organizational level has been on the emergence of social enterprises. These social enterprises are labelled as 'hybrid organizations' because they pursue both social and financial goals, attempting to combine organizational elements associated with divergent institutional logics.[1] 'Hybrid' is a term borrowed from biology to describe crossover in species. Hybrid organizations are often a crossover of the market, civil society, and/or public sectors (Jäger and Schröer, 2014). For example, Dees and Anderson (2003) see hybrid organizations as one type of 'sector-bending organization' that is blurring lines between non-profit and for-profit.

Hybrid organizing is defined as 'the activities, structures, processes and meanings by which organizations make sense of and combine multiple organizational forms' (Battilana and Lee, 2014, p. 397). While most studies examine the combining of two logics, there are increasing calls to examine how three or more elements or logics interact or integrate (Battilana et al., 2017). This makes the phenomenon of hybrid organizations of interest to many institutional scholars (Battilana et al., 2017) given their deviance from socially legitimate templates for organizing (Battilana and Lee, 2014; Dalpiaz et al., 2016; Pache and Santos, 2013; Smith et al., 2013; Smith and Besharov, 2019).

Battilana et al. (2017) show how hybrid organizations and organizing go beyond just social enterprises, and have existed for centuries. For example, health and education sectors are rife with organizational forms and organizing that seek both social and financial returns. Even biotechnology companies are shown to combine elements from academic and commercial sectors (Powell and Sandholtz, 2012). Situating social enterprises as hybrid organizations therefore provides a richer context from which to compare and theorize how they emerge, are managed, sustained and succeed.

Some institutional environments may be more conducive to the establishment of hybrids than others. For example, national economic and welfare system characteristics are likely to influence the emergence of hybrid organizations in social services. Regulatory change – such as the creation of new corporate legal models – can also open up opportunities for hybrids, as has occurred with the development of Community Interest Corporations in the UK, and Benefit Corporations in the USA. Broader cultural shifts can also influence which organizational practices are considered appropriate in a given field: for example, NFPs moving into commercial service delivery (Battilana et al., 2017). As discussed further below, intra-organizational factors can also influence the emergence of hybrids.

A growing stream of work investigates the challenges of managing hybrid organizations and organizational paradoxes, including social enterprises, and how the pressures of multiple logics are navigated and integrated (Kraatz and Block, 2008; Pache and Santos, 2010; Pratt and Foreman, 2000; see also Chapter 6 in this book). For example, external stakeholders may be confused as to the value proposition of the social enterprise, leading to legitimacy discounts. Internally, organizational members might find it hard to identify with their organization and their role in it, giving rise to a plurality of interpretations of organizational reality, leading to conflict and internal power struggles in trying to maintain alignment between identity and actions (Battilana et al., 2017; Battilana et al., 2012). Yet hybrid organizing, and associated management of paradoxes, also present opportunities and unique advantages, in fostering novel and creative combinations of elements or identities, leading to competitive advantage or greater social value than otherwise being delivered (Battilana et al., 2017; Santos et al., 2015; Smith and Besharov, 2019). For example, Jay (2013) finds that leaders' responses to tensions between multiple logics in a public–private partnership generated new approaches to promoting energy sustainability. Tracey et al. (2011) also highlight how the social enterprise Aspire spawned a new organizational form for addressing the societal problem of homelessness through commercial business ventures rather than non-profits.

Understanding the organizational challenges of managing hybrids such as social enterprises with their pursuit of financial and social returns is strengthened by also understanding the management of paradoxes (Schad et al., 2016). Schad et al. (2016, p. 10) define 'paradox' as 'persistent contradiction between interdependent elements'. This builds on earlier work of Smith and Lewis (2011) who defined paradox as contradictory yet interrelated elements that exist simultaneously and persist over time. Paradox is a useful meta-theoretical lens in organizational and management studies because as the world becomes more global, fast paced and hypercompetitive and requires cross-sector collaboration, competitive success may require organizations to pursue several paradoxical strategies rather than have a single-minded focus (Smith et al., 2010).

Paradox theory can inform examinations of social enterprises because, by definition, these hybrid organizations are managing tensions between social mission and business continuously and simultaneously (Smith et al., 2013). Paradox theory 'recognizes that their combination raises contradictory demands, it also explores how these demands are inter-related and mutually constitutive. Social missions and business ventures can reinforce one another, such that long-term success depends on attending to both' (Smith et al., 2013, p. 425). While paradox theory can be applied beyond social enterprises (for example, Andriopoulos and Lewis, 2009; Jarzabkowski et al., 2013; Smith, 2014), social enterprises provide a ripe setting to investigate these tensions. Smith et al. (2013, p. 410) summarize the paradoxical tensions that arise in social enterprises as relating to:

- Performing: How do organizations and leaders define success across divergent goals, particularly as the same event can simultaneously be a success in one domain and failure in the other? How can organizations sustain support for both social and financial metrics?
- Organizing: Who should organizations hire, and how can they socialize employees? How much should organizations differentiate versus integrate the social mission and the business venture? What legal designation should organizations adopt?
- Belonging: How can organizations manage divergent identity expectations among subgroups of employees? How can organizations manage divergent identity expectations among stakeholder groups? How can organizations present their hybrid social-business identity to external audiences?
- Learning: How can organizations attend to both the short term and long term? How can organizations manage increased short-term costs to achieve long-term social expansion?

These tensions are also canvassed in literature on hybrid organizing. For social enterprises, there are particular challenges (and opportunities) relating to selecting the appropriate legal structure (social enterprises can be NFP or for-profit), which also determines pathways for financing and scaling. There is also the challenge in distinguishing between customers and beneficiaries. This is especially the case when achieving social value and commercial revenue in a single transaction is not possible, such as when a social enterprise runs a financial service business to generate revenue to subsidize services for marginalized groups. Securing and developing people and organizational culture is also difficult, especially designing compensation systems that reinforce both social mission and effective operations (Battilana and Dorado, 2010; Battilana et al., 2012; Pache and Santos, 2013).

Battilana and Lee (2014, p. 404) propose a set of typologies that describe how organizations hybridize multiple elements including:

- dismissing: reject or rid the organization of one identity;
- separating: achieve partial conformity or compartmentalize so that multiple identities are maintained but quite separate;
- cumulative: retain all identities but forge links between them and balance competing demands;
- creative: manipulation of institutional demands or integration (fuse identities into a distinct new whole).

These examinations of hybrid organizing strongly support arguments to consider hybridity as a matter of degree, rather than as a type (Battilana et al., 2017). Managing this degree and shift between or amongst logics also raises an important issue for social enterprise hybrids in particular, that of mission drift (Battilana and Dorado, 2010; Ebrahim et al., 2014; Grimes et al., 2018; Smith et al., 2013). In navigating competing tensions, organizations may fall into routines where they reconcile conflicts by consistently favouring either business or social goals at the expense of the other. The organization then runs the risk of 'drift' toward better-established forms, so compromising its hybrid nature (Battilana and Lee, 2014). In Grimes et al.'s (2018) theorizing of mission drift, they note that 'an organization's mission serves as a socio-cognitive bridge between its identity and its actions by specifying why the organization *should* exist and how it *should* act (i.e., purpose)'.

Social enterprises often require the ongoing navigation and balancing of inherent paradoxes (an issue I return to in the following chapter). For example, in a ten-year study of a Cambodian social enterprise, Smith and Besharov (2019) develop a model of sustaining hybridity through structured flexibility, which is the interaction of stable organizational features and adaptive enactment processes. In short, this relies on two stable organizational features that support adaptation: paradoxical frames (a cognitive understanding of dual social and business elements as contradictory and interdependent) and guardrails (formal structures, leadership expertise, and external stakeholder relationships associated with each side of the hybrid). Both of these features must be present – together they make it possible for leaders to navigate strategic decisions by facilitating ongoing shifts in support between the social and business objectives.

Related to social innovation at the organizational level is the issue of social-intrapreneurship. This refers to social innovation occurring within existing organizations, as 'change makers' or perhaps institutional entrepreneurs, try to (re)direct existing organizational goals and operations towards social value as well as financial value (Tracey and Stott, 2017). While studies of CSR are related to this pursuit, they often occur in standalone units, or attempt to make amends for negative effects of organizational (corporate) activities. In contrast, I argue, social intrapreneurship is the attempt to change the mission and identity of the organization (as evaluated by both internal and external audiences), and to have this change in mission affect all organizational structures, processes and people.

While achieving this change in mission and identity could be analysed through existing literature on organizational change, it is also worth noting that in the context of social entrepreneurship and innovation, this change is increasingly supported by a range of mechanisms that certify the values of an organization. For example, in their study of BCorporations,[2] Gehman and Grimes (2017) investigate how and when (or when not) companies promote their membership of this values-based category. While this readily resonates with newly established social enterprises, it is also a mechanism to drive social value change in existing organizations. Such an exploration connects social intrapreneurship to other research on the role of categories and evaluations (Durand and Paolella, 2013; Glynn and Navis, 2013), and broader social movements (such as Fairtrade; see Nicholls, 2010); it also pertinently connects to organizational literature on identity work (Grimes et al., 2013). Furthermore, it emphasizes that hybrid organizing also occurs by degree, which in turn leads to consideration of the variation across social enterprises in terms of when, how and where they adhere to a (common) set of values, and the source of those values (and possible value complexity; see Gehman and Grimes, 2017). Personal identity and contextual factors shape social entrepreneurs' values, manifesting in varied choices and actions (Gehman and Grimes, 2017), as evidenced, for example, by women-run enterprises being more likely to certify as BCorporations (Grimes et al., 2018).

Fields: Social Innovation Within and Across Fields

An institutional field is defined as a community of organizations that interact together 'frequently and fatefully' (Scott, 1995, pp. 207–208) in a 'recognized area of institutional life' (DiMaggio and Powell, 1983, p. 148). As a cornerstone concept in institutional theory, field is used to describe an area of social life or a group of organizations 'that compete for the same resources as well as live by the same institutional frameworks in terms of laws, regulations, normative rules, and cognitive belief systems' (Wedlin, 2006, p. 4; DiMaggio and Powell, 1983; Greenwood et al., 2002; Wooten and Hoffman, 2008). Fields include key suppliers, resource and product consumers, regulatory agencies and other organizations that produce similar services or products (DiMaggio and Powell, 1983, p. 148). Importantly, fields are 'a collection of diverse, interdependent organizations that participate in a common meaning system' (Scott, 2014, p. 106). Fields are the social domain where societal logics are enacted and interpreted by actors, generating specific meanings, templates, form and practices that then govern field action (Zietsma et al., 2017); as such, it is an 'increasingly useful level of analysis' (Reay and Hinings, 2005, p. 351) generally and particularly for social innovation.

Understanding fields in regard to social innovation is important for three main reasons. First, it directs attention to the embeddedness of individuals and organizations in larger networks, systems and structures of meaning, recognizing that fields can constrain or support individual and organizational actors and are affected by them. Second, fields are sources of legitimacy, rules and norms, organizational templates and relational channels – this institutional infrastructure is the basis of the 'systems change' that many social enterprises and social entrepreneurs are seeking. Third, field-level approaches can help address new societal challenges and opportunities, as boundaries between sectors and social spheres have blurred (Zietsma et al., 2017), and societal and environmental problems such as climate change, pandemics, mass migrations, poverty and other grand challenges have emerged (George et al., 2016), affecting and requiring coordination among multiple fields. While a line of literature on public–private partnerships provides some practical insights into the difficulties of cross-sector arrangements (Gray and Purdy, 2018; Selsky and Parker, 2010), governing and organizing field-to-field intersections and their implications for change is a line of inquiry requiring further theorizing (Hinings et al., 2017; Zietsma et al., 2017).

In a classic study on issue-based fields, Hoffman (1999) demonstrates how fields may form around an issue, such as protection of the environment. He uses the concept of issue field to examine the chemical industry, which was challenged by environmentalists seeking to make industry practices more sustainable. Over a 30-year period he shows the changing relations and field configuration between industry, government, NGOs and insurance providers, and the eventual transformation of the chemical industry to be more environmentally sustainable. In another, yet distinct, field-level analysis, Fan and Zietsma (2017) analyse the issue of water and water governance, and how actors from very different fields (and so governed by divergent logics) came together and negotiated a new and sustainable water governance agreement in one of the driest regions in Canada. Studying these issues at a field level shows the process and effort to make transformational change within and across fields sustainable, or institutionalized.

Fields are also conceptually valuable for understanding markets and the emergence of markets. That is, from the fundamental position that markets are socially constructed and not 'naturally occurring' (Fligstein, 1996, 2001; Padgett and Powell, 2012; Polanyi, 1944[2001]). A markets-as-fields approach (Fourcade, 2007) is valuable given a field is the relational space in which market construction and activity occurs through the interaction of a variety of actors. In the analysis of markets, field analysts 'attempt to understand how the subjective orientations of actors mediate the effect of social structures to shape the functioning of markets' (Fourcade, 2007, p. 1042). 'The field is primarily a game whose rules actors both tacitly abide by and struggle to alter' (Fourcade, 2007, p. 1022).

Scholarly work has shown, for instance, that a well-functioning market relies on constructing social categories that create and express shared understandings between market participants (for example, Carroll and Swaminathan, 2000; Khaire and Wadhwani, 2010; Navis and Glynn, 2010; Pontikes, 2012; Rao et al., 2003). Other studies have shown the importance of social and relational structures in markets to enable their economic functioning (Mair et al., 2012; McKague et al., 2015; Venkataraman et al., 2016). For example, McKague et al. (2015) examine the actions of a non-governmental organization (NGO) in developing the dairy value chain in Bangladesh, working to build social and relational channels across the relevant actors in the value chain and market. Similarly, Venkataraman et al. (2016) examine how market-based activities of an NGO in Indian villages, seeking to improve economic and social conditions for rural women, had to alter the institutional infrastructure in the village for these novel economic activities to be adopted and sustained.

The institutional infrastructure of fields (Hinings et al., 2017) focuses on the structural elements that bind a field together and help to govern field interactions (Greenwood et al., 2011). Institutional infrastructure includes the cultural, structural and relational foundations that guide and structure exchange within and even across fields. These foundations thus give rise to and maintain the stability of the social environment – the normative, cognitive and regulative factors that specify, for instance, how organizations should interact and exchange.

However, such infrastructure varies in quality – specifically, in its degree of elaboration. For example, many studies show how the professional services field has a highly elaborated institutional infrastructure – a stable, tightly controlled and highly normative space of interaction, with unitary and established logics (Greenwood et al., 2002; Smets et al., 2012; Suddaby and Greenwood, 2005). In this field, firms, professional associations and education providers work together with formal regulators to produce a coherent or well-understood governance structure, underpinned by licensing, training, monitoring and disciplining of behaviour, which typically privileges a professional oligopoly.

Viewing organizational interaction through the lens of institutional infrastructure thus provides a way to understand how the 'rules of the game' in and across fields are generated, maintained and reinforced, and also changed. Institutional infrastructure is a way to understand, define and classify field conditions, and then also to compare across fields. It is also a valuable lens for examining the emergence of new fields (and so markets) or what are described as 'interstitial spaces' (Furnari, 2014) – uncultivated spaces between fields where interactions begin to occur, and that increasingly get structured and 'filled out' with all forms of institutional infrastructure such as categories, organizational models and templates, status differentiators, regulators, interest groups and events (Hinings et al., 2017).

The institutional infrastructure of fields is thus a useful lens to examine the emergence of new markets, and the impact investing market provides an example of this (Hinings et al., 2017). The practice of impact investing involves investing in companies, organizations and funds with the intention of generating measurable social and environmental impacts as well as financial returns. It attracts actors seeking new ways of mobilizing financial resources for the purpose of creating positive social change. As a new field, impact investing is emerging at the intersection of other fields – philanthropy, investment and finance, corporate social responsibility and social entrepreneurship. While the field itself may be emerging from the intersection of several fields, the dominant logic is that of the market, and the consequent materials required for this impact investing market are drawn from taken-for-granted assumptions and ideas about what a market needs to function – supply, demand, rankings, ratings and those to do the ratings (Logue, 2014). The market thus becomes the central, naturalizing analogy for organizing and building institutional infrastructure for this field, providing a powerful cognitive force (Logue et al., 2016).

In the early days of impact investing, there were field configuring events to draw actors together, a focus on building up definitions and categories, including organizational templates for achieving social impact, and education courses for NFPs to become 'investor ready'. Informal governance mechanisms emerged in the form of certifying mechanisms and firms for impact (such as BCorps). These categories, labels, certifications, practices, events and educational programmes begin to provide the necessary infrastructure for these actors frequently and fatefully to meet, connect and transact (Hinings et al., 2017). Applying an institutional lens in this way, at the field level, provides insights into how social innovations, such as impact investing, and social entrepreneurs, can pursue 'systems change', or rather institutional change.

Inter-field Relations

Understanding social innovation through the concept of fields is also valuable given that many of the social problems being addressed necessarily require collaboration across different fields. Complex social problems, such as inequality, poverty and climate change (George et al., 2016), exhibit no single definition or cause and effect, and are thus beyond the ability of public, private and non-profit sectors solely to address such challenges (Voorberg et al., 2015).

Indeed, many social problems are labelled as 'issue fields' consisting of actors from different fields who are all interested in a particular issue (Hoffman, 1999; Zietsma et al., 2017, p. 396). As such, participating actors have different norms, beliefs, practices and other institutions, as they often remain embedded in their (different) home fields. In cross-field collaborations, '[p]articipants in a collaborative process bring with them various institutional affiliations, and the institutionalized rules and resources' from their respective domains (Phillips et al., 2000, p. 29). Field-to-field relations and 'field overlaps' is an emerging line of inquiry in institutional theory studies (Schneiberg and Lounsbury, 2017; Zietsma et al., 2017), as scholars and practitioners grapple with understanding the management and governance of multi-stakeholder partnerships (Gray and Purdy, 2018). Field overlaps often create settings of institutional complexity because each field has a different set of interpretations or prescriptions of guiding logic regarding the area of overlap (Zietsma et al., 2017). It is also important to recognize that some complex 'wicked' problems (Rayner, 2006) need to be constantly 're-solved', their very nature making them unable to be completely resolved (Dorado and Ventresca, 2013; Rayner, 2006; Rittel and Webber, 1973). Furthermore, in examining and disentangling the forms of governance arrangements possible across the three domains of the state, private sector and civil society, Steurer (2013) concludes that aligning the interests of, say, business to social problems and issues 'takes place in a complex, poly-centred and multi-actor governance system that erodes the boundaries between societal domains (e.g. by means of co-regulation)' (2013, p. 403).

A line of literature on public–private partnerships (PPPs) provides some practical insights into the difficulties of cross-sector arrangements (Babiak and Thibault, 2009; Clarke and Fuller, 2010; Clarke and Mac-Donald, 2019; Gray and Purdy, 2018; Le Ber and Branzei, 2010; Selsky and Parker, 2010), yet does not completely address questions around how inter-field relations can be navigated and governed. There are challenges of aligning interests (O'Mahony and Bechky, 2008), achieving mutual prioritization of the problem (or solution) (Parmigiani and Rivera-Santos, 2011), and building shared governance and coordination models over common resources or common problems (Ansari et al., 2013; Casado-Asensio and Steurer, 2014; Mair et al., 2012; Ostrom, 2010; Steurer, 2013).

This may be overcome by developing a new common language to achieve consensus on problem definition and mediate between conflicting rationales (for example, Clarke and MacDonald, 2019; Westley and Vredenburg, 1991). At other times, new forms of meta-governance or hybrid regulations may be created (Steurer, 2013; Westley and Vredenburg, 1997), or entirely new organizations established to manage or coordinate a problem or shared resource (O'Mahony and Bechky, 2008). For example, to manage water resources in one of the driest regions in Canada, stakeholders agreed to establish a water stewardship council to govern activity (Fan and Zietsma, 2017).

The organizations that perform this 'work' of connecting different stakeholders and managing collaborations across fields are often described as brokers, network orchestrators (Paquin and Howard-Grenville, 2013), and more generally 'boundary organizations' (for example, Brown, 1991; Guston, 1999; O'Mahony and Bechky, 2008; Star, 2010; Waddock, 1991). Boundary organizations take different forms, yet are frequently formal structures that internalize the conflicting interfaces of different interests and organizations into a durable form of organizing in attempts to develop shared understandings (Carlile, 2002). For example, new financial products such as Social Impact Bonds (SIBs) require coordination across investors, NFP service providers and the government, as well as independent assessors. Fundamentally, SIBs bring together actors from different institutional domains governed by divergent rationales for action. In an SIB, private investors provide the capital necessary to develop and provide social services in a specific public policy field. If these services – commonly delivered by non-profit organizations or social enterprises – result in improved social outcomes (as verified by independent assessors using predetermined impact targets), investors receive success payments (that is, original investment and a percentage return) from a government agency (Arena et al., 2016; Bolton and Savell, 2010; Liebman, 2011;

Trotta et al., 2015; Von Glahn and Whistler, 2011). In response to these needs, intermediaries have emerged to broker the deal, develop the contract, get participants to all agree on measures of social and financial return, and manage the execution of the contract. Here, as boundary organizations, these intermediaries stabilize relations across actors from different fields, producing new routines and protocols for engagement, work across field boundaries (not necessarily changing them in this case), and often engage in much emotional work to develop a shared governance logic across stakeholders from diverse fields as part of ensuring longer-term commitment (Fan and Zietsma, 2017; Logue et al., 2019).

This raises important issues regarding the different types of navigation, orchestration and mediation work required in field-to-field relations, and how this may need to change over the duration of a collaboration or interaction in ensuring the longer-term sustainability of cross-sector collaborations, as different types of institutional complexity emerge (Jay, 2013; Meyer and Höllerer, 2014; see also Ansari et al., 2013; Paquin and Howard-Grenville, 2013; Vermeulen et al., 2016). This is also raised by Bryson et al. (2015) who, in theorizing about cross-sector collaborations, suggest a potential need for 'structural ambidexterity' of intermediaries and brokers to manage and respond to the changing tensions in such collaborations.

Field-level approaches can help address new societal challenges and opportunities, especially as boundaries between fields are increasingly blurred (Zietsma et al., 2017). Cross-field interactions can be both formal and informal, increasingly occurring in both physical and virtual inter-stitial spaces between fields (Furnari, 2014). For example, consider the role of digital platforms in coordinating actors from different fields virtually, redistributing roles and responsibilities as they weave new relational configurations and communities over time (McIntyre and Srinivasan, 2017; Nash et al., 2017). More formal intersections and overlaps of fields increasingly arise from the need to respond to coordination issues such as managing shared resources (Fan and Zietsma, 2017), leading to the need for different types of boundary organizations and intermediaries (Logue et al., 2019).

CHAPTER SUMMARY

In this chapter I suggested that social innovation, as social change, is usefully theorized as institutional change. A growing stream of insti-tutional theory literature examines social innovation and social problems, demonstrating its usefulness in focus, approach and across multiple levels of analysis. A focus on institutional change highlights how existing meaning systems and social structures may inhibit change (or contribute to existing problems), or be required to change in order to embed new ways of organizing and managing in addressing social and environmental problems, and how to sustain these solutions. At the individual level, literature on institutional entrepreneurship provides insights on the scale and type of change that many social innovators seek. At the organizational level, significant theorizing on hybrid organizing and managing paradoxes provides conceptual clarity on the many challenges facing organizations pursuing social innovation, especially those who identify as (or who are categorized as) social enterprises. At the field and inter-field level, as one of the more important and useful concepts in institutional theorizing, 'fields' provides significant analytical purchase in understanding cross-sector collaboration, governance, relational configurations and drivers of social innovation and change. This is an important theoretical lens for understanding social innovation and is reflective of all core characteristics of collectivity, diversity and relationality as identified in Chapters 1 and 2.

What is starting to emerge is that this and previous chapters reveal that any theorizing of social innovation is underpinned by certain institutionalized assumptions of morality and what it means to 'do good' and right by others and society. To explore and theorize further, I return to historical works of Adam Smith on the incorporation of morality in markets and the economy, and a line of literature in economic sociology on the construction of morality and legitimacy in markets. I expand this line of inquiry into the decision-making that occurs in social innovation, and relate this to moral-relational judgement as explained by phronesis, as a form of wisdom. I conclude by considering the implications of theorizing on morality, markets, organizations and decision-making for the articulation of a theory of impact.

NOTES

1. The practicality of 'managing hybridity' is a core tension for founders, owners, managers and employees of hybrid enterprises. This is discussed in further detail in Chapter 6.
2. BCorporations are a public certification programme enabling companies to affirm their commitments to positive environmental, social and governance (ESG) practices (and so the label 'benefit' corporations, BCorp for short).

REFERENCES

Amis, J.M., Munir, K.A. and Mair, J. (2017). Institutions and economic inequality. In R. Greenwood, C. Oliver, T.B. Lawrence and R. Meyer (eds), *The SAGE Handbook of Organizational Institutionalism* (2nd edn). London: SAGE Publications, pp. 705–36.

Andriopoulos, C. and Lewis, W. (2009). Exploitation–exploration tensions and organizational ambidexterity: managing paradoxes of innovation. *Organization Science*, **20**(4), 696–717.

Ansari, S., Wijen, F. and Gray, B. (2013). Constructing a climate change logic: an institutional perspective on the 'tragedy of the commons'. *Organization Science*, **24**(4), 1014–40.

Arena, M., Bengo, I., Calderini, M. and Chiodo, V. (2016). Social impact bonds: blockbuster or flash in the pan? *International Journal of Public Administration*, **39**(12), 927–39.

Babiak, K. and Thibault, L. (2009). Challenges in multiple cross-sector partnerships. *Nonprofit and Voluntary Sector Quarterly*, **38**(1), 117–43.

Battilana, J. (2006). Agency and institutions: the enabling role of individuals' social position. *Organization*, **13**(5), 653–76.

Battilana, J. and Dorado, S. (2010). Building sustainable hybrid organizations: the case of commercial microfinance organizations. *Academy of Management Journal*, **53**(6), 1419–40.

Battilana, J. and Lee, M. (2014). Advancing research on hybrid organizing: insights from the study of social enterprises. *Academy of Management Annals*, **8**(1), 397–441.

Battilana, J., Besharov, M. and Mitzinneck, B. (2017). On hybrids and hybrid organizing: a review and roadmap for future research. In R. Greenwood, C. Oliver, T.B. Lawrence and R. Meyer (eds), *The SAGE Handbook of Organizational Institutionalism* (2nd edn). London: SAGE Publications, pp. 128–62.

Battilana, J., Leca, B. and Boxenbaum, E. (2009). How actors change institutions: towards a theory of institutional entrepreneurship. *Academy of Management Annals*, **3**(1), 65–107.

Battilana, J., Lee, M., Walker, J. and Cheryl, D. (2012). In search of the hybrid ideal. *Stanford Social Innovation Review*, **10**(3), 50–55.

Bolton, E. and Savell, L. (2010). Towards a new social economy: blended value creation through social impact bonds. *Social Finance UK*. Accessed at: https://www.socialfinance.org.uk/sites/default/files/publications/towards-a-new-social-economy-web.pdf.

Brown, L.D. (1991). Bridging organizations and sustainable development. *Human Relations*, **44**(8), 807–31.

Bryson, J.M., Crosby, B.C. and Stone, M.M. (2015). Designing and implementing cross sector collaborations: needed and challenging. *Public Administration Review*, **75**(5), 647–63.

Carlile, P.R. (2002). A pragmatic view of knowledge and boundaries: boundary objects in new product development. *Organization Science*, **13**(4), 442–55.

Carroll, G.R. and Swaminathan, A. (2000). Why the microbrewery movement? Organizational dynamics of resource partitioning in the US brewing industry. *American Journal of Sociology*, **106**(3), 715–62.

Casado-Asensio, J. and Steurer, R. (2014). Integrated strategies on sustainable development, climate change mitigation and adaptation in Western Europe: communication rather than coordination. *Journal of Public Policy*, **34**(3), 437–73.

Clarke, A. and Fuller, M. (2010). Collaborative strategic management: strategy formulation and implementation by multi-organizational cross-sector social partnerships. *Journal of Business Ethics*, **94**(1), 85–101.

Clarke, A. and MacDonald, A. (2019). Outcomes to partners in multi-stakeholder cross-sector partnerships: a resource-based view. *Business & Society*, **58**(2), 298–332.

Dacin, M.T., Dacin, P.A. and Tracey, P. (2011). Social entrepreneurship: a critique and future directions. *Organization Science*, **22**(5), 1203–13.

Dalpiaz, E., Rindova, V. and Ravasi, D. (2016). Combining logics to transform organizational agency: blending industry and art. *Administrative Science Quarterly*, **61**(3), 347–92.

Dees, J. and Anderson, B. (2003). Sector-bending: blurring lines between nonprofit and for-profit. *Society*, May/June, 16–27.

DiMaggio, P. and Powell, W.W. (1983). The iron cage revisited: institutional isomorphism and collective rationality in organizational fields. *American Sociological Review*, **48**, 147–60.

DiMaggio, P.J. and Powell, W.W. (1991). *The New Institution in Organizational Analysis*. Chicago, IL: University of Chicago.

Dorado, S. and Ventresca, M.J. (2013). Crescive entrepreneurship in complex social problems: institutional conditions for entrepreneurial engagement. *Journal of Business Venturing*, **28**(1), 69–82.

Durand, R. and Paolella, L. (2013). Category stretching: reorienting research on categories in strategy, entrepreneurship, and organization theory. *Journal of Management Studies*, **50**(6), 1100–123.

Ebrahim, A., Battilana, J. and Mair, J. (2014). The governance of social enterprises: mission drift and accountability challenges in hybrid organizations. *Research in Organizational Behavior*, **34**, 81–100.

Elkington, J. and Hartigan, P. (2008). *The Power of Unreasonable People: How Social Entrepreneurs Create Markets that Change the World*. Boston, MA: Harvard Business Press.

Fan, G.H. and Zietsma, C. (2017). Constructing a shared governance logic: the role of emotions in enabling dually embedded agency. *Academy of Management Journal*, **60**(6), 2321–51.

Fligstein, N. (1996). Markets as politics: a political-cultural approach to market institutions. *American Sociological Review*, **61**(4), 656–73.

Fligstein, N. (1997). Social skill and institutional theory. *American Behavioral Scientist*, **40**(4), 397–405.

Fligstein, N. (2001). Social skill and the theory of fields. *Sociological Theory*, **19**(2), 105–25.

Fourcade, M. (2007). Theories of markets and theories of society. *The American Behavioural Scientist*, **50**(8), 1015–34.

Furnari, S. (2014). Interstitial spaces: microinteraction settings and the genesis of new practices between institutional fields. *Academy of Management Review*, **39**(4), 439–62.

Gehman, J. and Grimes, M. (2017). Hidden badge of honor: how contextual distinctiveness affects category promotion among certified B corporations. *Academy of Management Journal*, **60**(6), 2294–320.

George, G., Howard-Grenville, J., Joshi, A. and Tihanyi, L. (2016). Understanding and tackling societal grand challenges through management research. *Academy of Management Journal*, **59**(6), 1880–95.

Giddens, A. (1984). *The Constitution of Society*. Cambridge: Polity Press.

Glynn, M.A. and Navis, C. (2013). Categories, identities, and cultural classification: moving beyond a model of categorical constraint. *Journal of Management Studies*, **50**(6), 1124–37.

Gray, B. and Purdy, J. (2018). *Collaborating for Our Future: Multistakeholder Partnerships for Solving Complex Problems*. Oxford: Oxford University Press.

Greenwood, R. and Suddaby, R. (2006). Institutional entrepreneurship in mature fields: the big five accounting firms. *Academy of Management Journal*, **49**(1), 27–48.

Greenwood, R., Suddaby, R. and Hinings, C.R. (2002). Theorizing change: the role of professional associations in the transformation of institutionalized fields. *Academy of Management Journal*, **45**(1), 58–80.

Greenwood, R., Oliver, C., Lawrence, T.B. and Meyer, R.E. (2017). *The Sage Handbook of Organizational Institutionalism*. London: SAGE Publications.

Greenwood, R., Raynard, M., Kodeih, F., Micelotta, E.R. and Lounsbury, M. (2011). Institutional complexity and organizational responses. *Academy of Management Annals*, **5**(1), 317–71.

Grimes, M.G., Gehman, J. and Cao, K. (2018). Positively deviant: identity work through B Corporation certification. *Journal of Business Venturing*, **33**(2), 130–48.

Grimes, M.G., McMullen, J.S., Vogus, T.J. and Miller, T.L. (2013). Studying the origins of social entrepreneurship: compassion and the role of embedded agency. *Academy of Management Review*, **38**(3), 460–63.

Guston, D.H. (1999). Stabilizing the boundary between US politics and science: the role of the Office of Technology Transfer as a boundary organization. *Social Studies of Science*, **29**(1), 87–111.

Hardy, C. and Maguire, S. (2017). Institutional entrepreneurship and change in fields. In R. Greenwood, C. Oliver, T.B. Lawrence and R.E. Meyer (eds), *The SAGE Handbook of Organizational Institutionalism* (2nd edn). London: SAGE Publications, pp. 261–80.

Hinings, C.R., Logue, D.M. and Zietsma, C. (2017). Fields, governance and institutional infrastructure. In R. Greenwood, C. Oliver, T.B. Lawrence and R.E. Meyer (eds), *The SAGE Handbook of Organizational Institutionalism* (2nd edn). London: SAGE Publications, pp. 163–89.

Hoffman, A. (1999). Institutional evolution and change: environmentalism and the U.S. chemical industry. *Academy of Management Journal*, **42**(4), 351–71.

Jäger, U.P. and Schröer, A. (2014). Integrated organizational identity: a definition of hybrid organizations and a research agenda. *VOLUNTAS: International Journal of Voluntary and Nonprofit Organizations*, **25**(5), 1281–306.

Jarzabkowski, P., Lê, J.K. and Van de Ven, A.H. (2013). Responding to competing strategic demands: how organizing, belonging, and performing paradoxes coevolve. *Strategic Organization*, **11**(3), 245–80.

Jay, J. (2013). Navigating paradox as a mechanism of change and innovation in hybrid organizations. *Academy of Management Journal*, **56**(1), 137–59.

Khaire, M. and Wadhwani, R.D. (2010). Changing landscapes: the construction of meaning and value in a new market category – modern Indian art. *Academy of Management Journal*, **53**(6), 1281–304.

Kraatz, M.S. and Block, E.S. (2008). Organizational implications of institutional pluralism. In R. Suddaby and K. Sahlin-Andersson (eds), *The SAGE Handbook of Organizational Institutionalism*. London: SAGE Publications, pp. 243–75.

Lawrence, T.B. and Suddaby, R. (2006). Institutions and institutional work. In S. Clegg, C. Hardy, T.B. Lawrence and W.R. Nord (eds), *Handbook of Organization Studies*. London: SAGE Publications.

Le Ber, M.J. and Branzei, O. (2010). (Re)forming strategic cross-sector partnerships relational processes of social innovation. *Business & Society*, **49**(1), 140–72.

Levy, D. and Scully, M. (2007). The institutional entrepreneur as modern prince: the strategic face of power in contested fields. *Organization Studies*, **28**(7), 971–91.

Liebman, J.B. (2011). *Social Impact Bonds: A Promising New Financing Model to Accelerate Social Innovation and Improve Government Performance*. Washington, DC: Center for American Progress.

Logue, D.M. (2014). The 'stuff' of markets: an institutional analysis of impact investing. *Academy of Management Proceedings*, **2014**(1).

Logue, D.M., Clegg, S.R. and Gray, J. (2016). Social organization, classificatory analogies and institutional logics: institutional theory revisits Mary Douglas. *Human Relations*, **69**(7), 1587–609.

Logue, D.M., Höllerer, M.A., Millner, R., Jebali, J. and Clegg, S. (2019). Navigating institutional complexity in cross-sector collaboration: interweaving work and the case of social impact bonds. Working paper.

Maguire, S. and Hardy, C. (2006). The emergence of new global institutions: a discursive perspective. *Organization Studies*, **27**(1), 7–29.

Maguire, S. and Hardy, C. (2009). Discourse and deinstitutionalization: the decline of DDT. *Academy of Management Journal*, **52**(1), 148–78.

Maguire, S., Hardy, C. and Lawrence, T.B. (2004). Institutional entrepreneurship in emerging fields: HIV/AIDS treatment advocacy in Canada. *Academy of Management Journal*, **47**(5), 657–79.

Mair, J. and Martí, I. (2006). Social entrepreneurship research: a source of explanation, prediction, and delight. *Journal of World Business*, **41**(1), 36–44.

Mair, J., Martí, I. and Ventresca, M. (2012). Building inclusive markets in rural Bangladesh: how intermediaries work institutional voids. *Academy of Management Journal*, **55**(4), 819–50.

Mair, J., Wolf, M. and Seelos, C. (2016). Scaffolding: a process of transforming patterns of inequality in small-scale societies. *Academy of Management Journal*, **59**(6), 2021–44.

Martí, I., Courpasson, D. and Barbosa, S.D. (2013). 'Living in the fishbowl'. Generating an entrepreneurial culture in a local community in Argentina. *Journal of Business Venturing*, **28**(1), 10–29.

Martin de Holan, P., Willi, A. and Fernandez, P.D. (2017). Breaking the wall: emotions and projective agency under extreme poverty. *Business & Society*, **58**(5), 919–62.

McIntyre, D.P. and Srinivasan, A. (2017). Networks, platforms, and strategy: emerging views and next steps. *Strategic Management Journal*, **38**(1), 141–60.

McKague, K., Zietsma, C. and Oliver, C. (2015). Building the social structure of a market. *Organization Studies*, **36**(8), 1063–93.

Meyer, R.E. and Höllerer, M.A. (2014). Does institutional theory need redirecting? *Journal of Management Studies*, **51**(7), 1221–33.

Nash, V., Bright, J., Margetts, H. and Lehdonvirta, V. (2017). Public policy in the platform society. *Policy and Internet*, **9**(4), 368–73.

Navis, C. and Glynn, M.A. (2010). How new market categories emerge: temporal dynamics of legitimacy, identity, and entrepreneurship in satellite radio, 1990–2005. *Administrative Science Quarterly*, **55**(3), 439–71.

Nicholls, A. (2010). Fair trade: towards an economics of virtue. *Journal of Business Ethics*, **92**(2), 241–55.

O'Mahony, S. and Bechky, B.A. (2008). Boundary organizations: enabling collaboration among unexpected allies. *Administrative Science Quarterly*, **53**(3), 422–59.

Ostrom, E. (2010). Beyond markets and states: polycentric governance of complex economic systems. *American Economic Review*, **100**(3), 641–72.

Pache, A. and Santos, F. (2010). When worlds collide: the internal dynamics of organisational responses to conflicting institutional demands. *Academy of Management Review*, **35**(3), 455–76.

Pache, A. and Santos, F. (2013). Inside the hybrid organization: selective coupling as a response to competing institutional logics. *Academy of Management Journal*, **56**(4), 972–1001.

Padgett, J. and Powell, W. (2012). *The Emergence of Organizations and Markets*. Princeton, NJ: Princeton University Press.

Paquin, R.L. and Howard-Grenville, J. (2013). Blind dates and arranged marriages: longitudinal processes of network orchestration. *Organization Studies*, **34**(11), 1623–53.

Parés, M. (2015). Market-based social innovation: are business strategies and social change compatible? *Public Administration Review*, **75**(4), 628–31.

Parmigiani, A. and Rivera-Santos, M. (2011). Clearing a path through the forest: a meta-review of interorganizational relationships. *Journal of Management*, **37**(4), 1108–36.

Phillips, N., Lawrence, T.B. and Hardy, C. (2000). Inter-organizational collaboration and the dynamics of institutional fields. *Journal of Management Studies*, **37**(1), 23–43.

Polanyi, K. (1944[2001]). *The Great Transformation: The Political and Economic Origins of Our Time*. Boston, MA: Beacon Press.

Pontikes, E.G. (2012). Two sides of the same coin: how ambiguous classification affects multiple audiences' evaluations. *Administrative Science Quarterly*, **57**(1), 81–118.

Powell, W.W. and Sandholtz, K.W. (2012). Amphibious entrepreneurs and the emergence of organizational forms. *Strategic Entrepreneurship Journal*, **6**(2), 94–115.

Pratt, M.G. and Foreman, P.O. (2000). Classifying managerial responses to multiple organizational identities. *Academy of Management Review*, **25**(1), 18–42.

Rao, H., Monin, P. and Durand, R. (2003). Institutional change in Toque Ville: nouvelle cuisine as an identity movement in French gastronomy. *American Journal of Sociology*, **108**(4), 795–843.

Rayner, S. (2006). Wicked problems: clumsy solutions – diagnoses and prescriptions for environmental ills. *Jack Beale Memorial Lecture on Global Environment*, July, Sydney.

Reay, T. and Hinings, C.R. (2005). The recomposition of an organizational field: health care in Alberta. *Organization Studies*, **26**(3), 351–84.

Rittel, H.W. and Webber, M.M. (1973). Dilemmas in a general theory of planning. *Policy Sciences*, **4**, 155–69.

Santos, F., Pache, A. and Birkholz, C. (2015). Making hybrids work: aligning business models and organizational design for social enterprises. *California Management Review*, **57**(3), 36–58.

Schad, J., Lewis, M.W., Raisch, S. and Smith, W.K. (2016). Paradox research in management science: looking back to move forward. *The Academy of Management Annals*, **10**(1), 5–64.

Schneiberg, M. and Lounsbury, M. (2017). Social movements and the dynamics of institutions and organizations. In R. Greenwood, C. Oliver, T.B. Lawrence and R. Meyer (eds), *The SAGE Handbook of Organizational Institutionalism* (2nd edn). London: SAGE Publications, pp. 281–310.

Scott, R. (2001). *Institutions and Organizations*. Thousand Oaks, CA: SAGE Publications.

Scott, W.R. (1995). *Institutions and Organizations*. Thousand Oaks, CA: SAGE Publications.

Scott, W.R. (2014). *Institutions and Organizations* (4th edn). Thousand Oaks, CA: SAGE Publications.

Selsky, J.W. and Parker, B. (2010). Platforms for cross-sector social partnerships: prospective sensemaking devices for social benefit. *Journal of Business Ethics*, **94**(Suppl.1), 21–37.

Seo, M. and Creed, W.E.D. (2002). Institutional contradictions, praxis, and institutional change: a dialectical perspective. *Academy of Management Review*, **27**(2), 222–47.

Smets, M., Morris, T. and Greenwood, R. (2012). From practice to field: a multilevel model of practice-driven institutional change. *Academy of Management Journal*, **55**(4), 877–904.

Smith, W. (2014). Dynamic decision making: a model of senior leaders managing strategic paradoxes. *Academy of Management Journal*, **57**(6), 1592–623.

Smith, W.K. and Besharov, M.L. (2019). Bowing before dual gods: how structured flexibility sustains organizational hybridity. *Administrative Science Quarterly*, **64**(1), 1–44.

Smith, W.K. and Lewis, M.W. (2011). Toward a theory of paradox: a dynamic equilibrium model of organizing. *Academy of Management Review*, **36**(2), 381–403.

Smith, W.K., Binns, A. and Tushman, M.L. (2010). Complex business models: managing strategic paradoxes simultaneously. *Long Range Planning*, **43**(2–3), 448–61.

Smith, W.K., Gonin, M. and Besharov, M.L. (2013). Managing social–business tensions: a review and research agenda for social enterprise. *Business Ethics Quarterly*, **23**(3), 407–42.

Star, S.L. (2010). This is not a boundary object: reflections on the origin of a concept. *Science, Technology, & Human Values*, **35**(5), 601–17.

Steurer, R. (2013). Disentangling governance: a synoptic view of regulation by government, business and civil society. *Policy Sciences*, **46**(4), 387–410.

Strauss, A.L. (1978). *Negotiations: Varieties, Contexts, Processes, and Social Order*. San Francisco, CA: Jossey-Bass.

Suddaby, R. and Greenwood, R. (2005). Rhetorical strategies of legitimacy. *Administrative Science Quarterly*, **50**(1), 35–67.

Tracey, P. and Stott, N. (2017). Social innovation: a window on alternative ways of organizing and innovating. *Innovation*, **19**(1), 51–60.

Tracey, P., Phillips, N. and Jarvis, O. (2011). Bridging institutional entrepreneurship and the creation of new organizational forms: a multilevel model. *Organization Science*, **22**(1), 60–80.

Trotta, A., Care, R., Severino, R., Migliazza, M.C. and Rizzello, A. (2015). Mobilizing private finance for public good: challenges and opportunities of social impact bonds. *European Scientific Journal*, **1**, 259–79.

Van Wijk, J., Stam, W., Elfring, T., Zietsma, C. and Den Hond, F. (2013). Activists and incumbents structuring change: the interplay of agency, culture, and networks in field evolution. *Academy of Management Journal*, **56**(2), 358–86.

Van Wijk, J., Zietsma, C., Dorado, S., De Bakker, F.G. and Martí, I. (2019). Social innovation: integrating micro, meso, and macro level insights from institutional theory. *Business & Society*, **58**(5), 887–918.

Venkataraman, H., Vermeulen, P., Raaijmakers, A., and Mair, J. (2016). Market meets community: institutional logics as strategic resources for development work. *Organization Studies*, **37**(5), 709–33.

Vermeulen, P., Zietsma, C., Greenwood, R. and Langley, A. (2016). Strategic responses to institutional complexity. *Strategic Organization*, **14**(4), 277–86.

Von Glahn, D. and Whistler, C. (2011). Translating plain English: can the Peterborough Social Impact Bond construct apply stateside? *Community Development Investment Review*, **1**, 58–70.

Voorberg, W.H., Bekkers, V.J. and Tummers, L.G. (2015). A systematic review of co-creation and co-production: embarking on the social innovation journey. *Public Management Review*, **17**(9), 1333–57.

Voronov, M. and Vince, R. (2012). Integrating emotions into the analysis of institutional work. *Academy of Management Review*, **37**(1), 58–81.

Waddock, S.A. (1991). A typology of social partnership organizations. *Administration & Society*, **22**(4), 480–515.

Wedlin, L. (2006). *Ranking in Business Schools: Forming fields, Identities and Boundaries in International Management Education.* Cheltenham, UK and Northampton, MA, USA: Edward Elgar Publishing.

Westley, F. and Antadze, N. (2010). Making a difference: strategies for scaling social innovation for greater impact. *Innovation Journal*, **15**(2), 1–19.

Westley, F. and Vredenburg, H. (1991). Strategic bridging: the collaboration between environmentalists and business in the marketing of green products. *The Journal of Applied Behavioral Science*, **27**(1), 65–90.

Westley, F. and Vredenburg, H. (1997). Interorganizational collaboration and the preservation of global biodiversity. *Organization Science*, **8**(4), 381–403.

Wooten, M. and Hoffman, A.J. (2008). Organizational fields: past, present and future. In R. Greenwood, C. Oliver, K. Sahlin and R. Suddaby (eds), *The SAGE Handbook of Organizational Institutionalism* (2nd edn). London: SAGE Publications, pp. 55–74.

Zhao, E.Y. and Wry, T. (2016). Not all inequality is equal: deconstructing the societal logic of patriarchy to understand microfinance lending to women. *Academy of Management Journal*, **59**(6), 1994–2020.

Zietsma, C., Groenewegen, P., Logue, D. and Hinings, C.R. (2017). Field or fields? Building the scaffolding for cumulation of research on institutional fields. *Academy of Management Annals*, **11**(1), 391–450.

Zilber, T.B. (2006). The work of the symbolic in institutional processes: translations of rational myths in Israeli high tech. *Academy of Management Journal*, **49**(2), 281–303.

Zilber, T.B. (2007). Stories and the discursive dynamics of institutional entrepreneurship: the case of Israeli high-tech after the bubble. *Organization Studies*, **28**(7), 1035–54.

5. Social innovation: morality, markets and theories of impact

MORALITY IN THEORY AND PRACTICE

In this chapter I discuss how any theorizing of social innovation (and its impact) is underpinned by particular assumptions of morality and what it means to 'do good' and 'be good' for entrepreneurs, organizations and markets, and across sectors. It brings with it, explicitly or implicitly, notions of purpose (and so intentionality) and social value and change (and so morality). Yet, as I have shown in preceding chapters, social innovation and its fundamental relationship to morality is far less considered than expected: I summarize below.

In Chapter 1, in reviewing existing literature on social innovation, I identify six core aspects of social innovation that emerge from multi-disciplinary discussions: social value, source, significance or scale of change, and more recently a focus on collectivity, diversity and relationality. Yet there is little explicit theorization of social value beyond the idea that producing it is desired and a 'good' thing to do, and some consideration of the different values of the actors involved. This observation laid the groundwork to further theorize social innovation from a range of more positivist to constructivist positions on social value, and ultimately 'goodness'.

In Chapter 2, I theorize social innovation as it relates to social value specifically as it enables distinction between processes and outcomes of social value creation and capture, and builds off the historical anchoring of social innovation in ideas about value co-production (Ramirez, 1999). It can be seen that literature on social value creation, capture (and the little on value distribution), draws on a more positivist, value-free interpretation of the generation and allocation of 'value', social value being similarly organized and managed to economic value. What I find missing however is any theorizing of value distribution, an essential and distinct mechanism in social innovation for ensuring the value produced and captured is indeed shared. As such my novel development of value distribution is based on the notion that social innovation is about collectivity and sharing of rewards (and risk for that matter). In presenting three abstract models of value distribution, this assumes a pursuit of a fairer and more equitable distribution of value, or a distribution of value to address a particular social problem. Here, the decision-making around fairness and equity of distribution is connected to deeper understandings and positions of morality, and what is right and wrong.

In Chapter 3, I argue that understanding social innovation as polysemous means recognizing the different values – within different institutional logics – that guide different societal domains that often participate in socially innovative arrangements. In describing the domains of public sector, private or business sector, and not-for-profit sector, and their understandings of social innovation and rationales for participating, we can see how values may not align or how cross-sector partnerships try to align or integrate different moral values as to responsibility, roles and desired outcomes. This chapter details the plurality and complexity in navigating social values for social innovation, and presents an inherent conundrum: it is these differences in understanding that are both a source and barrier for social innovation. What I show is that recognizing the polysemous nature of social innovation affords a more critical inquiry of social innovation, requiring scholars to consider the multi-constructions of social problems and solutions (and their prioritizations) and the role of power in determining how multiple meanings (or views) of problems and solutions are established and what (and whose) values dominate.

In Chapter 4, I theorize social innovation as about social change and so institutional change; this means understanding and recognizing how certain values and ideas about 'right and wrong' are embedded in social structures, rules, routines and of course, meaning systems that constrain and enable (socially innovative) action. I describe how much social innovation activity across levels – individual, organization and field – reflects efforts to introduce or change social structures to exhibit and reinforce different or new social values. This is particularly apparent when examining hybrid organizations or when developing cross-field arrangements. I propose this particular lens to provide a social-cultural focus on theorizing social innovation across levels of analysis and as a process that often seeks change in social structures, relations and value systems, and to institutionalize these changes and new ways of organizing and managing.

In this chapter, in seeking to both bring to the fore and better theorize the fundamental relationship between social innovation, values and morality and implicit notions of 'doing good' and 'being good', I return to historical works of Adam Smith and early conceptions of morality in 'economy' and 'society'. I also consider more recent work (comparatively) in economic sociology and organization theory that examines morality in markets and the construction of moral legitimacy. Organizational and management scholars can do more than be contextually sensitive and appropriate (Lawrence et al., 2014) when it comes to theorizing social innovation. A '*wertfrei*' examination of social innovation is naïve and inconsistent with any social constructivist position.

In the second part of this chapter I take a different turn as I begin to explore how these theories and notions of social innovation and social value can be invoked in practice. There may be a number of fruitful ways to tackle this task, which will probably require another book, yet I will explore one as a start. In this second part of the chapter I will consider the phronetic path (phronesis) as a rich and relational approach to morality and decision-making. This is timely given the extreme inequality facing the world, multiple business and financial crises that escape accountability, and the failure of many neo-liberal economic approaches to providing and securing public goods and services and protecting shared resources. As I will describe, a more phronetic approach in management and organizational studies and practice (Flyvbjerg, 2001, 2006) could assist here. I suggest that articulating 'theories of impact' may support theoretical and empirical exploration of social innovation. I then suggest social innovation also be considered in practice as a process of moral-relational decision-making, grounding this in phronesis as described by Aristotle. Overall, this chapter aims to make explicit the relationship between social innovation and morality, and begins to assist organizational and management scholars in theorizing implications for future research and practice.

SOCIAL INNOVATION, MORALITY AND MARKETS

Underlying discussions of social innovation are fundamental understandings of purpose, morality and values. What is 'goodness'? What does it mean to 'do good' or 'be good' in terms of organizations, management and markets? While some fear the market has recoded 'doing the right thing' into a business opportunity and 'impact washing', doubting the genuine moral-sensitivities of business (Parker, 2002; Shamir, 2008), others suggest managers and business attempt to pursue 'moral good' in business decisions yet are circumvented by the market (or rather economy) restricting their moral pursuit (Aguilera et al., 2007). For example, Lewis and Juravle (2010) find that investment managers who valued and sought to make more ethical investments were constrained by market drivers that demand faster returns than many ethical, longer-term investments can provide. Research indicates that many investors are even willing to trade off market returns for principles of ethical investing, arguing that the 'rational economic man' is a useful assumption for [only] some forms of economic analysis rather than a universal reality' (Lewis and Mackenzie, 2000, p. 187).

Economic sociologists argue for the importance of studying markets, precisely because they are inescapable: 'They are the stuff our modern societies are made of. We simply cannot have a serious reflection on modernity without addressing processes of commodification, marketization, privatization, and ... the powerful role of economics in bringing about these transformations' (Fourcade, 2007, p. 1019). Indeed, examining formal and informal relationships in the commodification processes in markets provides detail as to the 'nature of the moral boundaries that are drawn around it' (Fourcade, 2007, p. 1028). Moral boundaries, and how they can be constructed and changed over time, is described by Anteby as 'a practice-based view of moral markets' (2010, p. 607), providing a lens on the social consequences of markets for social organization and change (Fourcade, 2007).

Similarly, in organizational studies as Kraatz and Block describe, values often refer to 'conceptions of the good – ideals about what is worth having, doing, and being' (2017, p. 540; see also Grimes et al., 2018). These conceptions – how they are created, maintained, legitimated, diffused or changed – are a critical feature of both organizations and institutional environments (Selznick, 2000; see also Grimes et al., 2018). How can we then understand social value – the sense of morality, or moral sentiments – associated with social innovation? In this section I briefly connect ideas of social innovation to the historical writings on economy and society, on morals and markets, of Adam Smith. This initial anchoring in Smith opens an agenda for future debates and theorizing on social innovation and its implications.

Morality in 'Economy', Morality in 'Society'

In returning to the work of Smith, both *The Wealth of Nations* and *The Theory of Moral Sentiments*, recent (scholarly and empirical) attention on social innovation can be seen as a manifestation of the undercurrents across the contemporary world on distinctions (and concern about the erosion) between society and economy. That is, that many political, governmental and civic decisions are made or framed as existing within the larger context of economy, the societal sphere (and social policy decisions) being subsumed into economy and so subjected to the workings of markets. Smith writes on the evolution of liberal market systems, positive law and civic ethics (Evensky, 2005) – all of which are fundamental to theorizing social innovation and afford opportunity for further exploration beyond the scope of this introductory book.

In making the case for connecting theories of social innovation to richer work of Smith, Norman (2018) provides a comprehensive historical review of the life, thought and impact of the collective works of Adam Smith, and its relevance for issues facing the world today. For example, while in *The Wealth of Nations* Smith may place the study of markets at the centre of economics, 'he does not idolize the market mechanism or see market exchange as a panacea for economic ills; and he is aware that much economic activity does not operate through markets at all' (Norman, 2018, p. 207). His idea of a 'natural system of liberty' was not about free markets or neo-liberal ideology, it was rather a counter system to feudalism. The 'commercial society' that emerged was a co-evolution of systems of institutions, laws and manners and moral self-awareness of mutual recognition and obligation (Norman, 2018, pp. 268–9). As Norman describes (2018), although 'commercial society' offered improved morals and manners, and a capacity to generate and distribute wealth and prosperity, it could also be corrupted in setting private interest against public virtue, requiring States that are strategic and strong, and independent institutions that can withstand State domination, as part of minimizing inequalities. A commercial society was thus:

> [A] society, not a clan or tribe, of people trading freely with each other under law; inclusive, at least in principle, of all and spreading wealth and opportunity to all; generating surpluses that can be used to protect the vulnerable; working with the grain of human instincts and human nature; and held together not by force, class hierarchy or rank but by mutual moral and social obligation. (Norman, 2018, p. 295)

How we organize society, the role of the State, the distribution of wealth, and the strength of relations and sense of responsibility – are all issues to explore further in settings of social innovation.

In another summary relevant for theorizing social innovation, Fitzgibbons (1995) argues that *The Wealth of Nations* was an applied moral theory with the central theme that 'a good moral climate would encourage good economic performance, and conversely that good economic performance could improve the moral climate' (1995, p. 154). 'The central theme of *The Wealth of Nations* was that respect for the cardinal virtues could both advance economic growth and minimize the alienation that liberalism and the creation of wealth entailed' (Fitzgibbons, 1995, p. 135). Smith proposed that 'the foundation of society was in fact justice ... the whole object of the laws, without which society could not exist, was to constrain the useful motives of greed and self-love' (Fitzgibbons, 1995, p. 141), and indeed focused much of his work on jurisprudence. Fitzgibbons interprets this as the idea that 'economic growth presupposed a compatible culture, and that this culture had to be rooted in moral notions' (Fitzgibbons, 1995, p. 146).

Shamir (2008, p. 6) suggests that core to Smith's work was a distinction between 'economy' and 'society': 'The political economy of Adam Smith constructed an economic sphere with its own laws. Accompanying this, civil society and its political institutions became the realm of moral sentiments and took on the management, control or elimination of the negative externalities generated by unregulated and under-regulated economic practices.' In more contemporary times, this distinction is perhaps not as distinct, or as Shamir argues has collapsed due to neo-liberalism. While in Smith's work the rationality of the economy and market is a 'distinct and limited form of social action', the rationality of the market in contemporary times is (or is increasingly) 'the organising principle for state and society as a whole' (Fourcade, 2007; Shamir, 2008, p. 6). This has led to the emergence of moral entrepreneurs of economic values (I think some critical management scholars would describe this as akin to the definition of social entrepreneur), and an expectation of business and markets to assume socio-moral obligations (Shamir, 2008). The collapse of these two distinct spheres of social action has arguably led to the 'economy' dominating 'society', with, as Shamir (2008) argues, moral issues and considerations losing their 'transcendental attributes' and emerging as business opportunities (Shamir, 2008). Is social innovation a contemporary manifestation of this re-splitting of 'economy' and 'society' as Smith initially theorized? Will the contemporary context of extreme global inequality reinvigorate the debate and drive to better balance 'economy' and 'society'?

Related arguments are taken up in Smith's *The Theory of Moral Sentiments*, an account of how moral and social norms are created and sustained by human communities (Norman, 2018). Evensky (2005) describes this tome as showing that Smith 'recognised that an unfettered freedom to pursue self-interest could undermine a constructive liberal society' (2005, p. 113); specifically that 'the *sine qua non* for a successful liberal system of free people and free markets is security for all participants' (Evensky, 2005, p. 113). This connects to the discussion above on law, justice and jurisprudence as foundational to Smith's works, with Evensky stating that the source of this security 'must be a system of justice that establishes and enforces principles of interpersonal behaviour that ensure individuals' security' (Evensky, 2005, p. 113). Importantly, that progress in one domain or sphere requires complementary progress in the other, so liberal market development and wealth accumulation requires simultaneous development in civic ethics and law. Indeed, as humankind progresses 'ever more complex social and political institutions play[ed] an essential instrumental role in making that progress possible' (Evensky, 2005, p. 118). Evensky (2005) summarizes Smith's position in these terms:

> But from the initial publication of *The Theory of Moral Sentiments* in 1759 to the last revision of that work in the year he died, 1790, the foundation of Smith's moral philosophical vision never changed. If a society of free people and free markets is to avoid the Hobbesian abyss, justice must be enforced not by institutions and police, but by self-government – that is, by citizens who share and adhere to a common, mature standard of civic ethics. (2005, pp. 128–9)

If we are to consider social innovation as social change, we need to consider the interaction between individuals and society, or fundamentally of structure and agency. Individuals existing in societal (and economic) structures can generate change and transcend existing norms (see Chapter 4); yet the process of progress is larger than any one individual. Social innovation is, in part, a contemporary manifestation of this distinction and struggle between economy and society, and is often attempting to rebalance progress across liberal markets, law (role of government) and civil society.

Markets as Embedded in Society

In anchoring social innovation to historical work such as Smith's, and understandings of economy and society, it is necessary to also anchor it in historical conceptions of the organization of society. Much of the work on social innovation either takes, or would benefit from taking, the position that markets are not naturally occurring entities. In Polanyi's (1944[2001]) monumental work, *The Great Transformation*, he makes exactly this point – that markets are constructed, and not the only way of organizing society or the distribution of resources, as history shows (consider tribes, clans, families). Furthermore, he argues that markets are embedded in society, this conception contrary to perhaps more recent (neo-liberal) theorizing that society is embedded in economy. He shows an intertwining of politics and economy, and so demonstrating the lack of historical evidence or support for popular doctrines of 'trickle down economics' (Stiglitz, 2001). He also highlights the deficiencies of self-regulating markets (and especially their consequences for the poor) and so the necessary role of government intervention (Stiglitz, 2001; Block, 2003).

Many trace the development of his work from the 1930s to 1944, which includes periods of time when Polanyi was lecturing in England, his early work influenced by Marxism (Block, 2003). In his own lecture notes on the Industrial Revolution he raises questions related to the balance between economic and social progress, such as: 'The Industrial Revolution presents us with a problem: The productive forces of the country increased enormously, yet the state and condition of the people was miserable. How to account for this?'

In Polanyi's (1944) discussions of different societal systems, feudalism and capitalism, he argues that both these involve a complex mix of political, cultural and economic practice in trying to extract surplus from direct producers, indeed that market economies are dependent upon the State to manage the supply and demand. Therefore there is no separate economic realm that operates on its own distinct logic (Block, 2003). He concludes his work with a discussion on the need to balance freedoms – that is, for example, freedom of speech, freedom to move capital, but also freedom from hunger, freedom from fear. While a full analysis of Polanyi's (1944) work is beyond the scope of this book (for example see Burawoy, 2003; Evans, 2008; Gemici, 2008), these ideas are extremely valuable and richly anchor social innovation in long-standing theorizing on the relationship between notions of economy and society.

Constructing Moral Legitimacy: Morality as Temporal

Organizational theorizing of social value, and more deeply morality, reveals the social construction of morality and rejection of absolute values or morals. What many economic sociology and organizational theory studies reveal is the moral boundaries of markets and the temporality of morality. They highlight how morality changes over time due to the actions of certain actors and processes (Fourcade, 2007; see also Healy, 2000; Haveman and Rao, 1997) and also certain devices and materials (Callon et al., 2007; Mackenzie and Millo, 2003). For example, Anteby (2010) offers a 'practice-based view' of morality in the business of US cadavers. He argues that *how* goods are traded contributes to morality as much as does the category of the traded goods themselves. In his examination of how the distribution and trade of cadavers for medical research changed over decades in the US, he seeks to explain the variation in the legitimacy for trades involving the same category of goods. Following legislative changes in the late 1960s, the trade in cadavers was given a legal basis and a framework within which to operate. Anteby examines how an industry emerged from this change, with two main competitors: academically-housed programmes and independent ventures. He finds that significant success of the academically-housed programmes was down to professionals' success in making claims around moral legitimacy: that academic programmes were a 'proper' and ethical way of trading as compared to 'improper commerce' (Anteby, 2010, p. 617). This highlights the concept of 'moral legitimacy' and efforts to obtain 'positive normative evaluations' by organizations of their activities (by various stakeholders), a rich point to explore in settings of social innovation.

Moral legitimacy 'is defined by what a community deems legitimate (Durkheim, 1973)' (Anteby, 2010, p. 608), drawing strength and stability from grounding in naturalizing analogies (Douglas, 1986; Logue et al., 2016). As such, 'moral legitimacy reflects not whether an organization and its activity benefit the evaluator or fit his or her plausible cognitive frames but whether they are perceived as the "right thing to do" (Suchman, 1995, p. 579)' (Anteby, 2010, p. 608). In a similar example of moral legitimacy changing over time, Haveman and Rao (1997) examine how a form of organization (thrift store or building society) was historically questioned on moral grounds, yet eventually accepted and institutionalized partly as it connected to changing conceptions of cooperation and savings rooted in the Progressive movement.

Moral legitimacy also connects to a growing body of work on valuation and valuation studies (for example, Fourcade, 2011; Lamont, 2012; Sauder et al., 2012). Many organizational studies have examined processes of valuation, or rather social orders and field structures, more so through the action and impact of ratings, rankings and certifying that occurs in financial markets (Beunza and Garud, 2007), higher education (Wedlin, 2011), consumer markets (Nicholls, 2010), and in regard to the impact of corporations, such as by BCorporation certification (Gehman and Grimes, 2017). These same practices, or rating, ranking and certifying, also shape social value assessments and perceptions, and are based on some agreed (or preferred) understanding of morality and what is good and right. The process of valuing determines what is 'proper or improper', or in the case of social innovation, what is 'good' or 'bad'. The very act or process of certifying or valuing shapes what is considered moral or good.

Overall, this section highlights a richer context in which to understand and theorize social innovation, critically evaluating understandings of goodness and morality, on which basis things might even be considered, labelled or categorized as a social innovation. In the next section I take a different turn in exploring how we might consider the 'practice' of social innovation when it comes to decision-making and making such moral-relational judgements. In considering Smith's ideas of how moral and social norms are created and sustained by individuals, I now turn to additional literature and theories on making decisions and judgements and understanding their intended and unintended impact.

A THEORY OF IMPACT: PRACTICE AND DECISION-MAKING

Social innovation is generative as a signifier, a polysemous term, that brings together, into a new network of meaning, diverse stakeholders who seek social change. As described above, there are deep assumptions of morality and 'goodness' in these motivations and activities, and yet a refined theory of impact is missing. It would be ironic in this setting not to consider more directly how theorizing can inform practice and vice versa. This is particularly so when much of the early discussions of social innovation and its meaning emerged from practitioners and their entrepreneurial efforts and policy decisions, providing opportunity to examine their moral-relational decision-making. In this section I explore how articulating a 'theory of impact' may be an opportunity to make this connection between theory and practice mutually informative, any theory of impact reflecting an underlying system of morality. I then take a slightly different turn and explore implications for individual decision-making in regard to social innovation, asking phronetic questions both in theory and practice, suggesting that social innovation also be considered as a process of moral-relational judgement.

Theories of Impact

Understanding and developing a 'theory of impact' in practice is a way to theoretically and empirically examine the underlying morality of a particular social innovation and its proponents. Social innovation is fundamentally about seeking social impact. Across the chapters, I have considered how social innovation, and for that matter, social impact, is both ambiguous (or rather polysemous) and contested (Choi and Majumdar, 2014; Ebrahim, 2003). The idea that social innovation provides social change or social impact is also prevalent across academic and grey literature. Measuring social impact is a socio-political process, as is the construction of moral legitimacy and the determination of social priorities and solutions. And yet management and organizational theories of 'impact' are underdeveloped (Gehman and Höllerer, 2019), understood as future 'societal consequences' (Greenwood et al., 2017, p. 15), or 'the long-term effects that an organization has on broad outcomes of interest' (Wry and Haugh, 2018, p. 566). It would be helpful for scholars alike to consider what explicit or underlying theories of impact may be at hand when empirically examining social innovation to uncover understandings of morality.

Articulating a 'theory of impact' reflects in some ways similar, long-standing, discussions in NFP literature, especially practitioner literature on 'theories of change' and 'logic models', to understand and to demonstrate organizational impact and that of interventions (Edwards et al., 2018). A 'theory of change' is a common methodology used by NFPs, donors and philanthropists to identify long-term goals and desired outcomes, and then map backwards to identify the necessary inputs and processes, producing an outcomes pathway (Brest, 2010). Similarly, a 'logic model' describes that chain of causes and effects towards a desired outcome, often used to plan, communicate, implement and evaluate interventions (Julian, 1997).

A theory of impact needs to consider both intended and unintended consequences (Gehman and Höllerer, 2019). This means evaluations and measures of social impact need to be both specific to an intervention or purpose, but also broader, over a longer duration and incorporate multiple stakeholders. What matters to one actor or stakeholder may differ substantially from what matters to another, leading to the challenge of diverse and sometimes conflicting demands for accountability (Ebrahim, 2003; Edwards et al., 2018). This also varies depending on how social innovation is theorized. If we return to the main theoretical lenses outlined in this book, for example, they each raise different questions as to understanding 'a theory of impact' and connecting to practice. These questions contribute to a future empirical research agenda in social innovation. For example, in using the lens of 'social value creation, capture and distribution', questions may include: What models of value distribution provide most immediate impact, or most transformational impact? How do these creation, capture and distribution processes and models work in cross-field collaborations? How do value creation, capture and distribution change democratic accountability and governance?

When considering social innovation as polysemous, articulating a theory of impact may raise the following questions for particular empirical settings: What and who gives social innovation meaning in a specific context? What view or measure of impact and so morality wins out over others and what is the consequence of this? What is the relationship between diverse interpretations and sustaining of impact? For how long can a vague interpretation be maintained and to what productive end? What materials or boundary objects and organizations are necessary in bridging moral codes?

Finally, when theorizing social innovation as institutional change, a theory of impact raises questions such as: How does pursuing social innovation change relational roles and systems which address social needs? How does institutional infrastructure within or across fields institutionalize a certain theory of appropriate impact? How does institutional complexity change over time and how is this navigated in cross-field collaborations?

Articulating 'theories of impact' across various theoretical lenses brings to the fore the intended and unintended consequences of social innovation, especially useful when examining empirical settings, and uncovers the underlying moral systems that are shaping action and decision-making.

Practising Social Innovation: Phronesis and Moral-relational Judgement

In this section, I describe what asking more phronetic questions means for theorizing and practising social innovation. This is only one possible path for examining morality and decision-making, selected given existing work on what a phronetic approach means for management and organizational studies (and education) more broadly (Jarvis and Logue, 2016).

There is now growing evidence that the neo-liberal experiment in the provision of public good in particular has failed – and failed globally (Norman, 2018). When one value regime results in so much inequality and harm, it is hardly surprising that more phronetic questions (Where are we going? Is this desirable?) are asked publicly by scholars and practitioners alike. The debates about 'what markets are and should be for, about the limitations of the ideas of "market failure" and the need to ensure effective competition, and about norms and culture and the role of the state' and 'what is to be done?' are alarmingly missing (Norman, 2018, p. 292).

Phronesis is a form of knowledge oriented towards practical-moral judgement articulated by Aristotle. As outlined by Jarvis and Logue (2016, p. 352):

> In *The Nicomachean Ethics*, Aristotle (384–322 BCE) drew distinctions between actions guided by different dispositions. Phronesis is a form of

knowledge (logos) oriented towards practical-moral judgement – that is, decisions about what constituted a (flourishing) 'good life' for an individual (living in the polis) which is central to Aristotle's Virtue Ethics (from Aristotle's *Nicomachean Ethics*) (Aristotle, 2009).

Phronesis provides a philosophical base for theorizing impact in social innovation for several reasons. First, it emphasizes practical wisdom, important given that much theorizing and action on social innovation emerged first from practice and policy makers. Second, it describes a form of moral-relational judgement, which I argue is heightened in settings of social innovation. Third, it opens up a set of scholarly questions that are unapologetically value-laden, placing morality and values as central to management and organizational theory, in contrast to the often value-neutral, scientific approach of much of the social sciences (Flyvbjerg, 2001, 2006).

Phronesis is distinguished from other forms of knowledge proposed by Aristotle, mainly *episteme* and *techne*. Flyvbjerg (2001, 2006) describes the distinction as: *episteme* as scientific knowledge, and so universal, invariable, context-independent and based on general analytical-rationality; *techne* as knowledge as craft or art, pragmatic, context-dependent, based on practical instrumental rationality governed by a conscious goal. In contrast, phronesis is knowledge of ethics, deliberation about values with reference to praxis, context-dependent, and oriented toward action. *Phronesis* is based on practical values rationality (Flyvbjerg, 2001, p. 57). In short: episteme is top-down deductive thinking, techne from rule-following procedures; in contrast phronesis is practical wisdom, built from deep experiences of life and a progressive formation of virtue (Jarvis and Logue, 2016; Sherman, 1997). This connects directly with Smith's work, *The Theory of Moral Sentiments*, and the idea that a 'commercial society' requires moral imagination – this being the ability to put oneself in another's shoes, to empathize (Norman, 2018).

Recently, Flyvbjerg (2001, 2006) has become a major proponent of phronesis as a theoretical and empirical approach across the social sciences. He argues that it is needed to balance episteme and techne, and that phronesis is only formed through experience; also that in Western cultures, societies have prized both episteme and techne above all else, neglecting the vital, balancing role of phronesis (see also Clegg, 2006, 2010).

CHAPTER SUMMARY

In conclusion, I have tried to address this in this book in particular, in theorizing social innovation across a range of ontological positions, and indeed arguing for less positivist stances toward social innovation and understandings of social value creation. Closely emulating the natural sciences hinders the ability of management and organizational scholars to engage in important and complex societal issues, which are value-laden and institutionalized by certain power structures and meaning systems. For scholars, adopting a phronetic approach to theorizing social innovation opens up questions as to its management and organization: is this development desirable? What, if anything, should we do about it (Flyvbjerg, 2001)? Social innovation needs to be understood as involving social action with moral and political consequences. In considering questions of impact and indeed developing theories of social innovation, greater attention needs to be given to values, virtue and context.

In the following and final chapter, Chapter 6, I describe in further detail three core tensions in the 'practice' of social innovation. It is fitting given that much of the discourse and the term itself emerged from practitioners and policy makers grappling with wicked problems, limited resources and entrenched systems of inequality, with academic work often lagging. In Chapter 6 I describe several challenges that provide worthy sites of further empirical investigation and theorizing: managing hybridity, measuring impact and governing (cross-sector) collaborations. The role of digital technologies in these issues adds another layer of complexity that also needs further exploration. I note data sources, emerging lines of inquiry and possible theoretical frameworks for pursuing both empirical and theoretical contributions.

REFERENCES

Aguilera, R., Rupp, D., Williams, C. and Ganapathi, J. (2007). Putting the S back in Corporate Social Responsibility: a multilevel theory of social change in organizations. *Academy of Management Review*, **32**(3), 836–63.

Anteby, M. (2010). Markets, morals and practices of trade: jurisdictional disputes in the US commerce in cadavers. *Administrative Science Quarterly*, **55**(4), 606–38.

Aristotle (2009). *The Nicomachean Ethics* (D. Ross, trans.). Oxford: Oxford University Press.

Beunza, D. and Garud, R. (2007). Calculators, lemmings or frame-makers? The intermediary role of securities analysts. *The Sociological Review*, **55**(s2), 13–39.

Block, F. (2003). Karl Polanyi and the writing of the Great Transformation. *Theory and Society*, **32**(3), 275–306.

Brest, P. (2010). The power of theories of change. *Stanford Social Innovation Review*, **8**(2), 46–51.

Burawoy, M. (2003). For a sociological Marxism: the complementary convergence of Antonio Gramsci and Karl Polanyi. *Politics & Society*, **31**(2), 193–261.

Callon, M., Millo, Y. and Muniesa, F. (2007). *Market Devices*. Oxford: Blackwell.

Choi, N. and Majumdar, S. (2014). Social entrepreneurship as an essentially contested concept: opening a new avenue for systematic future research. *Journal of Business Venturing*, **29**(3), 363–76.

Clegg, S. (2006). Why is organization theory so ignorant? The neglect of total institutions. *Journal of Management Inquiry*, **15**(4), 426–30.

Clegg, S. (2010). The state, power, and agency: missing in action in institutional theory. *Journal of Management Inquiry*, **19**(4), 4–13.

Douglas, M. (1986). *How Institutions Think*. Syracuse, NY: Syracuse University Press.

Durkheim, E. (1973). *Emile Durkheim on Morality and Society*. Chicago, IL: University of Chicago Press.

Ebrahim, A. (2003). Accountability in practice: mechanisms for NGOs. *World Development*, **31**, 813–29.

Edwards, M., Yerbury, H. and Burridge, N. (2018). Manifestations of social impact in civil society. *Third Sector Review*, **24**(1), 97–117.

Evans, P. (2008). Is an alternative globalization possible? *Politics & Society*, **36**(2), 271–305.

Evensky, J. (2005). Adam Smith's theory of moral sentiments: on morals and why they matter to a liberal society of free people and free markets. *Journal of Economic Perspectives*, **19**(3), 109–30.

Fitzgibbons, A. (1995). *Adam Smith's System of Liberty, Wealth and Virtue. The Moral and Political Foundations of the Wealth of Nations*. Oxford: Oxford University Press.

Flyvbjerg, B. (2001). *Making Social Science Matter: Why Social Inquiry Fails and How it Can Succeed Again*. Cambridge: Cambridge University Press.

Flyvbjerg, B. (2006). A Perestroikan straw man answers back: David Laitin and phronetic political science. In S. Schram and B. Caterino (eds), *Making Political Science Matter: Debating Knowledge, Research and Method*. New York: New York University Press.

Fourcade, M. (2007). Theories of markets and theories of society. *The American Behavioural Scientist*, **50**(8), 1015–34.

Fourcade, M. (2011). Cents and sensibility: economic valuation and the nature of 'nature'. *American Journal of Sociology*, **116**(6), 1721–77.

Gehman, J. and Grimes, M. (2017). Hidden badge of honor: how contextual distinctiveness affects category promotion among certified B corporations. *Academy of Management Journal*, **60**(6), 2294–320.

Gehman, J. and Höllerer, M. (2019). Venturing into the cultural future: research opportunities at the nexus of institutions, innovation, and impact. *Innovation: Organization & Management (IOM)*, forthcoming.

Gemici, K. (2008). Karl Polanyi and the antinomies of embeddedness. *Socio-Economic Review*, **6**(1), 5–33.

Greenwood, R., Oliver, C., Lawrence, T.B. and Meyer, R.E. (2017). *The SAGE Handbook of Organizational Institutionalism*. London: SAGE Publications.

Grimes, M.G., Williams, T.A. and Zhao, E.Y. (2018). Anchors aweigh: the sources, variety, and challenges of mission drift. *Academy of Management Review*, forthcoming.

Haveman, H.A. and Rao, H. (1997). Structuring a theory of moral sentiments: institutional and organizational coevolution in the early thrift industry. *American Journal of Sociology*, **102**(6), 1606–51.

Healy, K. (2000). Embedded altruism: blood collection regimes and the European Union's donor population. *American Journal of Sociology*, **10**(6), 1633–57.

Jarvis, W.P. and Logue, D. (2016). Cultivating moral-relational judgement in business education: the merits and practicalities of Aristotle's phronesis. *Journal of Business Ethics Education*, **13**, 349–72.

Julian, D.A. (1997). The utilization of the logic model as a system level planning and evaluation device. *Evaluation and Program Planning*, **20**(3), 251–7.

Kraatz, M.S. and Block, E.S. (2017). Institutional pluralism revisited. In R. Greenwood, C. Oliver, T.B. Lawrence and R.E. Meyer (eds), *The SAGE Handbook of Organizational Institutionalism* (2nd edn). London: SAGE Publications, pp. 532–58.

Lamont, M. (2012). Toward a comparative sociology of valuation and evaluation. *Annual Review of Sociology*, **38**, 201–21.

Lawrence, T.B., Dover, G. and Gallagher, B. (2014). Managing social innovation. In M. Dodgson, D. Gann and N. Phillips (eds), *The Oxford Handbook of Innovation Management*. Oxford: Oxford University Press, pp. 316–24.

Lewis, A. and Juravle, C. (2010). Morals, markets and sustainable investments: a qualitative study of 'champions'. *Journal of Business Ethics*, **93**(3), 483–94.

Lewis, A. and Mackenzie, C. (2000). Morals, money, ethical investing and economic psychology. *Human Relations*, **53**(2), 179–91.

Logue, D.M., Clegg, S.R. and Gray, J. (2016). Social organization, classificatory analogies and institutional logics: institutional theory revisits Mary Douglas. *Human Relations*, **69**(7), 1587–609.

Mackenzie, D. and Millo, Y. (2003). Constructing a market, performing theory: the historical sociology of a financial derivatives exchange. *American Journal of Sociology*, **100**(1), 107–45.

Nicholls, A. (2010). Fair trade: towards an economics of virtue. *Journal of Business Ethics*, **92**(2), 241–55.

Norman, J. (2018). *Adam Smith: What he Thought, and Why it Matters*. London: Penguin Random House.

Parker, M. (2002). *Against Management: Organisation in the Age of Managerialism*. Cambridge: Polity.

Polanyi, K. (1944[2001]). *The Great Transformation: The Political and Economic Origins of Our Time*. Boston, MA: Beacon Press.

Ramirez, R. (1999). Value co-production: intellectual origins and implications for practice and research. *Strategic Management Journal*, **20**(1), 49–65.

Sauder, M., Lynn, F. and Podolny, J.M. (2012). Status: insights from organizational sociology. *Annual Review of Sociology*, **38**, 267–83.

Selznick, P. (2000). Reflections on responsibility. *The Responsive Community*, **10**(2), 57–61.

Shamir, R. (2008). The age of responsibilization: on market-embedded morality. *Economy and Society*, **37**(1), 1–19.

Sherman, S. (1997). Promises, promises: credit as contested metaphor in early capitalist discourse. *Modern Philology*, **94**(3), 327–49.

Stiglitz, J.E. (2001). Foreword in The Great Transformation. In K. Polanyi (ed.), *The Great Transformation: The Political and Economic Origins of our Time.* Boston, MA: Beacon Press.

Suchman, M.C. (1995). Managing legitimacy: strategic and institutional approaches. *Academy of Management Review*, **20**, 571–610.

Wedlin, L. (2011). Going global: rankings as rhetorical devices to construct an international field of management education. *Management Learning*, **42**(2), 199–218.

Wry, T. and Haugh, H. (2018). Brace for impact: uniting our diverse voices through a social impact frame. *Journal of Business Venturing*, **33**(5), 566–74.

6. Social innovation: tensions in purpose and practice

In this chapter I examine three core tensions that are dominant in practitioner and policy discourse: (1) managing hybridity; (2) measuring impact; and (3) governing collaborations. In contrast to earlier chapters that outline ways of theorizing social innovation, in this chapter I take a reverse approach and consider three empirical and practitioner areas of focus/tensions associated with social innovation and explore how we can theorize to make both empirical and theoretical contributions. After all, social innovation as a term itself emerged from practitioner literature (see Chapter 1). While some of these tensions are introduced in earlier chapters, here I examine each in detail, covering the empirical debates and any initial or fruitful ways of theorizing where possible.

First, I discuss the tension of managing hybridity, a central area of concern for the growing numbers of social enterprises that are emerging globally, further complicated when traditional organizations (either private sector or not-for-profit sector) attempt to integrate social enterprises into existing structures. While introduced in Chapter 4, here I go deeper into this issue and discuss variations in degree and intensity of hybridity, legitimacy concerns (for internal and external stakeholders), design challenges and the key difficulties in trying to integrate processes and people.

Second, I discuss measuring impact and present an overview of the field of impact measurement, a dominant preoccupation in impact investing markets, in new social financing mechanisms (such as social impact bonds) and of policy makers more broadly (see also Chapter 2). There is a shift under way from social value to measuring impact, raising questions about previously institutionalized models and templates of organizing and their purpose. Increasingly, organizations (such as universities) are being asked to explicitly demonstrate (and so measure) their impact. I review social impact assessment and reporting, methods to compare social interventions and the emerging array of impact measurement tools. I suggest there is much opportunity in theorizing this central tension in social innovation by exploring the sociology of valuation and evaluation (Lamont, 2012).

The third practitioner tension I explore is that of governing collaborations, especially as so much social innovation relies on cross-sector activities or new cross-sector configurations as social innovations themselves. While the challenges of cross-sector collaborations are introduced in Chapter 3 and Chapter 4, here I expand further on ideas of polycentric governance, inclusive innovation and public entrepreneurship, as lines of inquiry that could assist in theorizing this practical tension. I also suggest an opportunity to draw on the national systems of innovation literature, and suggest conceptualizing a 'system of social innovation' to govern, coordinate and direct efforts towards specific social problems.

These three practical tensions offer much opportunity for theoretical and empirical contributions. This chapter does not set out to cover each tension in depth, but to highlight the aspects in each that are occupying practitioners and policy makers, and to suggest, where possible, lines of inquiry that could support efforts to better theorize social innovation.

MANAGING HYBRIDITY

In Chapter 4 ('Social innovation as institutional change'), I outlined approaches used to understand social innovation at an organizational level, and as such, the associated theorizing on hybrid organizing. The bulk of attention at the organizational level has been on the emergence of social enterprises. These social enterprises are labelled as 'hybrid organizations' because they pursue both social and financial goals, attempting to combine organizational elements associated with divergent institutional logics. Studies to date suggest the many difficulties in practice in managing hybridity (Smith et al., 2013) as further evidenced in emerging practitioner guides that delve into the issues of creating and organizing hybrids (Edwards et al., 2019). They also seek to provide greater clarity on the antecedents and outcomes of hybridity (Battilana et al., 2017; Shepherd et al., 2019). In this section I explore further the issues of managing hybridity and the opportunities for further theorizing. For the purposes of this discussion, I define 'hybrid' quite broadly to include not just the combination of social and commercial logics, but other combinations of logics as well.

Degree and Intensity of Hybridity

Edwards et al. (2019) argue that hybrids are not defined simply by their for-profit or non-profit status, but rather, that 'hybridity is determined and shaped by how, and to what degree, different forms of value creation and distribution are a core part of managing the organizational mission, strategy and measuring the attainment of goals' (p. 6). Battilana et al.'s (2017) review of the burgeoning volume of literature on hybridity, much of which examined social enterprises, identified three main streams of inquiry that have advanced our understanding. First, how conflicting institutional logics are inherent in hybrid organizing and so create management challenges across internal and external stakeholders; secondly, how these conflicts manifest and are managed within organizations; and thirdly, the implications this has for organizational identity.

While much of this earlier work positioned hybrids (in this case, mainly social enterprises) as a distinct organizational type, recently scholars have begun to argue that such a position overlooks the potential heterogeneity that exists among hybrids (Litrico and Besharov, 2018; Shepherd et al., 2019). Shepherd et al. (2019) agree with efforts to examine hybridity as a continuum, anchored by an economic logic at one end and a social logic on the other end, with greatest hybridity tending to be in the middle (Battilana et al., 2017). However, they extend this argument and suggest the need for theorizing on the degree of hybridity. This involves 'the relative importance of the economic logic vis-à-vis the social logic ... as well as the intensity of the logics' (Shepherd et al., 2019, p. 4). Shepherd et al. (2019) refer to hybrid relativity as the way in which economic and social logics are balanced or distributed within an organization in an attempt to account for the variation in attention that organizations can place on economic objectives or social objectives.

Shepherd et al. (2019, p. 9) describe a continuum for hybrid relativity in the following terms:

> a traditional social venture is relatively high in social logic and low in economic logic (low hybridity), a traditional economic venture is relatively high in economic logic and low in social logic (low hybridity), and a traditional hybrid venture is balanced – the social and economic logics are relatively equal within the venture (high hybridity).

An example of an organization with low relative hybridity would be a large corporation with CSR initiatives for their employees and the community.

However, in addition to describing this continuum for hybrid relatively, the authors suggest that it is also important to consider hybrid intensity, which 'refers to the vigor with which the economic logic is held within an organization and the vigor with which the social logic is held in the organization' (Shepherd et al., 2019, p. 9). They predict that organizations with high hybrid intensity (that is, strong social and economic logics) are more likely to seek to scale their operations to increase both their social and economic impact. In contrast, they predict organizations with low hybrid intensity (that is, weak social and weak economic logics) – potentially lifestyle businesses or small-scale family businesses – will not be as committed to growth.

This theorizing of the degree of hybridity in organizations provides a more nuanced approach and recognition of the heterogeneity possible in hybrid organizations and forms. It also opens up opportunities to better examine, manage and theorize the source of tensions and conflicts in hybrid organizations, and the competitive but also complementary inter-actions that may occur in the enactment of logics at the organizational level (Tobias et al., 2013; Meyer and Höllerer, 2014).

Legitimizing Hybridity

What many empirical examinations of social enterprises reveal is the challenge of achieving legitimacy when adopting a template or way of organizing that deviates from a traditional economic logic (for example manifested in a for-profit organizational model) or social logic (for example manifested in a not-for-profit organizational model) (Battilana and Dorado, 2010; Battilana and Lee, 2014; Dalpiaz et al., 2016; Pache and Santos, 2013; Smith and Besharov, 2017; see also Chapter 4 in this book). In classic organization theory, the pursuit of multiple institutional logics generates institutional complexity (Greenwood et al., 2011) and can threaten organizational legitimacy or 'cultural support' for the organization (Meyer and Scott, 1983). Organizations operate within the accepted norms and logics of their sector (DiMaggio and Powell, 1983) and they achieve legitimacy when they fit institutionalized norms, which hybrids do not (Battilana and Lee, 2014). The main forms of legitimacy are moral (the right thing to do) and cognitive (makes sense) legitimacy to both external and internal audiences (Blessing, 2015).

For example, a hybrid organization's cognitive legitimacy to external audiences may be lacking because there is not an institutionalized legal structure for hybrids and no associated funding processes (Battilana et al., 2012; Doherty et al., 2014). An ambiguous hybrid structure makes it difficult for financiers to categorize hybrid organizations (Doherty et al., 2014), and some evidence for this can be found in reports that pure charities are more successful at raising funds than hybrids (Battilana and Lee, 2014). There is also a threat to the hybrid's 'practical legitimacy' – external stakeholders such as customers and beneficiaries are concerned with receiving the same value from products and services produced by a hybrid with a social and business mission as those produced by a single mission organization (Blessing, 2015; Edwards et al., 2019). Further-more, a hybrid's moral legitimacy may be challenged by external audiences who question whether an organization with a social and business mission can adequately serve their social mission. For example, will a traditional charity running a social enterprise sacrifice social outcomes in order to achieve financial returns that donors demand or that the enterprise requires in order to remain commercially viable (Edwards et al., 2019; Logue and Edwards, 2013)? How will 'mission drift' be avoided in the face of pressure to conform to institutional norms and a single mission (Battilana and Lee, 2014; Grimes et al., 2018); see also Chapter 4 in this book)?

Practitioners and managers of hybrid organizations, specifically social enterprises, are also confronted by the issue of internal legitimacy – essentially a contestation over the organization's identity. Hybridity may heighten the differences in values and beliefs and contrasting conceptions of 'value' held by internal stakeholders (Smith and Besharov, 2017; Rhodes and Donnelly-Cox, 2014). For example, Edwards et al. (2019) suggest that hybrids that begin with a single social mission tend to have a strong 'social imprint' that, on the one hand, protects the social mission but, on the other hand, may work against the business mission when staff with a social background question the moral legitimacy of the business mission and how it impacts beneficiaries. The nature and pace of work associated with business (efficiency-driven with tight deadlines and carefully measured output) is vastly different to social services (values-driven with loosely measured outputs) and likely to cause tensions (Cooney, 2006). In a WISE (work integration social enterprise), where social impact is measured by employability of beneficiaries beyond the WISE, the social mission may impede the economic efficiency of the hybrid (Battilana et al., 2015). For example, a café with a social mission has real staffing needs associated with business efficiency that may not align with the social mission's objective of consistent employment for beneficiaries (Edwards et al., 2019). However, an alternative view in the literature is that by committing to multiple logics, hybrids may gain greater external legitimacy by appealing to multiple audiences, thereby increasing opportunities to access resources from external stakeholders, and that tensions between multiple logics can actually be productive and can be a source of innovation (Smith and Besharov, 2017). This becomes further complicated when considering hybridity as a question of degree (for example relativity and intensity).

Hybrid Organization Creation and Design

Shepherd et al. (2019) take the issue of organizational imprinting of hybrids further and suggest a future research agenda that investigates how an entrepreneur directly influences the degree of hybridity (Wry and York, 2017) in an emerging organization, based on their motivation and attention to and knowledge of social problems and challenges. Furthermore, they suggest that more research is needed into 'how communities of inquiry – collections of actors working towards a common objective – can influence the core logics of an organization during its emergence and evolution' (Shepherd et al., 2019, p. 1; see also Shepherd, 2015).

In classifying their design, hybrids can be further described as 'differentiated' or 'structural', and 'integrated' or 'blended' (Battilana and Lee, 2014; Ebrahim et al., 2014). This typology emerges from two key questions: Are your customers and beneficiaries the same people? Do beneficiaries automatically receive value from the core activities of the hybrid or does the hybrid have to provide additional activities or services to this group to achieve their goals? For example, when customers and beneficiaries are one and the same, the hybrid is integrated or blended. When social and commercial activities are separate, the hybrid is differentiated or structural and design decisions need to be made about how to treat the separate functions. These design types have varying implications when it comes to susceptibility to mission drift, financial instability, and securing legitimacy, with each hybrid type needing a different set of management practices and structures (Ebrahim et al., 2014). For example, Santos et al. (2015) suggest that blended or integrated hybrids are less likely to suffer from mission drift, are more financially sustainable and experience higher levels of internal and external legitimacy. These design types suggested by Santos et al. (2015) are summarized as follows:

- Market hybrid (integrated): social and commercial impact are not separated. For example, The Fred Hollows Foundation manufactures inexpensive intraocular lenses for sale in poor markets where they also train doctors to perform cataract surgery using these lenses. Market hybrids are unlikely to be prone to mission drift and experience high external and internal legitimacy.
- Blending hybrid (integrated): like the market hybrid, customers and beneficiaries are one and the same, but they need additional services, typically training. For example, to participate in a microfinance programme, customers must be mentored by the organization. The blending hybrid may be integrated (the same staff

service customers and provide training) or, where the training is very complex and specialized, the hybrid may be differentiated.

● Bridging hybrid (differentiated): customers and beneficiaries are from different groups. For example, an organization sells the same product to different groups but one group is paying a higher price and subsidizing the other. This structure carries the risk that higher paying customers will be prioritized, leading to mission drift.

● Coupling hybrid (differentiated): also separates customers and beneficiaries with the added complication that social impact is contingent on additional support services, such as training, which is separate from the commercial side of the business. This creates significant strain on the organization's resources and increases the likelihood of mission drift. There is also the risk of diminished allocation of resources to the social mission as financial sustainability is so challenging. For example, WISE hybrids aim to serve clients with competitive products/services whilst simultaneously providing training and counselling for the long-term unemployed with the desired social impact outcome of facilitating their graduation into jobs outside the organization.

Generally, hybrid organizations tend to identify as non-profits or for-profits or choose a differentiated model. A 2007 study of WISE organizations in France found that they were approximately equally split between operating as non-profits and for-profits (Pache and Santos, 2013). Hybrids that chose to operate as non-profits did so because it was the best way to avoid social mission drift and those who operated as for-profits chose this form to appear more 'professional' and 'business-like' (Pache and Santos, 2010, 2013). A more recent study of 70 social enterprises found that half were established as non-profits or for-profits and the other half combined several legal entities (Mair et al., 2015). Santos et al. (2015) recommends that 'coupling hybrids' might do best to establish separate entities for their social and business concerns, so as to develop expertise in both. In a guide on managing hybrids for practitioners in traditional not-for-profit organizations, Edwards et al. (2019) suggest those considering establishing a hybrid ask: What are the goals and priorities of your hybrid? Will you set up a hybrid as a separate entity to your existing organization or charity? What type of organizational form will best support the pursuit of your goals? Who are your customers, and who are your beneficiaries? Are these the same or different? Do all stakeholders (internal and external) share this understanding?

An alternative view of hybrid creation and design is the concept of 'hybrid spaces'. Extant research on differentiated hybrids has assumed different logics are structurally separated within different compartments in the organization (Perkmann et al., 2018). Perkmann et al. (2018) challenge this assumption and propose an alternative differentiated hybrid form: 'hybrid spaces'. This importantly moves conceptions of hybridity beyond social enterprises and combining social and economic logics, to considering where hybrid activity occurs. In a hybrid space, hybrid activity is contained within a bounded 'unit' within the organization which protects the organization from legitimacy problems and internal tensions. They argue that hybrid spaces are appropriate when an organization needs to leverage a dominant logic to fulfil a minority mission. For example, universities frequently have hybrid spaces called 'research centres' that utilize the university's dominant logic (non-profit research and publication) for commercial gain (applied research for profit). A traditional non-profit might consider using 'hybrid spaces' when engaging in for-profit activities that generate income for their social mission, but only if the hybrid leverages the activities associated with the (dominant) social mission (Perkmann et al., 2018).

Integration Processes and People

In Chapter 4 I discuss the different approaches that hybrids have taken in navigating institutional complexity and paradoxes inherent in their forms. For example, the work of Smith et al. (2013, p. 410) summarizes the paradoxical tensions that arise in social enterprises in relation to performing, organizing, belonging and learning, highlighting the tensions around: who should hybrid organizations hire; how can they socialize employees; and how might they manage divergent identity expectations among subgroups of employees. Understanding how divergent (competing or complementary or differently interpreted) logics are integrated within an organization reveals critical integration processes for managing hybridity.

In terms of employees, existing literature prescribes two types of staff competencies for hybrid organizations: 'pluralists', with extensive backgrounds in both social and business fields, or 'specialists', who work only on the business mission or only on the social mission. Whilst specialists are most appropriate when the hybrid is structurally differentiated, pluralists are considered ideal, though rare (Battilana et al., 2012; Smith and Besharov, 2017). Pluralist managers have been shown to develop and routinize integrating practices that facilitate other members' identification with the organization, thereby lessening conflict between members (Battilana and Lee, 2014; Perkmann et al., 2018). Other studies show that many hybrids adopt a strategy of 'blank slate' hiring: staffing the organization with people who have not already been 'institutionalized' in a specific logic (for example, new graduates) and socializing them to focus on operational performance, rather than hiring experts from business and social work who tend to become competitors within the hybrid (Battilana et al., 2012; Santos et al., 2015; Smith and Besharov, 2017; see also Edwards et al., 2019). However, this hiring strategy is not generally appropriate in the nascent stages of a hybrid organization (Battilana et al., 2012) where expertise in organizing templates is required. Related to this issue is the surprising lack of investigation into how to manage performance measurements for hybrid employees, despite the fact that having key performance indicators reflecting multiple goals would appear to be important in aligning organization members with the achievement of dual missions (Battilana and Lee, 2014).

Employees, managers and other internal stakeholders may experience tensions when working in a hybrid due to the differences in values and beliefs and contrasting conceptions of 'value' held by internal stakeholders (Smith and Besharov, 2017). As described by Edwards et al. (2019), such tensions arise when staff experience dissonance between seemingly different or even conflicting aims, values or ways of conducting a service. This is made particularly difficult when a hybrid organization is created by an existing organization (say, a traditional not-for-profit organization) that has an established, single and well-recognized social mission and specific legacy of enacting certain values. Edwards et al. (2019) suggest that

> for some staff, a perceived move away from the pure focus on social mission can cause tension. On one hand, imprinting protects the social mission, but on the other hand it may work against the business mission – especially when staff with a social (logic) background question the moral legitimacy of the business mission and how it impacts beneficiaries (p. 18).

(For a broader examination of the rationalization of the not-for-profit sector, see also Hwang and Powell, 2009.)

In terms of integrating processes, much of the literature examines 'conciliatory' processes for ameliorating tensions between staff from different sides of the dual missions. Managers may need to adjudicate tensions, yet studies suggest that more successful resolutions come from allowing staff to work through conflicts and find compromises (Battilana et al., 2015). This can be achieved by having 'spaces of negotiation', instituted via 'regulation meetings' where each staff group listens to the concerns of the other, and 'formal processes' of 'positive confrontation' where social workers and production supervisors coordinate their schedules (Battilana et al., 2015). These 'spaces of negotiation' serve to empower staff and (hopefully) preserve a 'productive tension' between the social and business mission and prevent tensions from escalating into conflicts (Battilana et al., 2015).

The success of the 'spaces of negotiation' practice is in line with the argument that social entrepreneurship is defined not only by the provision of 'care' to beneficiaries but also by organizational practices (Andre and Pache, 2016). For example, some scholars recommend the deliberate generation of a 'culture of caring' within hybrids by hiring 'caring' individuals and exposing non-frontline staff to the work that directly involves beneficiaries to create empathy for the hybrid's social mission (Andre and Pache, 2016; Rhodes and Donnelly-Cox, 2014).

While Smith and Besharov (2017) dismiss 'spaces of negotiation' as a short-term response to the challenges of a dual mission, they build on the concept of 'productive tensions' with their research on the use of 'paradoxical frames' – the understanding that the hybrid's dual missions are both contradictory and interdependent. Their longitudinal study of a 'sustaining hybrid' finds that when organizational leaders adopt paradoxical frames they are less likely to become mired in resolving tensions and more likely to look for workable solutions that allow the work to move forward (Smith and Besharov, 2017). At the same time, a second element of the hybrid, 'guardrails' – the structures, expertise and relationships associated with each side of the dual mission – form a boundary within which experimentation with alternative approaches can take place. Overall, this approach serves as an alternative to viewing 'tensions' as constraining, and logics as competing, reframing hybrids as adaptive organizations.

Conclusion

While there is a burgeoning collection of academic literature on social enterprises and hybrids, there is still much to investigate and a great need to inform practitioners' and policy makers' (pressing) concerns of how best to organize, operate and manage a hybrid. These types of discussions are important in shaping other issues, including impact measurement, which has substantial effects on the flow and directionality of capital and investment from both government and the private sector and the opportunities for scaling such organizational forms. I explore this issue of impact measurement further below.

MEASURING IMPACT

In this section, I further explore the growing practitioner debates on the need to measure (social) impact to build markets for social good – what, how, when and by whom should measurement be done – and argue for further theorizing. In their review of the state of the field of impact assessment, Ebrahim and Rangan (2014) suggest that academic study and theorizing was lagging behind practice in terms of impact assessment, particularly as the term 'impact' has become part of the everyday lexicon, especially for the social sector. Barraket and Yousefpour (2013) take a similar view although they see the field as being practitioner-led but academically informed; and Kroeger and Weber (2014) state that 'theoretical concepts for comparing social value creation are scarce' (p. 515). To conclude, I suggest theorizing impact measurement by drawing on the sociology of valuation and evaluation.

From Social Value to Measuring Impact

In recent years, a rapidly growing focus has emerged, across much of the policy and practitioner discourse on social innovation, on 'impact' – generating it from new activities and existing activities, measuring and comparing it, and developing new risk–return–impact paradigms, especially when it comes to investment decisions. It is this shift from (social) 'value' to 'impact' that is worthy of further problematization and investigation by scholars, as at first glance it would seem to indicate a shift from contributing toward collective good within existing systems to changing existing systems for both collective and individual benefit. It also suggests that taken-for-granted roles in society and purposes of organizations are now being challenged. For example, not-for-profit organizations now constantly need to demonstrate and measure their impact (and outcomes) to funders; universities now need to demonstrate (often immediate) impact of funded research and its benefits beyond the academy.

> We live in a time where the institutionalized purpose of various organizational forms and templates is now being questioned; value needs to be demonstrated, impact now needs to be measured.

In Chapter 2, the discussion on social value creation, capture and distribution raises the issue that 'value' is a decision about quality and an act of assessment. This is caught up in a myriad of related concepts such as blended value (Emerson, 2003), shared value (Dembek et al., 2016;

Porter and Kramer, 2011), subjective well-being, triple bottom-line accounting, corporate social responsibility, corporate social performance, and social return on investment. In investment spheres, growing impact investing rhetoric – which arguably currently surpasses impact investing activity – pushes the notion that there need not be any tradeoff between seeking social impact and financial returns. This movement and efforts to build impact investing markets (Tett, 2019; see also OECD, 2019) are seemingly subsuming earlier movements, such as ESG, which take into account environmental, social and governance aspects of investments, and 'responsible' investing, to a much looser, difficult to measure and generic idea of 'impact'. More broadly, I argue that this represents a shift from the role of the corporation in society from being responsible (that is, avoiding harm) to doing good (that is, using the corporate model to generate inclusive growth and produce greater social good). Interestingly, studies show that corporations do not suffer financially from positive social performance, but that this is only a mildly positive relationship and 'doing bad' has a greater negative effect than the positive effect of 'doing good' (Margolis and Walsh, 2003; Orlitzky et al., 2003).

One of the key empirical challenges in impact measurement is also defining the level of measurement given a lack of consistent definition. Ebrahim and Rangan (2014) point out that

> an established literature in international development and evaluation often uses the term to refer to 'significant or lasting changes in people's lives, brought about by a given action or series of actions'. More recently, impact has also come to be associated with results that target the 'root causes' of a social problem; while others use impact more narrowly to refer to an organization's specific and measurable role in affecting a social result (attribution) requiring a counterfactual for assessment. (Ebrahim and Rangan, 2014, p. 120)

Furthermore, I argue that a scholarly and phronetic approach is surely needed to ask publicly: what are the consequences of measuring impact in some ways? Is this appropriate? Is this desirable (Flyvbjerg, 2001)? Such an approach might then begin to reveal a changing logic of appropriateness in the way we organize to generate greater social good, or a more equal and equitable society and indeed economy, and the limits of quantifying qualitative outcomes and intangible good. In this section I further discuss the empirical debates on impact measurement and argue for the need to connect this to a sociology of valuation and evaluation (Lamont, 2012).

The Emergence of Social Impact Assessment and Reporting

Esteves et al. (2012) suggest that the genesis of social impact assessment is from environmental policy and linked to the requirement for environmental impact assessments to be conducted for large infrastructure projects. Contemporary social impact assessment (SIA) began along with environmental impact assessment in the early 1970s in response to the requirements of the National Environmental Policy Act (1969) in the USA. However, the field has now expanded. 'Now SIA researchers and practitioners are interested in the processes of analyzing, monitoring and managing the social consequences of planned interventions, and by logical extension the social dimensions of development in general' (Esteves et al., 2012, p. 34). According to Vanclay (2003), cited in Kroeger and Weber (2014), researchers in engineering and infrastructure understand SIA 'as an umbrella or overarching framework that embodies the evaluation of all impacts on humans and on all the ways in which people and communities interact with their socio-cultural, economic and biophysical surroundings'. Other authors state that social impact assessments for public (engineering) projects 'were oriented towards the technical collection of primarily quantitative data with which to determine "objectively" the nature of impacts, and those that were oriented towards providing a process through which the interests and aspirations of impacted communities could be represented in decision-making by facilitating community participation' (Lockie, 2001, p. 279).

However, although economic and environmental viability may be relatively easy to quantify, approaches for quantitative evaluation of social performance and underlying social value creation in public infrastructure projects from a community perspective remain challenging. In a recent example (within infrastructure and engineering), Doloi (2018) uses social network theory to compute mathematically the social performance index (SPI) for a project. Data collection is based on structured surveys of key stakeholder groups, asking for their perceptions across several project characteristics. Network characteristics across numerous relations between stakeholders and key project issues provide good indicators of how an actor (or a node) within the network is positioned relative to another actor. Doloi (2018, p. 144) states: 'The outputs of these social network models provide inputs for assessing the social value in the project mathematically. The threshold value for social performance is the stakeholders' initial expectations and interests across the project attributes and perceived benefits that flow into the society in short and long terms.' While public impact assessments have long been a part of public engineering and infrastructure projects, most pervasive has been its emergence and diffusion across the not-for-profit and social sectors.

The greater emphasis on reporting in these sectors is linked to changing approaches to governance and associated public policy regimes. New Public Management (Hood, 1995) and shifts from bureaucratic to contractual governance have recalibrated the funding environment for many not-for-profit organizations that rely on direct government funding or contracts to deliver social services. There is a shift away from funding core activities to funding, competitively, specific projects, outputs or outcomes (Barraket and Yousefpour, 2013). In their study of five small to medium Australian social enterprises, Barraket and Yousefpour (2013) found that, in practice, the primary driver of evaluation activities was to demonstrate legitimacy to external stakeholders. Similarly, Kroeger and Weber (2014) suggest that two issues that are compelling not-for-profit organizations to do more in relation to the measurement of social value creation are, first, many such organizations are wondering whether they minister to their beneficiaries as effectively as possible. These organizations want to know not only 'if they really are making progress and maximizing their potential positive social impact' but also 'how they are performing relative to their industry peers' (Lingane and Olsen, 2004, p. 124). Second, such organizations often depend on material and immaterial support from third parties, including foundations, governmental institutions, corporations and investors – sources that increasingly confront not-for-profit organizations with high expectations and demands regarding transparency and accountability (Campbell, 2002; Grimes, 2010; Miller and Wesley, 2010; Nicholls, 2009; Polonsky and Grau, 2011). These sources seek to evaluate and compare a variety of social interventions in order to fund only the most effective ones (Buckmaster, 1999; Miller et al., 2012). Others suggest that it is new models of funding such as venture philanthropy that demand 'increased attention toward evaluating the impact generated, as well as to certain management systems to be used in the organization funded' (Manetti, 2014, p. 447). There are many examples of explicit government approaches to impact measurement and the pressures placed on the social sector to demonstrate a programme's or intervention's worth. Examples of such overarching national developments include:

- In 2007, the Scottish Government implemented the Scottish National Performance Framework. Revised in 2011, the framework contains 16 national outcomes and 50 National Indicators.

- In the UK more generally, there has been increased focus on the measurement of social impact and outcomes to improve the effectiveness of public sector collaboration with non-government community sector providers. The Public Services (Social Value) Act 2012 requires public authorities to consider economic, social and environmental wellbeing in their public services contracts.
- At a federal level in the USA, the Government Performance and Results Act (GPRA) 1993 and the GPRA Modernization Act of 2010 were introduced with the purpose of embedding the use of outcomes-based decision-making in the federal budgeting process.
- The Canadian Government in the early 2000s switched to a project funding model for community organizations, resulting in increased results-based accountability.
- In Australia, the NSW Government has developed the Human Services Outcomes Framework, intended, amongst other things, to build a common understanding of the outcomes which are priorities across NSW Government agencies and non-government organizations, promote consistency of measurement and evaluation of human services outcomes and activities, and assist operational staff to understand how their roles contribute to broader human services outcomes.

While social sector organizations have engaged in measurement since the late 19th century, what is measured has changed. While the initial focus of social sector and community organizations was simply on measuring needs (for example how many people lived in poverty), this shifted to input and output measures in the 20th century as part of procurement and accountability needs, to now seeking to measure programme outcomes and overall lasting impact on society (Flateau et al., 2015). Growing stakeholder attention toward measurement, accountability and longer-term impact reflects a changed institutional context in which social sector organizations find themselves operating (Manetti, 2014).

Accounting for Impact

Unsurprisingly, the focus on quantifying impact leads to early discussions of actual accounting methods and programmes. Nicholls (2009, p. 758) identifies two key challenges in relation to reporting by organizations across the social sector: 'First, there is the question of what is to be measured and reported. There is a widespread perceived difficulty in establishing the relationship between complex input factors (grants, volunteers, market income, social capital, etc.) and the social impacts that correspond to the mission objectives of such organizations.' This contrasts with the more narrowly defined objectives of a traditional business. 'Second, there is the question of how to measure what is to be reported. As yet, there are no standardized calculative mechanisms for social value creation, nor any comparative unit of measurement' (Nicholls, 2009, p. 758).

In an early piece of work on this issue, Emerson (2003) puts forward the concept of blended value, being similar to shared value in that it is rooted in the activities of the firm. However, Emerson starts from the basis that corporations are already creating both social and economic value – the issue is one of measurement tools. He argues that better social management information and tracking systems are required, together with a new set of metrics or a common language for measuring and assessing value creation, whether the value being created is economic, social or environmental: 'All investments are understood to operate simultaneously in economic, social, and environmental realms. There is no "trade off" between the three, but rather a concurrent pursuit of value – social, financial, and environmental' (Emerson, 2003, p. 45).

Measuring blended value and quantifying a blended return on investment, then, requires a new approach to accounting and capital allocation. As both parts of value creation operate together, social and economic, measuring one or the other on its own becomes impossible or at least poses significant challenges (White, 2017). As one response, Nicholls (2009) builds on Emerson's blended value concept to develop a new construct – blended value accounting. Conventional accounting, with its emphasis on quantitative financial reporting, has failed to capture and value social and environmental goods and so blended value accounting represents a spectrum from quantitative reporting to more qualitative descriptions of social value creation. Yet it is important to note that Nicholls (2009) concludes that the measurement of social value still involves some bespoke reporting if it is to be fully expressed.

In practice, blended value accounting seems to have been overtaken by other methods such as Social Return on Investment, although some consider SROI as an example within a broader category of blended value accounting: 'SROI belongs to the field of blended value accounting since it largely has recourse to hybrid instruments of accounting and reporting, involving stakeholders in defining outputs, outcomes, and monetary proxies for measuring the impact of the organization' (Manetti, 2014, p. 451). Manetti (2014) describes the advantages of SROI as creating an effective dialogue between stakeholders as it requires stakeholder participation at all points, and contributes to internal controls. However, SROI is weaker in relation to providing data that fairly describes the situation, due to the obvious difficulty of monetizing many outcomes, especially intangible outcomes such as improvement in the self-confidence of participants. There is a risk that a disproportionate amount of organizational resources will be diverted into the attempt to monetize outcomes while the difficulty of measuring throws doubt on the reliability of SROI. For some social enterprises and not-for-profit organizations, there may also be a sense that, having to identify monetary proxies for every outcome achieved conflicts with their basic social aims. SROI is also described as an approach to impact measurement that combines social impact assessment with cost–benefit analysis. However, as the social value created is defined according to the intervention's customized theory of change, comparison across interventions is limited (Kroeger and Weber, 2014).

Comparing Interventions

One of the dominant drivers of impact measurement is the desire to compare the outcomes of different social interventions. This may be driven by governments seeking best value for taxpayer money for different interventions focusing on the same social problem, or by philanthropists and (impact) investors seeking to compare social returns across investment opportunities, funds and enterprises. As an example, and as mentioned in Chapter 2, Kroeger and Weber (2014) seek to address this challenge of impact reporting by developing an approach that permits the comparison of the social value creation of different, unrelated heterogonous interventions. They explain their quantitative approach and formula as follows:

> We use subjective satisfaction ratings to offer a uniform measurement unit that social interventions from different sectors can apply to gauge their performance and compare themselves with their industry peers. We then take the concept of mean life satisfaction (LS) in regions and countries, which conventionally indicates the living standard of regional or national economies, and combine it with insights from the not-for-profit literature. We conclude that social interventions primarily treat people below regional or national levels of mean LS. We can thereby easily calculate the social need for different treatment groups in different regions or countries. (2014, p. 513)

Kroeger and Weber (2014) also draw on organizational effectiveness theory, adopting a basic understanding of value creation 'to posit a social intervention's effectiveness as a relative construct' and so: '... define the effectiveness of a social intervention as the degree to which an organization reduces a treatment group's social need. This degree can then be meaningfully compared to the degree of an entirely different social intervention that also reduces a treatment group's social need' (2014, p. 513).

Ultimately, this formula creates what the authors describe as a uniform social value construct: 'subjective well-being' (SWB). This is composed of measures of overall life satisfaction and, within this, measures of domain satisfaction. While these all rely on subjective assessment, that is, personal reporting of satisfaction, Kroeger and Weber (2014) develop an approach that means that these measures can be used to compare across interventions and across different socioeconomic and institutional conditions in a region or country. A number of databases exist that provide a baseline or benchmark for these measures.

Again, I emphasize here that these impact measurement techniques may not be appropriate to all sorts of social problems, levels of analysis or organizational forms, and may lack applicability due to the (benchmarking) data required for calculation. While other sophisticated techniques such as experimental and quasi-experimental approaches, including the increasingly popular use of Randomized Control Trials (RCTs), are diffusing globally, these are also context-dependent in terms of problem and political and socio-economic conditions. For example, it may be rather morally inappropriate and politically unpalatable for governments to conduct RCTs in relation to social interventions with vulnerable or at-risk populations, such as children.

Using Impact Measurement Tools

Common empirical concerns across the application of impact measurement tools are level of analysis, attribution and additionality, and quality, availability and collection of data. Most of the impact measurement tools are seeking to move beyond outputs and outcomes to impact. Ebrahim and Rangan (2014) make the distinction that outcomes refer to 'lasting changes in the lives of individuals' and impact refers to 'lasting results achieved at a community or societal level', where the root causes of a social problem are addressed (p. 120). They note that attribution and additionality remain a challenge regardless of whether one is assessing outcomes or impacts, as these are often achieved by collections of actors working towards a shared goal making causality difficult to distinguish.

One of the key rationales for implementing impact measurement tools is to also improve organizational performance, yet there is mixed evidence that this is indeed the case (Barraket and Yousefpour, 2013; Ebrahim and Rangan, 2014). Sawhill and Williamson (2001), in a study of 30 leading non-profits, found that measurement was useful to the organizations for improving outcomes, particularly when they:

- set measurable goals linked to mission (rather than trying to measure mission directly);
- kept measures simple and easy to communicate; and
- selected measures that created a culture of accountability and common purpose in the organization, thus helping to align the work of disparate units and chapters.

However, the results were not all positive: a significant number of agencies reported that implementing outcome measurement:

- had led to a focus on measurable outcomes at the expense of other important results (46 per cent);
- had overloaded the organization's record-keeping capacity (55 per cent); and
- that there remained uncertainty regarding how to make programme changes based on identified strengths and weaknesses (42 per cent).

Public discourse and reviews of impact measurement applications across social enterprises, social programmes and impact investing models (for example, see Logue et al., 2017) suggest two particular challenges: (1) collecting quality data at a reasonable cost; and (2) selecting measures to measure against, that is, benchmarks. In terms of the first challenge, the impact of some 'pay for success' programmes in the USA has been evaluated using RCTs. However, this is an expensive approach that requires the evaluators to track those people who participate in the intervention and a control group that does not, to understand the impact of the intervention. And, as mentioned above, this approach may not be appropriate for all social problems. Lean data is an alternative approach being trialled, particularly in emerging economies. Here, the impact of social enterprises is assessed by surveying customers for feedback. Surveys take the form of interviews administered through mobile phones. This approach emphasizes using an impact measurement tool that aligns with the stage of the enterprise, and so as enterprises grow, they can consider measuring in more detailed or sophisticated ways.

For any impact measurement approach, having benchmarks and metrics with which to compare and measure progress is important, and challenging. Benchmarks may have to be compiled from multiple sources and from sources aggregated to a national level (as opposed to local or individual). In the case of homelessness, for example, benchmarking may require compiling health, justice, temporary accommodation and housing data from perhaps provincial and national sources. A number of indices or banks of measures are increasingly available, including:

- Impact Reporting and Investment Standards (IRIS);
- UN Sustainable Development Goals;
- Social Performance Taskforce Indicators for micro-finance providers;
- Grameen Progress Out of Poverty Index;
- The Global Value Exchange: a crowd sourced database of values, outcomes, indicators and stakeholders.

The Global Impact Investing Network (GIIN) is actively researching impact measurement. A recent study (GIIN, 2016) provides guidance around developing an impact framework for the clean energy sector. This study found that the most commonly measured impacts in that sector were:

- number of programme beneficiaries (output measure based on IRIS);
- number of people employed (output measure based on IRIS);
- reduction or avoidance of GHG emissions due to products or services sold (outcome measure based on IRIS);
- investments catalyzed by leveraging own capital (outcome measure);
- clean energy capacity of products or services sold (output measure based on IRIS);
- household cost savings resulting from shifts in spending on fuel (outcome measure);
- increased income resulting from higher productivity or additional income-generating opportunities (realized by end users) (outcome measure).

Improved impact measurement is seen as particularly important to the field of impact investing. For example, Impact Investing Australia has identified the strengthening of impact measurement and management as a key lever for growth in relation to impact investing (AAB, 2016), providing institutional infrastructure for the desired market (Hinings et al., 2017).

Ebrahim and Rangan (2014), in their state of the field review, provide a list of the current range of approaches to social performance measurement, often labelled as impact evaluation and outcome measurement, and many other public reports from international bodies provide further details also. As this chapter seeks to highlight the empirical tensions and developments that currently lack theorization, a brief review of some of the key approaches being used to measure and account for impact in settings of social innovation are included below.

Theory of change or logic model

This approach forms the foundation of much impact measurement. A programme logic model shows the intended relationship between inputs, outputs and outcomes for a programme. The 'outcomes' of community sector programmes are the differences these programmes make to the lives of the people they engage with. Typically, a set of indicators are developed to measure outcome and impact. Outputs are delivered in the short term, outcomes in the medium term, and impact is the longer-term widespread change.

Cost–Benefit Analysis (CBA)

CBA is a process for monetizing impact. It requires a financial value to be placed on the costs and benefits associated with a programme so that the two can be compared to see which one is greater. For this very reason it is a difficult approach to implement, as it requires the ability to place a monetary value on programme impacts across stakeholders. CBA is widely used across the public and private sector to help decision-makers prioritize among the use of funds for different programmes. However, Moonshot Global (2018) notes that: 'The insights that come from CBA are only as useful as the data used; many assumptions go into a CBA, which should be stated explicitly to help decision makers understand the context and limitations of the evidence they are using to inform strategies' (p. 6).

Results-based approaches

In the international development field, pay by results has been of increasing interest as an approach to development assistance for over a decade, especially in the health and education sectors but also increasingly in the environmental sector (Voigt and Ferreira, 2015). Pay by results is an approach characterized by several elements:

- the disbursement of funds is contingent on the delivery of predetermined results;
- the recipient has discretion over how results are achieved, under mutually agreed parameters; and
- independent verification acts as the trigger for disbursement.

Examples of results-based approaches include:

- the GAVI Immunization Services Support programme that paid countries for increases in routine immunization, measured as coverage rates of the diphtheria–tetanus–pertussis vaccine;
- social and development impact bonds; and
- challenge-linked financing, or awards and prizes for solutions to development problems.

Proponents of this approach argue that it can increase the effectiveness of aid as there is a greater focus on outcomes (rather than inputs) and recipients are encouraged to improve their efforts to meet targets as funding is contingent on achieving those targets. On the other hand, critics have drawn attention to issues such as:

- poorly designed measures can lead to unintended consequences or encourage coercive practices and gaming of the system;
- the costs of measuring and verifying results can be so high as to outweigh any benefits when compared to traditional grant funding.

Social Return on Investment (SROI)

Developed in 1997, SROI is designed to measure the performance of a given programme or investment by assessing impact. Like CBA, it assigns monetary values to outcomes. However, unlike CBA, stakeholder involvement is a key principle of SROI analysis. Stakeholders are closely involved in developing the theory of change for the project, which means that the theory of change is viewed as authentic and as providing 'a rich causal tapestry' of the change process (Faivel, 2018, p. 3). Others describe SROI as identifying 'quantified outcomes attributable to a project and then finding financial proxies that match these outcomes. By calculating in monetary terms the total value of benefits produced against the cost of investment, the final SROI ratio communicates at a glance the net value of a project' (Marden, 2011).

As in the case of CBA, monetization is the most complicated part of SROI. Below are three non-market methods for monetizing impacts.

- Cost-saving method: assigns a monetary value through the cost-savings a programme has achieved for the government or stakeholder. The challenge for this method is that it requires rigour and guidance on marginal costs and displacement.
- Stated preference: asks people what they would pay for a service or outcome to help infer willingness to pay. This approach is most

commonly used in estimating environmental values to date. The method involves both quantitative and qualitative data methods. This requires survey-based data collection, can be sensitive to framing bias and requires technical knowledge for design and estimation.

● Revealed preference: uses evidence of how people behave when making real choices and uses that to infer their willingness to pay (Moonshot Global, 2018).

Theorizing the Measuring of Impact: The Sociology of Valuation and Evaluation

In Chapter 2, I discussed how measuring devices for social value and impact contribute to developing the 'value infrastructure' (Barman, 2016, p. 206) or institutional infrastructure for various fields and markets and most importantly, shape the valuation of social good (Hinings et al., 2017, p. 179; see also Chapter 4 in this book). Important to an understanding of social innovation is the recognition that social value 'is multivocal in meaning and measure' with its proponents holding 'competing and contradictory conceptions of the meaning of that quality, how it can be achieved, and how judgment can be made' (Barman, 2016, p. 218).

In theorizing impact measurement – its assumptions, challenges, rhetoric, tools and applications – it is necessary and productive to situate it in a broader theoretical context of the sociology of valuation and evaluation. Lamont (2012, p. 204) describes a sociology of valuation and evaluation (SVE) as 'concerned with how value is produced, diffused, assessed, and institutionalized across a range of settings'. In this way, SVE is a social and cultural process because establishing value

> generally requires the following: (1) intersubjective agreement/disagreement on a matrix or a set of referents against which the entity (a good, a reputation, an artistic achievement, etc.) is compared; (2) negotiation about proper criteria and about who is a legitimate judge (often involving conflicts and power struggle (Bourdieu 1993)); (3) establishing value in a relational (or indexical) process involving distinguishing and comparing entities – as argued by many who have written on the topic, ranging from Ferdinand de Saussure and Karl Marx, to Georg Simmel, Roland Barthes and Pierre Bourdieu. (Lamont, 2012, p. 205)

There are of course additional and related lines of inquiry in the theorizing of markets and also market devices (Beckert, 2009; Callon et al., 2007; Fourcade, 2007) and a variety of disciplines across economic sociology, science and technology studies, management and organization studies, social and cultural anthropology, history, market studies, accounting studies, amongst others, that study valuation as a social practice (Helgesson and Muniesa, 2013). This has even resulted in recent years in the production of a dedicated journal entitled *Valuation Studies*.

In exploring SVE as a social and cultural process, it reveals important sub-processes of categorization and legitimation, identification and production of heterarchies, and issues around the devices of evaluation (such as the impact measurement tools described above) as non-human instruments of evaluation. In what follows I outline these aspects of SVE proposed by Lamont (2012) as an initial introduction to this approach to theorizing impact measurement.

There is a growing body of literature on the role of categories across organization and management theory, as they link to identities, cultural classification, practices, competition and institutions (for example, see Loewenstein et al., 2012; Glynn and Navis, 2013; Ocasio et al., 2015; Cattani et al., 2017; Kennedy and Fiss, 2013; Zuckerman, 1999). Lamont (2012) suggests categorization as an important sub-process in (e)valuation: 'At a minimum, (e)valuation requires categorization (or typification), i.e. determining in what group the entity (e.g. object or person) under consideration belongs.' This leads to an emphasis on boundaries and classification systems. Another important sub-process is legitimation, described as 'recognition by oneself and others of the value of an entity (whether a person, an action, or a situation)' (Lamont, 2012, p. 206). Here Lamont draws on and privileges Bourdieu (1993) given that his 'theory of symbolic fields emphasizes the role of critics and evaluators as gatekeepers in the production of symbolic capital for specific cultural goods'. Applying this lens to the practice of measuring impact leads to some important questions: Who decides what social problems are priorities? What and who decides what impact is desired, necessary, sufficient, and good? Who decides what devices are to be used to measure impact? How do these shape understandings of social value and power relations?

Another aspect of SVE is the notion of an actual or potential heterarchy, multidimensionality, or plurality of criteria of valuation and evaluation. Unveiling evaluation criteria and bringing to light the devices, institutions or cultural and social structures that support or enable them is a core focus of SVE (Lamont, 2012). Much existing literature in organization studies shows how institutions support different systems of value, and the distinct role of institutional logics (Friedland and Alford, 1991; Thornton et al., 2012) in producing and shaping orders of worth in and across societies, fields and organizations (see also Chapter 4 in this book). For example, Lamont describes the power and influence of the logic of the market in regard to what and how things (and life) are valued: 'neo-liberalism [provides] a context in which definitions of worth that are not based on market performance tend to lose their relevance and where market fundamentalism is exercising strong homogenizing pressures on collective identities and on shared definitions of what defines a worthy life' (Lamont, 2012, p. 208).

It is also important and necessary to examine the (e)valuative micro-practices that also support these heterarchies. These include the 'technologies of evaluation, criteria of evaluation, the customary rules or conventions of the field, the self-concept of evaluators, and the role of non-humans and instruments of evaluation' (Lamont, 2012, p. 211). The role of evaluators is particularly important, and particularly 'how strongly they are invested in what defines a proper evaluation, and ultimately, on their self-concept as an evaluator, which is necessarily implicated in the act of evaluation' (Lamont, 2012, p. 211). This is interesting in emergent fields such as impact investing where there are not yet customary rules and the nascent market is currently in a state of conflict and contestation over which measurement tools, devices and indices should dominate or become standard. This will have significant implications for power structures in this field and its role in shaping social value and the production of 'social good'.

A case in point here is Arjaliès and Durand's (2019) exploration of the valuation of product categories and, specifically, the development of socially responsible investment (SRI) in France. The French investment industry, working with the French public authorities, was the first in the world to define the SRI category based on the moral purposes of the product, not its technical features. According to Arjaliès and Durand, in the early 2000s, SRI was described in France as simply 'integrating non-financial concerns into investment processes'. It was considered that this would lead to a more holistic view of a fund, and thereby generate both greater investment and better financial performance (pp. 16–17). However, post-GFC, there was significant questioning of the role of banks and accusations of greenwashing by existing SRI funds. This led to a tightening of the definition of SRI: in 2016, the Ministry for the Economy and Finance endorsed the first industry website created to explain the SRI label to the general public, which included the following definition:

> SRI is a form of investment that aims to reconcile economic performance with social and environmental impact by financing companies and public organizations that contribute to sustainable development, whatever their activity sector. The SRI label, attributed through a strict labeling process led by

independent organizations, is a unique milestone for savers who wish to participate in a more sustainable economy.

Using this as a case study, the authors analyse product categories as a function of market actors' faculty of *judging* (categories and their normative attributes). This compares to market actors' faculty of *knowing*, which refers to understanding categories through their physical and functional features. The authors define 'normative attributes' of categories that reveal a purpose, or specific values stemming from and referring to the faculty of judging: 'Categories also include normative attributes that comprise values and intentionality, although the latter are most often silenced. Product categories hence are not only organizing devices but also function as questioning devices that encourage market actors to reflect on their purposes when producing or buying a specific product' (p. 4).

One of the key findings and arguments made by Arjaliès and Durand (2019) is that while studies in economic sociology have shown that product categories are classification devices that organize markets, 'they are also judgment devices conveying particular norms and ideals' (2019, p. 34). Relevant to this chapter, the authors conclude that: 'Increased questioning of market functioning, including its underpinnings and purposes, is transforming the roles and responsibilities of producers, and the functions of product categories. When faced with these changes, scholars need to find new ways of understanding the normative component of markets and its impact on consumption and society' (2019, p. 35).

Conclusion

In reflecting upon the discussions in Chapter 2 on social value (creation, capture and distribution), Vatin (2013) points out an important distinction between evaluation as a process of assessment and valorization as the process of adding value:

> The notion of valuation often blurs a distinction that is crucial to the understanding of economic processes: the distinction between processes of assessment (in which things undergo judgements of value) and processes of production (in which things are produced so as to be of value) ... Evaluation no longer appears as a simple preliminary to valorization, as the economics of conventions would have it. All along the chain of production, valorization is present in acts of evaluation, in that they are provisional modalities for establishing a value that is under construction. (p. 45)

Measuring impact is a growing practitioner and policy maker preoccupation, and one that is shifting the allocation of large amounts of capital and reshaping how we prioritize and solve social and environmental problems globally. A sociology of valuation and evaluation provides a rich theoretical lens to understand the social and cultural practices that are defining and producing 'impact' and 'social value'. The various practitioner tensions outlined in this section demonstrate the need and opportunity for improved theorizing of these contemporary issues that are of both theoretical and empirical import. A sociological view of valuation and evaluation will provide a better understanding of the conditions that sustain definitions of worth and value, and also the impact of devices and technologies on evaluation.

GOVERNING COLLABORATIONS

In this section, I further explore the challenges around governing cross-sector collaborations given that much of the theoretical and empirical studies on social innovation call for a greater diversity of actors in producing social value or impact, or consider new relational arrangements across diverse actors and sectors as a necessary form of social innovation to address entrenched social problems. I also focus on governing collaborations due to the substantial and growing practitioner and policy maker interest in how to conduct effective and productive cross-sector collaborations (Quelin et al., 2017; Gray and Purdy, 2018).

Similar to the topics on managing hybridity and measuring impact, academic theorizing is lagging behind practitioner needs and development (mainly because it is occurring in disciplinary silos), and missing the opportunity to develop knowledge on how to engage effectively in cross-sector work. This is important not just for the many social problems that are wicked and require the input of diverse stakeholders, but also because contemporary societies are struggling with reforming deeply rooted systems, such as financial, educational and health care, where effective cross-sector work holds promise.

In Chapter 3, I establish the source of the difficulties in governing cross-sector collaborations when considering social innovation as polysemous, and note Ostrom's idea of polycentric governance systems for common goods. In Chapter 4, I further explore the difficulties in establishing and managing field-to-field interactions. Here I discuss the range of studies that consider the difficulties in bringing together actors from different fields and domains and the challenges of aligning interests (O'Mahony and Bechky, 2008), achieving mutual prioritization of the problem (or solution) (Parmigiani and Rivera-Santos, 2011), and building shared governance and coordination models over common resources or common problems (Ansari et al., 2013; Casado-Asensio and Steurer, 2014; Mair et al., 2012; Ostrom, 2010; Steurer, 2013).

In what follows, I highlight practitioner concerns with cross-sector collaborations (Gray and Purdy, 2018). I then expand on several ideas as they relate to governing collaborations. First, the idea of polycentric governance systems (see also Chapter 3) that, while initially proposed to govern the commons, provide helpful insights into producing governance arrangements to address social problems (that involve a wide range of actors from across public, private and not-for-profit domains). Polycentric governance systems require the participation of all relevant actors, and so I consider what recent work on 'inclusive innovation' means for theorizing social innovation in highlighting the need to include marginalized actors. I then consider recent work that specifically focuses on the role of the state and public entrepreneurship in such collaborative governance arrangements. In developing a more systematic approach to governance arrangements, I conclude by exploring insights from literature examining national systems of innovation and suggest how this might assist in conceptualizing 'national systems of social innovation'.

The Challenges of Governing Cross-sector Collaborations

It is now well established that responding to the world's largest and most intractable social problems requires cross-sectoral responses and engagement of multiple and diverse actors to pursue more sustainable development. Yet this is difficult to organize and sustain because, as I have outlined across Chapter 3 and Chapter 4, the norms, logics, values, practices, accountabilities and regulations that guide each sector (be it the public, for-profit, not-for-profit or social enterprise sector) generate conflict and complexity. Given this, the starting assumption should be that success in cross-sector collaborations will be very difficult to achieve (Bryson et al., 2006). As noted above, it often complicates efforts to measure impact given that attribution is particularly difficult in collective arrangements.

Collaboration is defined as 'a process that engages a group of autonomous stakeholders interested in a problem or issue in an interactive deliberation using shared rules, norms, and structures, to share information and/or take coordinated actions' (Gray and Purdy, 2018, p. 11). Going further, Gray and Purdy (2018, p. 11) suggest that 'this process may simply involve stakeholders informing each other about the issue of interest, but more often it includes negotiating a set of norms and routines that will govern their future interactions and remain open to revision as they renegotiate their relationships over time'. More cross-sector collaborations are emerging, as complex and wicked social problems are not bound within a single institutional domain (Rittel and Webber, 1973), and are beyond the capacity of government alone, instead requiring the pooling of resources across stakeholders. Gray and Purdy (2018) suggest the following contextual factors that generate an urgent and growing need for cross-sector collaboration:

- deepening income inequality;
- growing importance of health in the economy;
- environmental degradation including climate change, water crises, and the need for sustainability;
- large-scale involuntary migration;
- increases in extreme weather events;
- continued decline in the ability of governments to handle complex problems.

While Gray and Purdy (2018) examine collaborative partnerships as a form of organizing, they are keen to point out the challenges and limits of partnerships in addressing complex social problems, as just agreeing to collaborate is no guarantee for success. In bringing together diverse stakeholders to address these issues, there will be conflicts over desired outcomes and methods that arise from historical relations, distrust, differing frames, identity or value differences, differences in risk perceptions, resource constraints, and power differences. To overcome this requires skilful leadership and design in developing a shared vision, and in dealing with power imbalances and changing conditions (Gray, 1989).

Reflective of discussions in Chapter 4 is Gray and Purdy's (2018) institutional theory view of collaborative partnerships that highlights the role of legitimacy, the construction of boundaries, and the negotiation of norms, practices and beliefs. Also important is the recognition of the 'home fields' in which participating stakeholders are based, providing insights into their guiding logics of action (Thornton et al., 2012; Toubiana and Zietsma, 2017). This provides theoretical insight into understanding existing 'rules of the game' and institutionalized ways of relating and organizing, and how new institutional infrastructure might be developed to establish and govern a cross-sector collaboration.

Ideas of how to govern cross-sector collaborations, and who should do so, are drawn from a range of literature. In what follows I explore some of these ideas, such as Ostrom's idea of polycentric governance and rules that need to be considered in constructing cross-sector collaborations. I then explore further the role of the State in these growing collaborations that cross institutional domains, where the State is a public entrepreneur and central stakeholder in ensuring inclusive responses to complex problems. I then look at how these inform broader understandings of relational configurations and system approaches to social innovation.

Polycentric Governance

Elinor Ostrom, political economist and Nobel Prize winner, produced a portfolio of work across her career on the governance of the commons and institutional arrangements to develop and sustain the management of natural resources (Klein et al., 2010). For Ostrom, the problem of providing and producing public goods – for example, health, education, safety – as well as the problem of devising governance mechanisms for sustaining natural resources requires institutional arrangements that are beyond those of the market. It is inherently difficult to regulate the commons because it 'involves making tough decisions under uncertainty, complexity, and substantial biophysical constraints as well as conflicting human values and interests' (Dietz et al., 2003). These public goods are often at the core of what social innovators and innovations are trying to improve, expand or indeed protect. Governing use of the commons is relevant for social innovation in several ways:[1]

- systems for governing use of the commons could be social innovations in and of themselves – overcoming the tragedy of the commons, encouraging a collective approach to use and a long-term view;
- embedded in this is the notion of the common good and shared social value as opposed to individuals pursuing their own self-interest;
- the tragedy of the commons is a wicked problem.

How citizens, public officials and private sector providers are coordinated, incentivized and participate initially and on an ongoing basis in the co-production of public goods and services generates what Ostrom refers to as a polycentric system. As described in Chapter 3, understanding how stakeholders from public, private and community fields come together is 'crucial for achieving higher levels of welfare in developing countries, particularly for those who are poor' (Ostrom, 1996, p. 1083). Ostrom (1999) outlines the components of the 'commons problem' as follows:

- A common-pool resource is a natural or man-made resource from which it is difficult to exclude or limit users once the resource is provided, and one person's consumption of resource units makes those units unavailable to others.
- When the resource has a high value and there are no institutional constraints on its use, there are strong incentives for individuals to appropriate more and more units, leading to congestion, over-use and ultimately depletion of the resource.
- There is also a free-rider problem. When it is difficult to exclude users, then those users who would willingly ration their use of the resource are reluctant to do so because of the potential for others (free-riders) to take advantage of this and consume more than their share.

In earlier work based on laboratory experiments and reviews of empirical field studies, Ostrom (1999) makes the case as to why polycentric governance systems are superior to centralized, top-down authority models of governance and also the variety of alternative governance arrangements that are possible (Ostrom, 2010). Her investigation finds that: 'Field studies in all parts of the world have found that local groups of resource users, sometimes by themselves and sometimes with the assistance of external authorities, have created a wide diversity of institutional arrangements for coping with common-pool resources' (1999, pp. 494–5).

Ostrom argues that resource users are mistakenly considered as being incapable of cooperating for longer-term benefits or in building and reciprocating trustworthy relationships, and instead are thought of as norm-free maximizers of immediate gains. She also argues that incentive schemes and rules can be redesigned and that organizing requires central direction. That is, the multitude of self-organized resource governance systems are mere collections of individual agents out to maximize their own short-term returns. In contrast, Ostrom suggests that

> a better foundation for public policy is to assume that humans may not be able to analyze all situations fully but that they will make an effort to solve complex problems through the design of regularized procedures and will be able to draw on inherited capabilities to learn norms of behavior, particularly reciprocity. (1999, p. 495)

These regularized procedures or rules can be designed, changed and enforced by users themselves – a process that we would perhaps now describe as co-creation or co-production by a diverse range of relevant participants – rather than through (for example) top-down creation by officials. For example, Ostrom's studies on the water industry in California in the 1960s showed that multiple smaller agencies could regulate the supply of water very efficiently, contrary to the belief that one central agency would always be more effective (Ostrom, 2010). In a similar institutional theory study of water distribution in a Canadian province, Fan and Zietsma (2017) also show how diverse local stakeholders contributed to the development of a water stewardship council, developing trustworthy relationships and seeking longer-term gains (see also Chapter 4).

Interestingly, Ostrom identified different types of rules to assist in designing mechanisms for governing the commons. These rules also reflect similar discussions on institutional infrastructure (see Chapter 4), whereby certain types of infrastructure in fields (or in field-to-field relations) shape activity and define who can participate, how and so on. These rules are a useful listing for scholars studying the emergence and construction of fields, and how institutional infrastructure is developed within and across fields (with the sequencing of these rules and activities as an as yet under-developed line of inquiry). The major types of rules suggested by Ostrom are listed below.

- Boundary rules – and deciding who can participate. Research has shown that 'one way of coping with the commons is ... to change the composition of those who use a common-pool resource so as to increase the proportion of participants who have a long-term interest in sustaining the resource, who are likely to use reciprocity, and who can be trusted' (1999, p. 513).
- Authority rules: what participants may, must or must not do. In practice, appropriators use a wide variety of rules that affect the actions available to participants and thus affect their basic strategies.
- Position rules: the different capabilities and responsibilities of those in particular positions.
- Payoff rules: penalties (or costs) and benefits attached to actions. Ostrom suggests that locally organized groups are in a better position to monitor and enforce rules. They can also create incentive systems that support shared use and can be adapted as required.
- Information rules: the kind of information present or absent in a situation.
- Scope rules: these affect the outcomes that are allowed, mandated or forbidden.
- Aggregation rules: how individual actions are transformed into final outcomes.

Ultimately, these rules become design principles and 'synthesize core factors that affect the probability of long term survival of an institution developed by the users of a resource' (2010, p. 653). Ostrom argues that, for any given common-pool resource, smaller, localized and self-organized groups or, as she describes them, 'complex adaptive systems' have a greater chance of devising a set of effective rules for governing a common resource than any single central authority because a set of rules devised to manage one situation may no longer fit as conditions change and evolve. This is a polycentric system of governance, 'where citizens are able to organize not just one but multiple governing authorities at different scales' (1999, p. 528), such as special districts, private associations, or parts of a local government. Ostrom argues that this is preferable because governance of the commons – and arguably attempts at addressing complex social problems – requires an adaptive process. Many studies have shown the importance of involving local communities in governance of common-pool resources, no matter whether the governance structure is otherwise private or public in nature. In regard to the role of government, Ostrom suggests that: 'Moving away from the presumption that the government must solve all common-pool resource problems while recognizing the important role of governments is a big step forward. Hopefully, in the future, more national officials will learn to work with local and regional officials, nongovernmental organizations, and local groups of citizens' (2010, p. 664).

In reflecting on her Nobel prize-winning work from across her career, Ostrom concludes that more is to be done on developing institutions that positively motivate humans to solve social dilemmas:

> The most important lesson for public policy analysis derived from the intellectual journey I have outlined here is that humans have a more complex motivational structure and more capability to solve social dilemmas than posited in earlier rational-choice theory. Designing institutions to force (or nudge) entirely self-interested individuals to achieve better outcomes has been the major goal posited by policy analysts for governments to accomplish for much of the past half century. Extensive empirical research leads me to argue that instead, a core goal of public policy should be to facilitate the development of institutions that bring out the best in humans. We need to ask how diverse polycentric institutions help or hinder the innovativeness, learning, adapting, trustworthiness, levels of cooperation of participants, and the achievement of more effective, equitable, and sustainable outcomes at multiple scales (2010, p. 665)

These ideas and insights have informed streams of inquiry in ecological management sustainability, and public entrepreneurship and administration, yet are less prominent in organization and management theory of late. In one recent exception, Fournier (2013) has drawn on Ostrom's work to propose 'commoning' as an autonomous form of social organization and argues for 'the significance of the commons for offering essential spaces, outside our increasingly failing markets and states, in which to reconstruct social relations' (Fournier, 2013, p. 438). This organizing for a collective good or to share (social) value may emerge as what Fournier (2013) describes as three types of commoning, relevant for scholars of social innovation:

- organizing in common: collective allocation of common resources and users' responsibilities;
- organizing for the common: collective use of common resources;
- organizing of the common: collective production of common resources.

Fournier (2013) suggests that we need to draw on Ostrom's work but also go further and theorize beyond the responsible allocation of rights in a resource system, examining governance mechanisms as they endure (or not). I also encourage scholars to consider the relevance and value of Ostrom's work for theorizing social innovation (both process and outcome) and take seriously the notion of polycentric governance models, the inclusiveness of these governance mechanisms, and the role of the state within this in terms of setting direction. In what follows, I discuss further the topic of inclusiveness, and in particular inclusive growth and inclusive innovation, in terms of how it relates to and complements theories of social innovation. I then discuss the role of the state in these polycentric governance systems and processes of social innovation.

Inclusive Innovation

In a perhaps more tangential but nonetheless related line of work, inclusive innovation is also a concept of interest to scholars theorizing social innovation (and now polycentric governance), as it again supports the idea of increased and diverse stakeholder participation in innovation, especially when addressing difficult social problems. Inclusive development is defined by Johnson and Andersen as: 'a process of structural change which gives voice and power to the otherwise excluded groups. It redistributes the incomes generated in both the formal and informal sectors in favour of these groups, and it allows them to shape the future of society in interaction with other stakeholder groups' (2012, p. 25).

Relatedly, inclusive innovation is defined as the 'development and implementation of new ideas which aspire to create opportunities that enhance social and economic well-being for disenfranchised members of society' (Johnson and Andersen, 2012, p. 25). This definition relies strongly on Sen's (1985) work around development as having the twin aspects of 'freedom' and 'capabilities', and emphasizes the need to empower the poor and marginalized members of society, and also the need for structural change. Sen's capabilities approach also features in some work and debates on impact measurement and improving social outcomes (this chapter). Sen (1985) argues that social value is best understood through the concepts of 'functionings' and 'capabilities' rather than through more traditional economic concepts, such as choice, desire or fulfilment, the reason being:

> The essence of focusing on capability is to expand the beneficiaries' freedom to choose amongst their functionings those that they value the most – these then become their achieved functionings if they so choose. What is then important is that beneficiaries have the capabilities to lead the kind of lives they want to lead, to do what they want to do and be the people they want to be. Once they effectively have these capabilities, they can choose to act on them in line with their own ideas of the kind of life they want to live. Therefore, the notion of social value can be improved if both the possibilities for what beneficiaries can do are expanded and, more importantly, the ability to realise those possibilities is developed. (Sen, 1985 in Johnson and Anderson, 2012, p. 786)

What is important in these definitions of inclusive growth is that both process and outcomes are important. Inclusive innovations can be delivered by for-profit and not-for-profit organizations: the important issue is the aspiration to increase social and economic wellbeing, and beneficiary capabilities. Indeed, Chaminade et al. (2018) argue that inclusive innovations could be considered as a form of social innovation, as the value of the innovation accrues primarily to society as a whole rather than to private individuals. Further, 'an interesting fact about social innovations is that implementing a social innovation implies creating new social relations between different individuals and groups, that is, they intrinsically change the innovation system by transforming the relations between actors' (2018, p. 85).

In organization and management studies, inclusive innovation has arguably been subsumed into a larger body of work on social entrepreneurship and new business models (especially at the bottom of the pyramid), and more recently social innovation (perhaps because it conveys a wider remit than only inclusivity per se). Reflective of many of the characteristics of social innovation, in George et al.'s (2012) review of inclusive innovation, the authors highlight the need for participation (of marginal actors), the need to recognize the community (governance) structures and context in which the innovation is trying to occur, and also consider inclusive innovation as both process and outcome. They note how inclusive growth is a widely recognized goal of public policy and also rely on Sen's work in considering inclusive growth as

> improvements in the social and economic wellbeing of communities that have structurally been denied access to resources, capabilities, and opportunities. Inclusive growth can be viewed as a desired outcome of innovative initiatives that target individuals in disenfranchised sectors of society as well as, at the same time, a characteristic of the processes by which such innovative initiatives occur, (2012, p. 661)

George et al.'s (2012) focus is on the central role of organizations in inclusive innovation in connecting disenfranchised individuals and communities with opportunities that foster social and economic growth. In this business-focused approach, 'inclusive growth diminishes trade-offs between growth and inequality because the poor become enfranchised as customers, employees, owners, suppliers, and community members' (George et al., 2012, p. 661). What is interesting is that the many questions that are raised in their review (and their special issue more broadly) reflect the questions raised across various theories of social innovation. For example:

> Which types of organizations initiate inclusive innovation, and how do they harness and internalize these initiatives successfully? Are maverick individuals who refuse to accept institutional and resource constraints the engine of growth? Do important breakthroughs occur through institutional entrepreneurship in which individuals reframe the rules and norms for business activity in an established context [see also Chapter 4]? What drives the success or failure of top-down versus bottom-up types of innovations – do ideas that emerge from and integrate with the local context have better chances of adoption or success than those planned elsewhere and subsequently imported into a resource-limited setting? Alternatively, does inclusive innovation more often depend on the attributes of the innovations themselves rather than the source of the ideas that give rise to the innovative activity? Which performance outcomes constitute success [see Chapter 2, and this chapter on measuring impact]? When organizations search for inclusive innovation, perhaps the fundamental question one should ask is cui bono (who benefits) [see Chapter 5]?' (2012, p. 661)

The conceptions of inclusive innovation range from it being a corporate social responsibility to an economic or political objective (George et al., 2012).

Importantly, George et al. (2012) recognize the link to Ostrom's work and the need to understand existing social structures and community networks when attempting inclusive innovation. They note the possible differences in community structures in rural settings and in settings that are resource poor. Here there may be alternative models of community governance and communal principles of organization to manage communal water and land. This brings up the issue of how to build inclusive innovation systems (Chaminade et al., 2018). While governments have a role to play in supporting innovations and policies that will benefit the poor, Chaminade et al. (2018) argue that governments need to do much more and focus on interventions that aim for institutional change, improved market conditions, market institutions and the redistribution of welfare through labour market reforms, reforms of the financial markets, improvements of the business environment, reduction of red tape, enforcement of property rights and so on. Chaminade et al. (2018) argue that building inclusive innovation systems is an issue in both developing and developed countries as increased inequality creates problems across both types of societies. However, in their view, more research is needed on how innovation systems can become more inclusive, how changes in the system can be triggered and steered and by whom. In what follows I take up this challenge and examine the role of the state in further detail (in terms of public entrepreneurship) and later suggest the need to conceptualize national systems of social innovation.

Public Entrepreneurship

As introduced in Chapter 3, a major line of argument throughout Ostrom's work was how insights from private sector entrepreneurship could be transferred into the public sector. In this way, public entrepreneurship might lead to new forms and methods of allocating resources over time for the collective good, establishing new rules of the game (or changing them), possibly establishing new public organizations, and the creative management of public resources (Bernier and Hafsi, 2007; Klein et al., 2010). For theorizing social innovation, an understanding of public entrepreneurship repositions the role of the State in the broader neoliberal environment, in setting direction for growth and changing the nature of regulation as well as the delivery of public services. The two main empirical issues I explore here are the regulatory context for new forms of cross-sector partnerships and also the role of the State in directing activity and scaling innovations in addressing complex social problems.

In the era of New Public Management, Steurer (2013) looks at how governmental deregulation has been accompanied by soft governmental regulation as well as 'societal re-regulation', focusing on the areas of corporate social responsibility (CSR) and sustainable development that require significant governance changes. 'Policy makers as well as researchers recognized early on that sustainable development is not only concerned with first-order policy issues of "what to do", but also with second order governance issues of "how to do it"' (2013, p. 390). In looking at the different ways in which partnerships can form across business, government and civil society, providing new forms of regulation, Steurer (2013) develops a governance typology based on 'who steers' and 'how'.

In each of these institutional domains (see Chapter 3 and Chapter 4), there are familiar forms of regulation and governance mechanisms. For the government, they are the ultimate regulators, with options to implement hard (legislative) or soft (guidelines, benchmarks, endorsements and so on) regulation (Steurer, 2013). For business, there is self-regulation as a governing mechanism, where businesses self-specify rules, self-monitor their conduct and self-enforce compliance without direct and explicit interference from the State or civil society – making it difficult to delineate at times from management. For civil society organizations, attempts to regulate are made through formal standard setting and pressuring and lobbying. What is most relevant for theorizing social innovation is Steurer's (2013) development of 'domain-spanning co-regulation'. This is 'an umbrella term for co-operative forms of steering in which actors from different societal domains aim to achieve common objectives or supply public services jointly', often including those who are to be regulated and the beneficiaries of the regulation in the arrangement (Steurer, 2013, p. 397). This is particularly relevant when theorizing social innovation and particularly for many more recent social innovations (such as social impact bonds) that are embarking on new forms of relational configuration and so new forms of governing mechanisms (see also Klein et al., 2010; Chapter 3). Steurer (2013) describes several forms of co-regulation, depending on the institutional domains involved.

- Public co-management, which involves civil society and government actors. It is usually concerned with the joint management of common pool resources (see earlier discussion on Ostrom; see Chapter 3).

- Public co-regulation (government and business) through certification schemes, negotiated agreements and public–private partnerships.
- Private co-regulation (business and civil society) involving certification schemes and private–private partnerships.
- Tri-partite co-regulation involving standards (such as ISO), certification schemes and partnerships.

What is important here is to recognize that the volume of activity addressing complex social problems is necessarily occurring in poly-centred and multi-actor contexts, where traditional boundaries between institutional domains (see Chapter 4) are eroding, and there is a need for the State to consider different types of governance mechanisms to steer and direct such activity.

This leads to the next important point on public entrepreneurship and the role of the State – that of setting the direction. It is insufficient to consider the role of the State as only intervening to fix markets or systems failure. This is particularly true for settings of social innovation where the State is needed to both innovate and also guide and govern other activity towards producing social value. When it comes to producing innovation more generally, Mazzucato (2015) reminds us that the State has been behind most breakthrough radical technologies from the Internet to nanotechnology. She demonstrates how much of the technology in the iPhone has depended on government-funded research and technological developments – counter to much of the narrative around the role of private sector entrepreneurs and the attribution of technological advancements. In her now classic book embraced by policy makers globally, Mazzucato identifies four key challenges to be resolved in understanding the role of the state in innovation:

> The first key problem is that any framework that focuses on policy only in terms of fixing problems, especially (but not only) market failures, does not embody any explicit justification for the kind of market creation and mission-oriented directionality (and 'routes' within directions) that was required for innovations such as the Internet and nanotechnology and is required today to address societal challenges (Mazzucato 2015). Secondly, by not considering the state as a lead investor and market creator, such failure-based approaches do not provide insights into the type and structure of public sector organizations that are needed in order to provide the depth and breadth of high-risk investments. Thirdly, as long as policy is seen only as an 'intervention', rather than a key part of the market creation and shaping

process, the type of evaluation criteria used to assess mission-oriented investments will inevitably be problematic. Fourthly, by not describing the state as a lead risk-taker and investor in this process, the failure-based approaches have avoided a key issue regarding the distribution of risks and rewards between the state and the private sector. (Mazzucato, 2016, p. 142)

In terms of public entrepreneurship and innovation, Mazzucato goes furthest in arguing for an entrepreneurial State – that the government must take a leading role and that it should be able to take risks and invest in those areas where the private sector will not.

In recent work, and relevant for the State's role in identifying and directing activity, Mazzucato (2016) suggests the need for mission-oriented innovation policy, which can be readily applied to social problems, and is indeed already applied to environmental problems such as climate change. For example, Mazzucato has informed European Union policy approaches in this regard where bold and ambitious 'missions' and desired outcomes drive diverse participants, across levels, through a variety of mechanisms and approaches. By setting missions, such as 'zero homeless people' that require different sectors to work together, it is possible to create instruments that reward those businesses that are willing and able to co-invest alongside public investments. Mazzucato (2018) suggests that missions should be broad enough to engage the public and attract cross-sectoral investment and should remain focused enough to involve industry and achieve measurable success. By setting the direction for a solution, missions do not specify how to achieve success. Rather, they stimulate the development of a range of different solutions to achieve the objective (Mazzucato, 2018). This is a different systematic approach to addressing complex problems.

Towards 'Systems of Social Innovation'

For all the policy and practitioner discussions on governing collaborations with diverse stakeholders from across sectors as part of pursuing social innovation, it seems relevant to consider how broader national innovation systems are also organized and conceptualized. In this section I explore insights from literature examining national systems of innovation and suggest how this might assist in conceptualizing national systems of *social* innovation.

The concept of a 'national innovation system' (NIS) developed in the late 1980s and 1990s, and was novel in that it reconceived innovation as occurring through interactions and networking across a range of organizations, as opposed to just technology-driven perspectives and scientific invention. Context and institutional infrastructure was important and knowledge generation involved many different types of organizations and crossed organizational boundaries (Chaminade et al., 2018). Lundvall et al. describe a national innovation system as an 'open, evolving and complex system that encompasses relationships within and between organizations, institutions and socio-economic structures which determine the rate and direction of innovation and competence-building emanating from processes of science-based and experience-based learning' (Lundvall, 2009, cited in Chaminade et al., 2018, p. 2). According to Edquist, 'a more general definition of (national) systems of innovation includes "all important economic, social, political, organizational, institutional and other factors that influence the development, diffusion and use of innovation"' (2005, p. 183). When the OECD began to adopt the concept at the beginning of the 1990s, it became widely used by international organizations and by national governments. An important tenet of the NIS concept is the rejection of the idea 'that the market is a fine-tuned system that must not be disturbed by state interventions' (Chaminade et al., 2018, p. 17). Another strong focus was on user–production interactions and learning from these and other interactions, and also learning by doing.

In the early 2000s, the concept of the 'Triple Helix' innovation system emerged from the NIS literature. This described innovation as occurring through the overlapping institutional domains of the State, industry and academia (Etzkowitz and Leydesdorff, 2000). In this Triple Helix model, a knowledge infrastructure is generated across domains, with hybrid organizations often emerging at the interfaces, with markets and technological innovations sub-dynamics of this broader system. Edquist (2005) developed the following list of activities as those that can be expected to be important in an innovation system.

- Provision of research and development, creating new knowledge primarily in engineering, medicine and the natural sciences.
- Competence building in the labour force.
- Formation of new product markets.
- Articulation of quality requirements emanating from the demand side with regard to new products.
- Creating and changing organizations needed for the development of new fields of innovation (for example enhancing entrepreneurship to create new firms and intrapreneurship to diversify existing firms, creating new research agencies).
- Networking through markets and other mechanisms, including interactive learning between different organizations.

- Creating and changing institutions – for example tax laws, R&D investment routines – that provide incentives or obstacles to innovation.
- Incubating activities for new innovative efforts.
- Financing of innovation and other processes that can facilitate the commercialization of knowledge and its adoption.
- Provision of consultancy services around (for example) technology transfer, commercial information and legal advice.

While this NIS concept emphasizes the need for activities, relationships and institutional infrastructure to reach across domains in order to generate new knowledge and innovation, Mazzucato criticizes the systems perspective of innovation on the basis that it 'has focused primarily on the need to build horizontal linkages between actors. While this contributed important insights into the framework conditions required for innovation, it has ignored those more vertical policies required for setting the direction of change, and the characteristics of public agencies required to set such a direction' (2016, p. 141). Reconfiguring the role of the State is a focus in recent work on NIS, with a much more proactive role envisaged (Chaminade et al., 2018). Consistent with Mazzucato's (2018) arguments on mission-driven innovation policy and more public entrepreneurship, Chaminade et al. (2018) describe a crucial and active role for the State in the following areas, which I would argue are also essential for social innovation:

- directionality: or the need to articulate collective priorities and the direction of change;
- demand articulation: the need to anticipate user needs and articulate public procurement;
- reflexibility: the ability of the system's agents to anticipate changes and to mobilize actors;
- coordination: the need to manage policies in different realms (labour, education, industry and trade) to steer the system in the right direction.

These 'vertical' activities suggest a clear and important role for the State within a national system of social innovation. However, a national system of social innovation must find ways to encourage and coordinate the participation of actors from across sectors.

Conclusion

So, is the idea of national systems of social innovation useful? For one thing, it emphasizes the need for much activity and infrastructure to connect and build relationships across different institutional domains. It also highlights the role of the variety of sources of (social) innovation and knowledge of solutions to social problems than just the social sector or just industry. What it also does is strongly position the role of the State in setting direction and pace in addressing social and environmental problems, by coordinating and brokering relationships, and trialling new forms of governing and policy implementation. It also considers markets as just one mechanism to address (social) innovation challenges, and so while discussions on the role of impact investing markets are important, they are not the only mechanism that is needed to address the variety and complexity of problems facing societies today. In addition to mission-oriented innovation policy (such as around climate change), could we also have bold goals around social problems, such as zero homelessness, or children's education? What might having this mission mean for creating a new and inclusive system of relationships and knowledge around it? What might policy look like if we conceptualized 'systems of social innovation'?

CHAPTER SUMMARY

While this book outlined and developed several theories of social innovation, this concluding chapter aimed to return to several empirical tensions that are challenging practitioners and policy makers: managing hybridity, measuring impact, and governing collaborations. These are rich and complicated tensions, and in this chapter I have only begun to outline key areas of practitioner concern, application and examples – all of which provide future research opportunities. Where relevant, I have highlighted associated lines of theoretical inquiry to aid in these possible empirical investigations, as part of broader efforts to better theorize social innovation. There is much opportunity for organizational and management scholars to do so, making substantial empirical and theoretical innovations as many institutions, organizations and managers grapple with some of the most complex challenges of our time.

NOTE

1. I especially thank Dr Gillian McAllister here.

REFERENCES

Andre, K. and Pache, A.C. (2016). From caring entrepreneur to caring enterprise: addressing the ethical challenges of scaling up social enterprises. *Journal of Business Ethics*, **133**, 659–75.

Ansari, S., Wijen, F. and Gray, B. (2013). Constructing a climate change logic: an institutional perspective on the 'tragedy of the commons'. *Organization Science*, **24**(4), 1014–40.

Arjaliès, D-L. and Durand, R. (2019). Product categories as judgment devices: the moral awakening of the investment industry. *Organization Science*, forthcoming.

Australian Advisory Board on Impact Investing (2016). Views from the impact investing playing field in Australia on what's happening and what's needed next. Accessed at: https://impactinvestingaustralia.com/wp-content/uploads/20171215_Views-from-the-Field-2017_FINAL-1.pdf.

Barman, E. (2016). *Caring Capitalism*, Cambridge: Cambridge University Press.

Barraket, J. and Yousefpour, N. (2013). Evaluation and social impact measurement amongst small to medium social enterprises: process, purpose and value. *Australian Journal of Public Administration*, **72**(4), 447–58.

Battilana, J. and Dorado, S. (2010). Building sustainable hybrid organizations: the case of commercial microfinance organizations. *Academy of Management Journal*, **53**(6), 1419–40.

Battilana, J. and Lee, M. (2014). Advancing research on hybrid organizing: insights from the study of social enterprises. *The Academy of Management Annals*, **8**(1), 397–441.

Battilana, J., Besharov, M. and Mitzinneck, B. (2017). On hybrids and hybrid organizing: a review and roadmap for future research. In R. Greenwood, C. Oliver, T.B. Lawrence and R.E. Meyer (eds), *The SAGE Handbook of Organizational Institutionalism* (2nd edn). London: SAGE Publications, pp. 133–69.

Battilana, J., Lee, M., Walker, J. and Dorsey, C. (2012). In search of the hybrid ideal. *Stanford Social Innovation Review*, **10**, 51–5.

Battilana, J., Sengul, M., Pache, A.C. and Model, J. (2015). Harnessing productive tensions in hybrid organizations: the case of work integration social enterprises. *Academy of Management Journal*, **58**, 1658–85.

Beckert, J. (2009). The social order of markets. *Theory and Society*, **38**(3), 245–69.

Bernier, L. and Hafsi, T. (2007). The changing nature of public entrepreneurship. *Public Administration Review*, **67**(3), 488–503.

Blessing, A. (2015). Public, private, or in-between? The legitimacy of social enterprises in the housing market. *Voluntas*, **26**, 198–221.

Bourdieu, P. (1993). *The Field of Cultural Production: Essays on Art and Literature*. New York: Columbia University Press.

Bryson, J.M., Crosby, B.C. and Stone, M.M. (2006). The design and implementation of cross-sector collaborations: propositions from the literature. *Public Administration Review*, **66**, 44–55.

Buckmaster, N. (1999). Associations between outcome measurement, accountability and learning for non-profit organisations. *International Journal of Public Sector Management*, **12**(2), 186–97.

Callon, M., Millo, Y. and Muniesa, F. (2007). *Market Devices*. Oxford: Blackwell.

Campbell, D.T. (2002). Outcomes assessment and the paradox of nonprofit accountability. *Nonprofit Management and Leaders*, **12**, 243–59.

Casado-Asensio, J. and Steurer, R. (2014). Integrated strategies on sustainable development, climate change mitigation and adaptation in Western Europe: communication rather than coordination. *Journal of Public Policy*, **34**(3), 437–73.

Cattani, G., Porac, J.F. and Thomas, H. (2017). Categories and competition. *Strategic Management Journal*, **38**(1), 64–92.

Chaminade, C., Lundvall, B-Å. and Haneef, S. (2018). *Advanced Introduction to National Innovation Systems*. Cheltenham, UK and Northampton, MA, USA: Edward Elgar Publishing.

Cooney, K. (2006). The institutional and technical structuring of nonprofit ventures: case study of a U.S. hybrid organization caught between two fields. *Voluntas*, **17**, 137–61.

Dalpiaz, E., Rindova, V. and Ravasi, D. (2016). Combining logics to transform organizational agency: blending industry and art at Alessi. *Administrative Science Quarterly*, **61**(3), 347–92.

Dembek, K., Singh, P. and Bhakoo, V. (2016). Literature review of shared value: a theoretical concept or a management buzzword. *Journal of Business Ethics*, **137**, 231–67.

Dietz, T., Ostrom, E. and Stern, P. (2003). The struggle to govern the commons. *Science*, 12 December, p. 1907.

DiMaggio, P.J. and Powell, W.W. (1983). The iron cage revisited: institutional isomorphism and collective rationality in organizational fields. *American Sociological Review*, **48**, 147–60.

Doherty, B., Haugh, H. and Lyon, F. (2014). Social enterprises as hybrid organizations: a review and research agenda. *International Journal of Management Reviews*, **16**(4), 417–36.

Doloi, H. (2018). Community-centric model for evaluating social value in projects. *Journal of Construction Engineering and Management*, **144**(5), 04018019.

Ebrahim, A. and Rangan, V. (2014). What impact? A framework for measuring the scale and scope of social performance. *California Management Review*, **56**(3), 118–41.

Ebrahim, A., Battilana, J. and Mair, J. (2014). The governance of social enterprises: mission drift and accountability challenges in hybrid organizations. *Research in Organizational Behavior*, **34**, 81–100.

Edquist, C. (2005). Systems of innovation: perspectives and challenges. In J. Fagerberg, D. Mowery and R. Nelson (eds), *The Oxford Handbook of Innovation*, Oxford: Oxford University Press.

Edwards, M., Logue, D. and McAllister, G. (2019). Managing hybrids: a practitioner guidebook. University of Technology Sydney and The Wayside Chapel. Available at: www.cbsi.uts.edu.au.

Emerson, J. (2003). The blended value proposition: integrating social and financial returns. *California Management Review*, **45**(4), 35–51.

Esteves, A.M., Franks, D. and Vanclay, F. (2012). Social impact assessment: the state of the art. *Impact Assessment and Project Appraisal*, **30**(1), 34–42.

Etzkowitz, H. and Leydesdorff, L. (2000). The dynamics of innovation: from National Systems and 'Mode 2' to a Triple Helix of university–industry–government relations. *Research Policy*, **29**(2), 109–23.

Faivel, S. (2018). SROI evolution or revolution? *SVA Quarterly*, April. Available at: https://www.socialventures.com.au/sva-quarterly/sroi-revolution-or-evolution/?utm_medium=email&utm_campaign=SVAQ%20August%202018%20New&utm_content=SVAQ%20August%202018%20New+CID_4763af133004d3603e4e79415d25c14b&utm_source=Campaign%20Monitor&utm_term=READ%20FULL%20ARTICLE.

Fan, G.H. and Zietsma, C. (2017). Constructing a shared governance logic: the role of emotions in enabling dually embedded agency. *Academy of Management Journal*, **60**(6), 2321–51.

Flateau, P., Zaretzy, K., Adams, S., Horton, A. and Smith, J. (2015). *Measuring Outcomes for Impact in the Community Sector in Western Australia*. Bankwest Foundation Social Impact Series No. 1, Bankwest Foundation, Western Australia.

Flyvbjerg, B. (2001). *Making Social Science Matter: Why Social Inquiry Fails and How it Can Succeed Again*. Cambridge: Cambridge University Press.

Fourcade, M. (2007). Theories of markets and theories of society. *American Behavioral Scientist*, **50**(8), 1015–34.

Fournier, V. (2013). Commoning: on the social organisation of the commons. *M@n@gement*, **16**(4), 433–53.

Friedland, R. and Alford, R.R. (1991). Bringing society back in: symbols, practices, and institutional contradictions. In W.W. Powell and P.J. DiMaggio (eds), *The New Institutionalism in Organizational Analysis*. Chicago, IL: University of Chicago Press.

George, G., McGahan, A.M. and Prabhu, J. (2012). Innovation for inclusive growth: towards a theoretical framework and a research agenda. *Journal of Management Studies*, **49**(4), 661–83.

GIIN (2016). Impact measurement in the clean energy sector. Global Impact Investing Network. Available at: https://thegiin.org/assets/FINAL_GIIN_cleanenergyreport_PRINTREADY_singles_nocropsFINALFINAL.pdf.

Glynn, M.A. and Navis, C. (2013). Categories, identities, and cultural classification: moving beyond a model of categorical constraint. *Journal of Management Studies*, **50**(6), 1124–37.

Gray, B. (1989). *Collaborating: Finding Common Ground for Multiparty Problems*. San Francisco, CA: Jossey-Bass Publishers.

Gray, B. and Purdy, J. (2018). *Collaborating for Our Future: Multistakeholder Partnerships for Solving Complex Problems*. Oxford: Oxford University Press.

Greenwood, R., Raynard, M., Kodeih, F., Micelotta, E.R. and Lounsbury, M. (2011). Institutional complexity and organizational responses. *Academy of Management Annals*, **5**(1), 317–71.

Grimes, M. (2010). Strategic sensemaking within funding relationships: the effects of performance measurement on organizational identity in the social sector. *Entrepreneurship Theory and Practice*, **34**, 763–83.

Grimes, M., Williams, T.A. and Zhao, E.Y. (2018). Anchors aweigh: the sources, variety, and challenges of mission drift. *Academy of Management Review*, doi.org/10.5465/amr.2017.0254.

Helgesson, C.F. and Muniesa, F. (2013). For what it's worth: an introduction to valuation studies. *Valuation Studies*, **1**(1), 1–10.

Hinings, C.R., Logue, D.M. and Zietsma, C. (2017). Fields, governance and institutional infrastructure. In R. Greenwood, T. Lawrence, C. Oliver and R. Meyer (eds), *The SAGE Handbook of Organizational Institutionalism* (2nd edn). London: SAGE Publications, pp. 163–89.

Hood, C. (1995). Contemporary public management: a new global paradigm? *Public Policy and Administration*, **10**(2), 104–17.

Hwang, H. and Powell, W.W. (2009). The rationalization of charity: the influences of professionalism in the nonprofit sector. *Administrative Science Quarterly*, **54**, 268–98.

Johnson, B. and Andersen, A.D. (2012). *Learning, Innovation and Inclusive Development: New Perspectives on Economic Development Strategy and Development Aid*. Aalborg: Aalborg Universitetsforlag.

Kennedy, M.T. and Fiss, P.C. (2013). An ontological turn in categories research: from standards of legitimacy to evidence of actuality. *Journal of Management Studies*, **50**(6), 1138–54.

Klein, P., Mahoney, J., McGahan, A. and Pitelis, C. (2010). Toward a theory of public entrepreneurship. *European Management Review*, **7**, 1–15.

Kroeger, A. and Weber, C. (2014). Developing a conceptual framework for comparing social value creation. *Academy of Management Review*, **39**(4), 513–40.

Lamont, Michèle (2012). Toward a comparative sociology of valuation and evaluation. *Annual Review of Sociology*, **38**(1), 201–21.

Lingane, A. and Olsen, S. (2004). Guidelines for social return on investment. *California Management Review*, **46**(3), 116–35.

Litrico, J.B. and Besharov, M.L. (2018). Unpacking variation in hybrid organizational forms: changing models of social enterprise among nonprofits, 2000–2013. *Journal of Business Ethics*, 1–18.

Lockie, S. (2001). SIA in review: setting the agenda for impact assessment in the 21st century. *Impact Assessment and Project Appraisal*, **19**(4), 277–87.

Loewenstein, J., Ocasio, W. and Jones, C. (2012). Vocabularies and vocabulary structure: a new approach linking categories, practices, and institutions. *The Academy of Management Annals*, **6**(1), 41–86.

Logue, D. and Edwards, M. (2013). Across the digital divide. *Stanford Social Innovation Review*, Fall.

Logue, D., McAllister, G. and Schweitzer, J. (2017). Social entrepreneurship and impact investing report. Report prepared for innovationXchange, Department of Foreign Affairs and Trade by the University of Technology Sydney. Accessed at: https://www.uts.edu.au/sites/default/files/article/downloads/UTS %20SEIII%20Research%20Report_2017.pdf.

Mair, J., Martí, I. and Ventresca, M.J. (2012). Building inclusive markets in rural Bangladesh: how intermediaries work institutional voids. *Academy of Management Journal*, **55**(4), 819–50.

Mair, J., Mayer, J. and Lutz, E. (2015). Navigating institutional plurality: organizational governance in hybrid organizations. *Organization Studies*, **36**(6), 713–39.

Manetti, G. (2014). The role of blended value accounting in the evaluation of socio-economic impact of social enterprises. *Voluntas*, **25**, 443–64.

Marden, R. (2011). Can SROI help the voluntary sector measure value. *The Guardian*, 18 July.

Margolis, J.D. and Walsh, J.P. (2003). Misery loves companies: rethinking social initiatives by business. *Administrative Science Quarterly*, **48**(2), 268–305.

Mazzucato, M. (2015). *The Entrepreneurial State.* London: Anthem Press.

Mazzucato, M. (2016). From market fixing to market-creating: a new framework for innovation policy. *Industry and Innovation*, **23**, 140–56.

Mazzucato, M. (2018). *Mission-Oriented Research & Innovation in the European Union: A Problem-solving Approach to Fuel Innovation-led Growth.* Accessed 20 August 2018 at: https://ec.europa.eu/info/sites/info/files/mazzucato_report_2018.pdf.

Meyer, J. and Scott, W.R. (1983). *Organizational Environments: Ritual and Rationality.* Beverly Hills, CA: SAGE Publications.

Meyer, R.E. and Höllerer, M.A. (2014). Does institutional theory need redirecting? *Journal of Management Studies*, **51**(7), 1221–33.

Miller, T.L. and Wesley, C.L. (2010). Assessing mission and resources for social change: an organizational identity perspective on social venture capitalists' decision criteria. *Entrepreneurship Theory and Practice*, **34**, 705–33.

Miller, T.L., Grimes, M.G., McMullen, J.S. and Vogus, T.J. (2012). Venturing for others with heart and head: how compassion encourages social entrepreneurship. *Academy of Management Review*, **37**(4), 616–40.

Moonshot Global and Living Collaborations (2018). Contextualising impact measurement and monetisation: a review of literature and trends. Report developed for the Scaling Frontier Innovation Program, DFAT innovationXchange.

Nicholls, A. (2009). 'We do good things, don't we?': 'Blended Value Accounting' in social entrepreneurship. *Accounting, Organizations and Society*, **34**, 755–69.

Ocasio, W., Loewenstein, J. and Nigam, A. (2015). How streams of communication reproduce and change institutional logics: the role of categories. *Academy of Management Review*, **40**(1), 28–48.

OECD (2019). *Social Impact Investment 2019: The Impact Imperative for Sustainable Development*, Paris: OECD Publishing.

O'Mahony, S. and Bechky, B.A. (2008). Boundary organizations: enabling collaboration among unexpected allies. *Administrative Science Quarterly*, **53**(3), 422–59.

Orlitzky, M., Schmidt, F.L. and Rynes, S.L. (2003). Corporate social and financial performance: a meta-analysis. *Organization Studies*, **24**(3), 403–41.

Ostrom, E. (1996). Crossing the great divide: coproduction, synergy, and development. *World Development*, **24**(6), 1073–87.

Ostrom, E. (1999). Coping with tragedies of the commons. *Annual Review of Political Science*, **2**, 493–535.

Ostrom, E. (2010). Beyond markets and states: polycentric governance of complex economic systems. *American Economic Review*, **100**, 641–72.

Pache, A.C. and Santos, F. (2010). When worlds collide: the internal dynamics of organizational responses to conflicting institutional demands. *Academy of Management Review*, **35**, 455–76.

Pache, A.C. and Santos, F.M. (2013). Inside the hybrid organization: selective coupling as a response to competing institutional logics. *Academy of Management Journal*, **56**, 972–1001.

Parmigiani, A. and Rivera-Santos, M. (2011). Clearing a path through the forest: a meta-review of interorganizational relationships. *Journal of Management*, **37**(4), 1108–36.

Perkmann, M., McKelvey, M. and Phillips, N. (2018). Protecting scientists from Gordon Gekko: how organizations use hybrid spaces to engage with multiple institutional logics. *Organization Science*, forthcoming.

Phills, J., Deiglmeier, K. and Miller, D. (2008). Rediscovering social innovation. *Stanford Social Innovation Review*, **6**, 34–43.

Polonsky, M. and Grau, S.L. (2011). Assessing the social impact of charitable organizations: four alternative approaches. *International Journal of Nonprofit and Voluntary Sector Marketing*, **16**(2), 195–211.

Porter, M. and Kramer, M. (2011). Creating shared value. *Harvard Business Review*, **89**(1–2).

Quelin, B., Kivleniece, I. and Lazzarini, S. (2017). Public–private collaboration, hybridity and social value: towards new theoretical perspectives. *Journal of Management Studies*, **54**(6).

Rhodes, M.L. and Donnelly-Cox, G. (2014). Hybridity and social entrepreneurship in social housing in Ireland. *Voluntas*, 25(6), 1630–47.

Rittel, H.W. and Webber, M.M. (1973). Dilemmas in a general theory of planning. *Policy Sciences*, **4**(2), 155–69.

Santos, F., Pache, A.C. and Birkholz, C. (2015). Making hybrids work: aligning business models and organizational design for social enterprises. *California Management Review*, **57**(3), 36–58.

Sawhill, J.C. and Williamson, D. (2001). Mission impossible? Measuring success in nonprofit organizations. *Nonprofit Management and Leadership*, **11**(3), 371–86.

Sen, A. (1985). *The Standard of Living*. Cambridge Tanner Lectures, 11–12 March, Cambridge: Cambridge University Press.

Shepherd, D.A. (2015). Party on! A call for entrepreneurship research that is more interactive, activity based, cognitively hot, compassionate, and prosocial. *Journal of Business Venturing*, **30**(4), 489–507.

Shepherd, D.A., Williams, T.A. and Zhao, E.Y. (2019). A framework for exploring the degree of hybridity in social entrepreneurship. *Academy of Management Perspectives*, forthcoming.

Smith, W.K. and Besharov, M.L. (2017). Bowing before dual gods: how structured flexibility sustains organizational hybridity. *Administrative Science Quarterly*, 0001839217750826.

Smith, W.K., Gonin, M. and Besharov, M.L. (2013). Managing social–business tensions: a review and research agenda for social enterprise. *Business Ethics Quarterly*, **23**(3), 407–42.

Steurer, R. (2013). Disentangling governance: a synoptic view of regulation by government, business and civil society. *Policy Sciences*, **46**(4), 387–410.

Tett, G. (2019). Governments won't step in to fund sustainable development. Will private finance step in? *Financial Times*, 24 January. Accessed at: https://www.ft.com/content/82ef5e8e-1ea1-11e9-b126-46fc3ad87c65.

Thornton, P.H., Ocasio, W. and Lounsbury, M. (2012). *The Institutional Logics Perspective: A New Approach to Culture, Structure, and Process*. Oxford: Oxford University Press.

Tobias, J.M., Mair, J. and Barbosa-Leiker, C. (2013). Toward a theory of transformative entrepreneuring: poverty reduction and conflict resolution in Rwanda's entrepreneurial coffee sector. *Journal of Business Venturing*, **28**(6), 728–42.

Toubiana, M. and Zietsma, C. (2017). The message is on the wall? Emotions, social media and the dynamics of institutional complexity. *Academy of Management Journal*, **60**(3), 922–53.

Vatin, F. (2013). Valuation as evaluating and valorizing. *Valuation Studies*, **1**(1), 31–50.

Voigt, C. and Ferreira, F. (2015). The Warsaw Framework for REDD+: implications for national implementation and access to results-based finance. *Carbon & Climate Law Review*, **9**(2), 113–29.

White, L. (2017). A cook's tour: towards a framework for measuring the social impact of social purpose organisations. *European Journal of Operational Research*, **268**(3), 784–97.

Wry, T. and York, J.G. (2017). An identity-based approach to social enterprise. *Academy of Management Review*, **42**(3), 437–60.

Zuckerman, E.W. (1999). The categorical imperative: securities analysts and the illegitimacy discount. *American Journal of Sociology*, **104**(5), 1398–438.

Index